Louisiana
Real and Rustic

Louisiana
Real and Rustic

Emeril Lagasse

with Marcelle Bienvenu

Photographs by Brian Smale

WILLIAM MORROW AND COMPANY, INC. ——•—— NEW YORK

Library of Congress Cataloging-in-Publication Data

Lagasse, Emeril.
Louisiana real and rustic / Emeril Lagasse : photographs by Brian Smale.—1st ed.
p. cm.
Includes index.
ISBN 0-688-12721-5
1. Cookery, American—Louisiana style. I. Title.
TX715.2.L68L35 1996

641.59763—dc20   95-46653
CIP

Printed in the United States of America

First Edition

13 14 15 16 17 18 19 20 21 22 23 24 25

BOOK DESIGN BY NANCY STEINY

To the people of Louisiana who shared with us their

heritage and love of food. To those

who are presently continuing these traditions

and to those who will continue to preserve

what has been passed down for generations

Acknowledgments

A tremendous thanks to Anne Kearney, a very talented cook who was at Emeril's but who is now owner-chef of Peristyle's in New Orleans. She tirelessly gathered, shopped, chopped, measured, and cleaned up after us. Without her, this book would not have happened. Thanks to Felicia Willett, one of the baker's at Emeril's, who tirelessly helped us in the final recipe testing and revisions. My hat goes off to the photographer, Brian Smale, who boarded boats, ran through burning cane fields, perched atop levees, sweated in pepper fields, and even spent a long, cold night at a duck camp to capture the people and scenes of Louisiana. Thanks, too, to his assistant, Shelly Thomas. Big, big pats on the back for the staffs at Emeril's and NOLA and especially Michael Jordan, Bernard Carmouche, and Lou Lynch. To Marty Dalton, my incredible assistant, for her constant dedication to making things happen. To Marcelle's husband, Rock Lasserre, we shall be forever indebted. He was always there for support when we needed it. We also say thank you to Marcelle's mama, Rhena, who offered advice and historical information. To the folks at William Morrow, for having the faith and foresight to publish this book, and to Harriet Bell who began the project. Without Mom and Dad (Hilda and John), well, I wouldn't be here. Ruth and Hugh Hohn, Tari's parents, are always around to lend a hand. To all of you, I shall always be grateful for your love and encouragement. And finally, to my wife, Tari, who not only shared our home and her kitchen, but also for her constant love and support in life. We also want to thank the following people who shared their knowledge and lent their assistance: Paul McIlhenny at Avery Island • Lawrence "Boo" Levert III at Levert–St. John, Inc. • Branan B. Beyt, Jr., at St. Mary Sugar Cooperative • Mark Swanson at Natchitoches Pecans, Inc. • Mike Davis at the Conrad Rice Mill • Gerald "Hammy" Patin at the Ace Hunting Club • Adner Ortego, who played his fiddle and shared his wine with us • Russel Leger at Ned Leger Grocery and Meat Market • Bryan Bourque at Black's Oyster House • Tommy Dantin and Lonie Bell of the MV Wyoming • Dallas "Canou" Toups, who welcomed us aboard his oyster boat • Fred's Lounge in Mamou • Dan and Margie Regard, who extended to us their warm hospitality • Joe and Julie Regard, who guided us through pecan country

Contents

Introduction

When I moved to New Orleans to take over the reins as executive chef at Commander's Palace, I knew very little about the rest of Louisiana. Like many people, I thought it was nothing more than a soggy water-filled swamp. But it didn't take me long to get caught up in the passion and enthusiasm of the Brennan clan, owners of Commander's, who continually search for the freshest and best ingredients for their restaurant. I began going out into the state visiting quail farms, crawfish ponds, strawberry fields, butcher shops, and fishing ports. And that's how I discovered the rest of Louisiana. I found the swamps and marshes, bayous and streams, lakes, bays, and a great web of waterways that were teeming with a great variety of fish, blue crabs, sweet shrimp, plump oysters, and succulent crawfish. I drove along country roads bounded by fields of sugarcane, rice, and sweet potatoes in the southern part of the state and majestic pecan and peach orchards in the north. During the spring and summer months, I saw roadside gardens filled with okra, tomatoes, bell peppers, and eggplant. I visited the pepper fields at Avery Island, home of McIlhenny Co., the makers of Tabasco pepper sauce. In small towns, here and there, I discovered busy butcher shops where andouille, boudin, fresh pork sausage, and grattons were sold as quickly as they were made. And I learned about the geographical differences. North Louisiana begins somewhere around Alexandria, located almost dead center in the middle of the state, where the soil turns from rich brown to red clay. Many people will tell you that north Louisiana and south Louisiana are almost like two different states, and that is, for the most part, correct. I heard this difference very aptly explained by a Louisiana journalist, who said that the best way to understand this phenomena is to think of southern America, or what most people might call the Deep South, slamming right down on an imaginary line in the center of the state and meeting up with a culture that is more European with a touch of the Caribbean thrown in. While north Louisianians are unlike other Southerners, that is, those from Arkansas, Mississippi, Alabama, and such, in that they eat gumbo and a few other Louisiana dishes, they do have a twang that is associated with those neighboring states. In the southern part of the state is Acadiana, a region composed of 22 parishes (unlike the rest of the United States, counties here are called parishes) where the people speak a melodious patois that combines an ancient French dialect with touches of English, German, Spanish, and African. Then there's the section of the state east of the Mississippi River that includes Baton Rouge, the state capital, and New Orleans as well as fishing ports leading to the mouth of the river south of New Orleans. The common denominator that has enchanted me is that just about everywhere I ventured something good is always simmering on the stove or popping out of the oven. During my wanderings, I came to realize, too, that to understand and appreciate the cuisine, it's best to know how it evolved. First of all, because Louisiana was claimed by the French explorer Robert La Salle, its roots are strongly French. In 1718, another French explorer by the name of Bienville came up the mouth of the Mississippi River to what is now New Orleans, and named it for the Duc d'Orléans. A great influx of French colonists followed to carve a city out of the mosquito-infested watery land, and a great port of entry opened. The first French settlers with their knowledge and love of food inevitably set the wheels in motion for the development of a new cuisine. They found themselves at a loss for the traditional ingredients of French cooking to

which they were accustomed. The spices and herbs, the vegetables, the meats of their homeland were not available in the beginning. Native ingredients and Indian herbs soon combined with French cooking skills to form the foundation of what has come to be known as Creole cooking. The word "Creole" has many different meanings. During colonial times, it simply denoted French or Spanish colonists and their descendants, particularly those who maintained some of the customs and language of the mother country. But over time, Creole has taken on other definitions. Some French-speaking blacks of southwest Louisiana, like the formerly French-speaking blacks of New Orleans, refer to themselves as Creole, meaning of mixed ancestry. In addition, some whites of French descent in New Orleans are called Creoles. To add to the confusion, a Creole language, based on French and African vocabulary and grammar, is spoken in Haiti, Martinique, and Guadeloupe—and in Louisiana. When referring to the cuisine, though, Creole has come to describe the French style that developed in New Orleans. Through the years, with the arrival of the Spanish,

Africans, Germans, Italians, and English who came to Louisiana, most by way of New Orleans, the cuisine was influenced by all of those cultures as well. Trade with the West Indies, Haiti, Mexico, and Cuba had its impact. A new culinary form began to evolve. Yet another culture, another influence, came from a group of settlers who began to arrive in Louisiana in the mid-eighteenth century, the Acadians. These hardy people had first come to the New World from France as early as the seventeenth century and settled in Canada, in what is now called Nova Scotia, but was then known as Acadie. Though their numbers were small, the Acadians apparently constituted a cultural and political threat to the British colonists, who drove them out of their homes in the eighteenth century. The Acadians lived off the land and the sea; they bothered no one and still spoke French as it had been spoken when they left France. When the English took over Canada, the Acadians refused to swear allegiance to the English flag, and they refused to give up Catholicism. In 1755, they were deported. The women and children were cruelly separated from the men, and the exiles were sent in every direction with no regard for family ties. The saga of the Acadians' search for a new home was immortalized by Henry Wadsworth Longfellow in his epic work *Evangeline*, which tells of the tragic plight of a young betrothed couple separated during the mass deportation. Longfellow's characters, Evangeline and Gabriel, arrive in Baltimore and Georgia, respectively. They both come eventually to the Louisiana territorial settlement of Poste des Attakapas, a French and Indian trading post later to become St. Martinville. In Longfellow's poem, Gabriel

arrives first, becomes restless, and leaves in search of Evangeline.
Subsequently she arrives, learns of Gabriel's departure and continues her search, ending at a Philadelphia almshouse where Gabriel
lies gravely ill. As she kneels beside him, he draws his last breath
with Evangeline's name on his lips. According to Acadian
lore, based mostly on fact, Louis Arceneaux (Gabriel) arrived in
Poste des Attakapas before Emmeline Labiche (Evangeline).

Convinced he would never again see his lost fiancée, he
marries another Acadian maiden. Some years later, as a
group of Acadian exiles steps from a boat onto the shore
of Bayou Teche, Louis sees Emmeline, her eyes still
searching for him. Louis rushes to her and takes her in
his arms. But after Emmeline learns that he has married,
she suffers a breakdown and never regains her health.
Within months, she dies and is buried behind the church
in St. Martinville. Like these tragic figures, the
Acadians wandered for ten years or more looking for
each other and searching for a new home. Many died; some simply disappeared. Many settled along the eastern seaboard, while
others returned to France. Some survivors found their way to New
Orleans, where they were accepted by the French and Spanish
Catholics who lived there. But city life was not for them, and many
gradually settled in the swamps and waterways of south Louisiana.
Life in the wetlands was not the Eden they expected,
but the Cajuns, as Acadians came to be called, were used to living
off the land. They quickly adapted to their environment. They
learned to make do with what ingredients were on hand and what

they could grow in the rich alluvial soil along the bayous and streams. They traded secrets with one another, and they developed a Cajun cuisine that was mostly French inspired, but was also influenced by the other settlers who found their way to Louisiana. Perhaps because of their sufferings and probably because of their sheer tenacity, the descendants of those wanderers are fiercely proud, with a strong appreciation of their heritage. Cajuns need little or no reason for a party, and they share a twenty-four-hour-a-day love affair with food. This legacy has become the focus of what Louisiana cuisine means to me. This strong determination to preserve the Cajun culture is found primarily in Acadiana, but you will also find it in varying degrees throughout the state. Cajuns bring with them their joie de vivre wherever they go. Within this culture exist certain subcultures, each with its own style, each with its own charm, its own accent. Take for instance, the Acadians who settled on *la prairie tremblante*, the trembling prairie, their name for the marshlands that are neither land nor water, but a combination of both. The gumbos and other dishes of that area will more than likely contain a variety of seafood. Cajuns to the north and inland use more beef and poultry in their cooking because that is what is more closely at hand. The bayou Cajuns, those who live on the Teche and on Lafourche, each have a different kind of gumbo or jambalaya. Differences and overlapping between the Creole style and the Acadian traditions have also evolved. Acadians tend to favor pot cooking, where practically the whole meal is cooked in one pot, most likely as an accommodation to their rural way of life. They use ingredients from their farms and gardens, and perhaps because they were used to living under strenuous conditions, they tend to serve strong country food, pungent and peppery, often softened with rice. In Acadiana, you will find widespread use of ducks, frogs, pork, homemade sausages, beans, yams, and pecans. The Creole cuisine is a more refined one, due to the aristocratic influences of the French and Spanish settlers who lived in New Orleans.

Ingredients are market oriented, and meals are served in distinct courses. In the Creole kitchen, oysters Rockefeller could be created at Antoine's, breakfast could become a feast at Brennan's. Creole cooking aspires to a grand cuisine, with delicate blends, subtle combinations, and separate sauces. It has made New Orleans a mecca for food enthusiasts. At the same time, poor boys, oysters on the half shell, and red beans and rice are common daily fare in New Orleans. Here is where the overlapping occurs. Rice is used in both cuisines, showing up in jambalayas, gumbos, and in puddings. Seafood, both saltwater and freshwater, appears and reappears like a refrain in a song. In both cuisines dishes are jazzed up with spices and pepper. Gumbos are served in both the country and the city. I liken the development of these two cuisines to jazz, which has its roots in New Orleans. You can add a note here, and a note there. It's the same in their pots. Add a little more pepper, oui? Let it cook a little longer? Pourquoi pas? Change this, change that. If you can't find a shrimp, use a crab. If you don't like okra, use filé to thicken your gumbo. Do whatever it takes to tingle the taste buds. These lusty Acadians and sophisticated Creoles know no limits. I once heard someone say that though the Creoles lived in luxury in New Orleans and along the Mississippi River while the Acadians settled in the swamps and backcountry, the two groups met at least long enough to agree on one rule in all matters of food. The rule was that there is no rule. There is no one way of doing things. You can always be sure that whatever is prepared, the cooks have put heart and soul into their pots and pans. Nowhere else have I found this passion for flavor that encompasses the lives of people day in and day out. The locals discuss in great detail what they enjoyed at a meal yesterday, the quality of the meal they are eating today, and the anticipation of what they may have tomorrow. Listen in on conversations at any fine restaurant, corner café, grocery store, or butcher shop, and you will get the lowdown on the best sausage around, news of a mess of fish caught in the Gulf, or a new recipe using crawfish. What I find even more intriguing is how involved Cajun men are in cooking and in preserving the traditions of the cuisine. They hunt, fish, garden, and spend a great deal of time in the kitchen, not only at the camp but also at home. At most festivals, teams of men are in charge of tending great pots of gumbo and caldrons of jambalaya and boiling up hundreds of pounds of crawfish. These men can prepare a five-course meal fit for a king. Everywhere my travels led me, I was struck by the simpleness of life. Acadians are loose and relaxed, gracious and outgoing. Everything they do, they do with gusto. They laugh heartily, they eat, dance, play, and pray with great enthusiasm. They are eager to share food with strangers or show a visitor how to make a roux. Acadians love to have a good time, and their good times usually include food, lots of it. This legacy runs very deep. It has been passed from generation to generation, and I hope there is no end in sight. This is the Louisiana I want you to experience. I hope you will come to enjoy the rich and tantalizing dishes—crawfish bisque, panfried oysters, bread pudding, gâteau de sirop, and other classics, as well as some new dishes—of this state. Keep in mind that everyone will tell you that his or her recipe is the best, and well it might be. In the same spirit, I will say the ones in this book are among the best. I feel strongly that this very special cuisine should be preserved, and so I welcome you to Louisiana Real and Rustic.

Louisiana
Real and Rustic

CHAPTER 1

The Garde-Manger

WORCESTERSHIRE SAUCE, SEASONING MIXES, PICKLED PEPPERS, AND MORE

ears ago, Louisiana homemakers favored the garde-manger, or food safe. Similar to a pie safe, it was a large wood cabinet where staple ingredients such as flour, salt, rice, oil, and herbs and spices were kept. When foods were put by (canned, preserved, or pickled), they, too, were stored in the garde-manger. Today, mirlitons, okra, peppers, and pears are still pickled, preserved, and canned, and used during winter. With refrigeration, cooks can set aside a day or two several times a year to make broths and stocks and stash them in the freezer for making gumbos, stews, and soups. Seasoning blends, the individual stamp of Louisiana cooks, can be made in batches and stored in airtight containers. Once you try my recipe for Worcestershire sauce, you'll never go back to the commercial kind. Here are recipes to fill a garde-manger that no good Louisiana cook would do without. Pickled mirliton, okra, and peppers are great to munch on and fig preserves are a favorite.

The Louisiana
Real and Rustic Pantry

Andouille A smoked sausage made with lean pork and seasoned with garlic, salt, and hot peppers. Used to flavor many Louisiana dishes, it is similar to the Polish sausage kielbasa, which can be used as a substitute.

Bell Pepper A main ingredient in many of the dishes in Louisiana. Green peppers are used unless otherwise specified.

Boudin Literally means "pudding," but in Louisiana it's a sausage stuffed with bits of pork, cooked rice, green onions, and other seasonings.

Butter Unsalted butter is used in all recipes unless otherwise specified.

Cane Syrup Made by evaporating sugarcane juice. This thick, intensely sweet syrup is favored by south Louisianians, who use it on biscuits, toast, and other breakfast foods. It is also often used in baking and cooking. Steen's 100% Pure Cane Syrup is the most readily available brand, but if you can't find cane syrup, substitute two parts dark corn syrup with one part dark molasses.

Crawfish Freshwater crustaceans resembling miniature lobsters. They are found in rivers and lakes as well as raised commercially in ponds in south Louisiana.

Creole Cream Cheese Made from skim milk that is clabbered, then ladled into perforated molds or cheesecloth to drain overnight. After it is drained, the curds are covered with fresh cream.

Creole Mustard Pungent prepared mustard made from spicy brown mustard seeds rather than the more familiar, but blander, yellow ones. The seeds are steeped in distilled white vinegar, then coarsely ground and left to marinate for up to twelve hours before packing. As a substitute, use any whole-grain prepared brown mustard.

Eggs Large eggs are used in all recipes unless otherwise specified.

Filé Powder Ground sassafras leaves from trees that grow wild along the coast of the Gulf of Mexico. First used as a seasoning by the Choctaw Indians, it is used to flavor and thicken gumbo. Filé powder becomes stringy when boiled, so should be added to a gumbo only after the pot is removed from the stove.

Flour Bleached all-purpose flour is used in the recipes unless otherwise noted. To measure all flour, use the scoop-and-level method.

Garlic Powder Used with fresh garlic in some dishes. The combination gives the food a more pronounced flavor.

Green Onions Scallions anywhere else but in Louisiana. They impart a sharp and fragrant taste to many local dishes. Unless otherwise specified, the entire green onion, both green and white parts, is used.

Gumbo Crabs Hard-shell crabs with the top half removed, the claws and legs still attached. They are used to flavor seafood gumbo.

Ham Hock The three-inch pieces of bone and meat between the foot and the picnic ham. Cured and smoked, hocks are used to flavor dishes like smothered cabbage or cabbage soup.

Mirliton Also known as chayote, vegetable pear, christophine, or cho-cho. The firm crisp flesh, surrounding a single flat seed, has a delicate flavor. It can be pickled or cooked as a vegetable.

Onion Powder Often used with fresh onions to intensify the flavor in a dish.

Pecan The "crown prince of nuts," sold in halves or in pieces. If they are to be chopped or ground, it is so noted in the recipe.

Pickled Pepper Hot peppers (cayenne, tabasco, banana), pickled and used to flavor salads, stuffings, meats, and poultry, especially in south Louisiana.

Pickled Pork The toes and feet of the front legs or the shoulders of the pig, pickled and used to flavor greens, vegetables, and beans. Similar to salt meat.

Poor Boy Also called po boy. A gigantic sandwich made with French bread split down the middle and filled with either roast beef, ham, sausage, or fried seafood—among other things. Believed to have been created by two poor boys, or streetcar workers, Benny and Clovis Martin, and sold for ten cents apiece during the 1914 New Orleans streetcar strike, when several thousand striking poor boys could afford little more.

Rice Long-grain or extra-long-grain white rice (not converted rice) is the choice of Louisiana cooks. It is usually steamed, not boiled.

Salt Table salt is used except where noted as kosher.

Seafood Boil A mixture of dry herbs and spices, wrapped in cheese-cloth or netting, added to the pot of water when seafood, such as crabs, shrimp, and crawfish, is boiled. You can purchase seafood boil in the spice section of most supermarkets or make your own.

Tasso A heavily seasoned smoked ham used for flavoring vegetables, stews, gumbos, and sauces.

Emeril's Worcestershire Sauce

ouisianians, known for liking their food flavorful and piquant, often use Worcestershire sauce. In the mid-1980s while I was executive chef at Commander's Palace in New Orleans, the American Beef Council, looking for a new image for beef, asked some chefs to come up with new recipes. I decided to create my own Worcestershire sauce. It's a rich tangy sauce, wonderful not only on beef but also with chicken and fish. Fresh horseradish root can be found mainly in Asian markets.

2 tablespoons olive oil

6 cups coarsely chopped onions

4 jalapeños, with stems and seeds, chopped (3/4 cup)

2 tablespoons minced garlic

2 teaspoons freshly ground black pepper

4 cans (2 ounces each) anchovy fillets

1/2 teaspoon whole cloves

2 tablespoons salt

2 whole medium lemons, skin and pith removed

4 cups dark corn syrup

2 cups Steen's 100% Pure Cane Syrup

2 quarts distilled white vinegar

4 cups water

3/4 pound fresh horseradish, peeled and grated (about 3 cups)

1. Combine the oil, onions, and jalapeños in a large heavy stockpot over high heat. Sauté for 2 to 3 minutes, or until slightly soft. Add the garlic, pepper, anchovy fillets, cloves, salt, lemons, corn syrup, cane syrup, vinegar, water, and horseradish and bring to a boil. Reduce the heat and simmer, stirring occasionally, for about 6 hours, or until the mixture barely coats a wooden spoon. Strain.

2. Spoon the hot mixture into 3 hot sterilized pint-size jars, filling to within 1/2 inch of the top. With a clean damp towel, wipe the rim and fit with a hot lid. Tightly screw on the metal ring. Process in a hot-water bath (see page 18) for 15 minutes.

3. Using tongs, remove the jars, place on a towel, and let cool. Test the seals. Tighten the rings. Store in a cool, dark place. Let age for at least 2 weeks before using. Can be stored in the refrigerator in a covered jar or bottle indefinitely. Refrigerate after opening.

About 6 cups or 3 pints

Green Jalapeño Sauce

o question about it. People in the Bayou State like their food spicy and hot—not so hot that you can't taste the food, but with a little heat to warm the mouth. In cafés, a condiment tray filled with a variety of local pepper sauces has the place of honor in the center of the table. Customers choose their personal favorite to heat up their dishes according to their own preferences. In recent years there has been a trend of using green sauce made with jalapeño peppers for flavoring local dishes. At Avery Island, near New Iberia, in the southern part of the state, the McIlhenny family has added such a sauce to their Tabasco Brand Products and it's good. But when I get my hands on garden-grown jalapeño peppers, I make my own. A few shakes brighten up grilled fish, chicken, and beef, or adds a little tang to a bowl of soup. Since the volatile oils in the flesh and seeds of the jalapeños, or any hot peppers for that matter, can make your skin tingle and your eyes burn, wear rubber gloves when handling them. Be careful not to touch your face or eyes while working with the peppers.

20 jalapeños, stemmed and cut crosswise into ⅛-inch slices (about 2½ cups)

3 cloves garlic, sliced

½ cup thinly sliced onion

¾ teaspoon salt

1 teaspoon vegetable oil

2 cups water

1 cup distilled white vinegar

1. Combine the jalapeños, garlic, onions, salt, and oil in a nonreactive saucepan over high heat. Sauté for 3 minutes. Add the water and continue to cook, stirring often, for about 20 minutes. Remove from the heat and allow to steep until mixture comes to room temperature.

2. In a food processor, puree the mixture for 15 seconds, or until smooth. With the processor run-

ning, pour the vinegar through the feed tube in a steady stream. Pour into a sterilized pint jar or bottle and secure with an airtight lid. Refrigerate.

3. Let age for at least 2 weeks before using. Can be stored in the refrigerator up to 6 months.

2 cups

Rustic Rub

he secret to Louisiana cuisine is in the seasonings we use. They are the heart and soul of our cuisine. We always judge someone's ability to cook by what his or her food tastes like, not what it looks like. Every Louisiana kitchen, be it Mama's or the local butcher shop's, is stocked with a personal spice blend. Many of the recipes in this book include some of this spice mix. The recipe can be doubled or tripled. This seasoning mix is similar to the one in my first book. I like this version for a real and rustic taste.

8 tablespoons paprika	3 tablespoons onion powder
3 tablespoons cayenne	6 tablespoons salt
5 tablespoons freshly ground black pepper	2½ tablespoons dried oregano
	2½ tablespoons dried thyme
6 tablespoons garlic powder	

1. Combine all the ingredients in a mixing bowl. Blend well.

2. Can be stored in an airtight container in your spice cabinet for up to 3 months.

2 cups

Seafood Boil Seasoning Mix

hen I moved to New Orleans, I was invited to a seafood boil. Like the clambakes I grew up with in Massachusetts, seafood boils are held outdoors and there's always a crowd, plenty of food, and a ritual to the day. Down here, the order of the day begins with gathering the ingredients. The freshest crawfish and/or crabs are bought, usually packed in sacks or hampers. The vegetables—new red potatoes, sweet tender corn, and lots of yellow onions—are at the ready. Links of smoked sausage and whole artichokes have been assembled to throw into the pot. The tables are spread with old newspapers and huge caldrons are filled with herb-flavored water. A Cajun band provides chanky-chank music to keep toes tapping. I like to listen to the old-timers argue about seasoning mix. Some insist that the bagged mix bought at the local market is best, while others prefer bottled liquid seasoning. Of course, lots of salt and cayenne is added along with whatever is used. Here's a mix that I like. This amount is enough to cook five pounds of crabs or crawfish. (See page 94 for boiling procedure.)

1/4 cup mustard seeds

3 tablespoons coriander seeds

2 tablespoons whole allspice

2 tablespoons dillseeds

1 teaspoon whole cloves

6 small dried red chilies crumbled, or 1 tablespoon crushed red pepper

8 bay leaves

1. Combine all of the ingredients together in a jar. Cover and shake well to mix.
2. When ready to use, place the mixture in a square of cheesecloth, draw up the corners and secure with kitchen twine. Add this bag to the pot of boiling water.
3. Can be stored in an airtight jar in your spice cabinet for up to 3 months.

About 1 cup

Chicken Broth

hen making gumbos, stews, and gravies, or any kind of soup, good broth makes all the difference. Discerning cooks in Louisiana pride themselves on their broths and stocks. Always thrifty, they never let anything go to waste. The meat from the chicken that is boiled makes Great Chicken Salad (page 271). And if you're going to fire up the stove to make chicken broth, throw in two birds since it takes no more time to cook more.

2 fryers, rinsed in cool water (2½ to 3 pounds each)

8 quarts water

2 cups coarsely chopped carrots

1½ cups coarsely chopped celery

2 cups coarsely chopped onions

8 garlic cloves

5 bay leaves

2 teaspoons salt

2 teaspoons black peppercorns

1 teaspoon dried rosemary

1 teaspoon dried oregano

1 teaspoon dried basil

1 teaspoon dried tarragon

1. Put the chickens in a large stockpot and cover with the water. Add the carrots, celery, onions, garlic, bay leaves, salt, peppercorns, and dried herbs and bring to a rolling boil over high heat. Reduce the heat to medium and simmer for 1½ hours.

2. Remove from the heat and let cool for about 1 hour.

3. Remove the chickens from the pot. Remove the skin and debone. Cover and refrigerate the meat until ready to use. Return the bones to the pot. If your refrigerator is large enough, put the pot in the refrigerator. If not, pour the broth and bones into smaller containers. Cover and refrigerate for 8 hours.

4. Remove the fat that has risen to the surface. Bring the broth and bones to a boil over high heat. Reduce the heat to medium and simmer for 1 hour. Cool and strain. Store in pint or quart containers in the freezer.

About 5 quarts

Brown Chicken Broth

 hen I want richer taste and deeper color, this is the chicken broth I use. Raw bones, necks, and backs are full of flavor. They are roasted, then boiled to extract every last drop of taste.

1½ pounds raw chicken bones, including necks and backs, skin removed and rinsed in cool water

1 tablespoon vegetable oil

1 cup coarsely chopped onions

½ cup coarsely chopped celery

½ cup chopped carrots

1 teaspoon salt

½ teaspoon freshly ground black pepper

¼ cup tomato paste

1 tablespoon black peppercorns

½ teaspoon dried thyme

½ teaspoon dried oregano

½ teaspoon dried basil

5 bay leaves

10 cups water

1 cup red wine

1. Preheat the oven to 400°F.

2. Toss the chicken bones with the vegetable oil. Season the onions, celery, and carrots with ½ teaspoon salt and ¼ teaspoon pepper. Spread the bones and vegetables evenly on a baking sheet. Roast for 45 minutes.

3. Remove from the oven and spoon the tomato paste evenly over the bones and vegetables. Return to the oven and roast for 15 minutes.

4. Remove from the oven and turn the bones and vegetables into a large stockpot over high heat. Scrape the baking sheet to loosen any browned particles and add to the pot. Add the peppercorns, thyme, oregano, basil, bay leaves, the remaining ½ teaspoon salt, the remaining ¼ teaspoon pepper, the water, and red wine. Bring to a boil. Reduce the heat to medium-low and simmer, uncovered, for about 2 hours. Let cool.

5. Remove any fat that has risen to the surface. Strain. Store in 1- or 2-cup containers in the freezer.

1 quart

Turkey Broth

hen you have a turkey carcass after a holiday meal, use it to make a broth. Highly prized by cooks in south Louisiana, it is used to make Turkey Bone Gumbo (page 68).

1 turkey carcass

3 ribs celery, cut into 4-inch pieces

2 medium onions, quartered

4 quarts water, or enough to cover the carcass

2 teaspoons salt

1 tablespoon black peppercorns

4 bay leaves

1. Place the carcass in a large stockpot. Add the celery, onions, water, salt, peppercorns, and bay leaves.

2. Bring to a boil, reduce the heat to medium, and simmer, uncovered, for 2 hours. Remove from the heat. Skim any fat that has risen to the surface.

3. Strain through a large fine-mesh sieve. Reserve any meat that has fallen off the bones and pick off any meat that may still remain on the carcass. Reserve the onions and celery for gumbo. Use right away or store the broth in quart containers in the freezer.

About 2 quarts

Veal Stock

ere is a hearty stock to use in robust dishes of beef, lamb, or veal. Your butcher can supply you with good marrow bones.

7 pounds veal marrow bones, sawed into 2-inch pieces

1 can (6 ounces) tomato paste

2 cups coarsely chopped onions

1 cup coarsely chopped celery

1 cup coarsely chopped carrots

2 cups dry red wine

1 teaspoon salt

20 black peppercorns

5 garlic cloves

5 bay leaves

1 teaspoon dried thyme

½ teaspoon dried rosemary

6 quarts water

1. Preheat the oven to 450°F.

2. Put the bones in a shallow roasting pan and roast for 1 hour. Remove from the oven and spread evenly with the tomato paste. Combine the onions, celery, and carrots and lay on top of the bones. Return to the oven and roast for 30 minutes. Remove from oven and drain off any fat.

3. Place the roasting pan over medium heat on the stove and pour the wine over the bones and vegetables. Using a wooden spoon, deglaze, scraping the bottom of the pan for browned particles. Put everything into a large stockpot. Add the salt, peppercorns, garlic, bay leaves, thyme, rosemary, and water. Bring to a boil over high heat. Reduce the heat to medium and simmer for 4 hours. Let cool.

4. Remove any fat that has risen to the surface. Strain. Store in 1- or 2-cup containers in the freezer.

2 quarts

Onion Marmalade

his quick marmalade made of caramelized onions with a dose of zippy cayenne is delicious on Country Pâté (page 208) or Rabbit Sausage (page 215).

4 cups finely chopped onions

2 tablespoons vegetable oil

1 teaspoon salt

¼ teaspoon freshly ground black pepper

¼ teaspoon cayenne

¼ cup sugar

2 tablespoons distilled white vinegar

2 tablespoons chopped parsley

1. Sauté the onions in hot oil in a skillet over medium-high heat with the salt, pepper, and cayenne. Cook, stirring often, for about 10 to 12 minutes, or until the onions are golden. Add the sugar and cook for 2 minutes, stirring constantly. Add the vinegar and parsley and cook for 1 minute. Remove from the heat, cool, and serve.

2. Can be stored in an airtight container in the refrigerator for up to 1 week.

1 ½ cups

Quick Pickled Okra

uring the summer months, okra bushes grow thick and tall in roadside gardens. Because okra is used in so many Louisiana dishes (gumbos, salads, and as a side dish), no one wants to be caught with none on hand. At the French Market in New Orleans or at farm stands throughout the southern part of the state, people who do not grow their own, poke around the bins for the youngest, most tender pods, about three inches in length. When I pick up a basket or two at the produce market, I set some aside to pickle. Marcelle likes them in her martinis (page 339) or to garnish a Bloody Mary (page 338), but they're also good just for munching.

1 pound okra pods, washed and sliced in half lengthwise

6 tablespoons kosher salt

2 cups water

3 cups distilled white vinegar

2 tablespoons sugar

2 bay leaves

½ teaspoon cayenne

1 teaspoon brown mustard seeds

2 cups sliced onions

1. In a colander, toss the okra with 3 tablespoons of the salt. Let drain in the sink or over a bowl for 1 hour.

2. Combine the water, vinegar, the remaining 3 tablespoons salt, the sugar, bay leaves, cayenne, and mustard seeds in a nonreactive saucepan over medium heat. Stir to dissolve the sugar and salt. Bring to a boil. Add the onions and cook for 1 minute, until they are slightly soft.

3. Rinse the okra in cool water to remove the salt and any slime that has accumulated. Put the okra in a large plastic bowl or other nonreactive container. Pour the brine mixture over the okra and stir. Cool to room temperature.

4. Cover and refrigerate for at least 6 hours before using. Can be stored in airtight containers in the refrigerator for up to 1 month.

3 quarts

Pickled Mirliton

hroughout late summer and into fall, mirliton vines, heavy with fruit, can be found on many backyard trellises. Ripe mirlitons range from three to eight inches long. The flesh is firm, crisp, and white, with a delicate flavor. Louisiana cooks prepare mirlitons in many ways, and pickling is not the least of these. Once pickled, mirlitons can be used in salads, as a relish, or to garnish a martini.

8 medium mirlitons	6 bay leaves
4 medium carrots, cut into 3-inch julienne	½ cup salt
	¼ cup sugar
1 large onion, halved and cut lengthwise into 1-inch slices	¼ cup whole black peppercorns
20 garlic cloves	1 teaspoon cayenne
4 quarts distilled white vinegar	2 teaspoons dry mustard

1. Cut the mirlitons in half lengthwise. Remove the seeds. Cut each half lengthwise into slices about ¹/₂ inch thick. Put the mirlitons, carrots, onion, and garlic in a large bowl. Cover with ice and cold water. Let sit for 2 hours to perk up the vegetables. Drain thoroughly.

2. In a large nonreactive stockpot, combine the vinegar, bay leaves, salt, sugar, peppercorns, cayenne, and mustard. Bring to a boil. Add the vegetables, reduce the heat, and simmer for 5 minutes. Remove from the heat. Sterilize 7 quart-size preserving jars and keep hot. Soak the lids and keep hot. Pack each jar tightly with the vegetables, dividing them evenly, and enough of the hot liquid to come within ¹/₂ inch of the top. With a clean damp towel, wipe the rim and fit with a hot lid. Tightly screw on the metal ring and process in a hot-water bath (see page 18) for 15 minutes.

3. Using tongs, remove the jars, place on a towel, and let cool. Test seals. Tighten the rings. Store in a cool dry place. Let age for 4 to 5 weeks.

7 quarts

Canning Pickles and Preserves

Sterilizing jars and lids Wash the jars in hot suds and rinse in scalding water, or put through the sanitizing cycle of a dishwasher. Immediately place them on a rimmed baking sheet or put into a preheated 225°F. oven at least 20 minutes before filling. The jars also may be kept in a saucepan of barely simmering water, then dried with a clean towel. The jars must be hot when filled with hot liquid to avoid breakage. Separate the lids from the metal rings. Place the lids in a shallow bowl and pour boiling water over them to soften the rubber seal. Allow to soak for 3 minutes before using. Do not soak over direct heat.

Filling the jars Pack vegetables or fruits tightly into the jars and pour hot or boiling liquid or syrup over them to within $1/2$ inch of the top of the jar. This allows headspace, which is necessary for the expansion of food.

Sealing the jars With a clean, damp towel, wipe the rim of the jar to remove any drips, which would interfere with sealing, and fit with a hot lid. Tightly screw on a metal ring.

Hot-water bath Preserved fruits and vegetables generally need to be processed in a hot-water bath, which destroys microorganisms that cause spoilage. Place the jars on a rack, without touching, in a deep canning kettle with water to cover by one inch. Cover the kettle and boil for the amount of time specified in each recipe. Remove the jars with a plastic-coated lifter to a cooling rack and allow to cool completely before storing. During the heat processing, the contents of the jars expands, forcing some of the air out. The remaining air inside contracts as it cools to create a partial vacuum, which pulls the lids tight against the jar rims. The vacuum and the lid's sealing compound maintain the seal. A popping noise after the contents have cooled is an indication that the seal is complete. To test, press the center of the cooled lid. If it stays depressed, the jar is sealed. If not, refrigerate and eat the contents within two to three weeks or reseal with a new flat lid and repeat the hot-water bath.

Labeling and Storing Write the name of the product and the date it was canned on a label that will adhere to the jar after it has cooled. Canned foods stored in a cool (below 70°F.), dark, dry place will retain their flavor, color, and nutritional value for one year.

Pickled Banana Peppers

 outh Louisiana cuisine relies heavily on peppers. Hot peppers like cayenne and tabasco give food the heat we love. Sweet green bell peppers bring a subdued flavor to a long list of dishes. Banana peppers, which grow on lush bushes from Lake Charles to New Orleans during the hot summer months, are sweet and flavorful and used in salads and relishes. They are pickled for later use, which is how I like them best. When I was growing up in Fall River, Massachusetts, Dad always pickled his yearly crop. He liked them on bread and in his drinks and often used them when he cooked Sunday dinner.

1½ pounds banana peppers

2 quarts distilled white vinegar

1 tablespoon black peppercorns

3 tablespoons salt

1 tablespoon sugar

¼ teaspoon cayenne

6 bay leaves

1 large onion, halved and cut into 1-inch slices

24 garlic cloves

1. With a sharp knife, make a slit in the peppers from stem to tip, do not cut all the way through.

2. In a nonreactive pot, combine the vinegar, peppercorns, salt, sugar, cayenne, and bay leaves and bring to a boil. Add the peppers, onion, and garlic. Cook for 3 to 4 minutes until the vegetables wilt slightly. Remove from the heat.

3. Using tongs, pack the peppers snugly in 6 hot sterilized quart-size preserving jars. Evenly divide the onion, bay leaves, and garlic among the jars, tucking them in between the peppers. Fill each jar with the hot vinegar mixture to within ½ inch of the top. With a clean damp towel, wipe the rim and fit with a hot lid. Tightly screw on the metal ring. Process in a hot-water bath (see page 18) for 15 minutes.

4. Using tongs, remove the jars, place on a towel, and let cool. Test the seals. Tighten the rings. Store in a cool dry place. Let age for at least 1 week before using.

6 quarts

Bread-and-Butter Pickles

arcelle told me about childhood summers with her two elderly aunts, May and Belle, who spent their mornings canning, preserving, and pickling. They had a stove housed on the back porch that was used just for "putting up." Her uncles would set out early in the morning to pick corn and beans. When cucumbers were abundant, Tante May did her magic and put up jars of bread-and-butter pickles. Marcelle was given her own jar to do with as she pleased. She just loved the pickles on ham sandwiches.

6 pounds medium cucumbers, cut crosswise into ¼-inch slices

1 cup salt

1 cup thinly sliced onions

3 cups distilled white vinegar

2 cups sugar

1 cup water

2 teaspoons mustard seeds

1 tablespoon black peppercorns

20 garlic cloves

10 whole allspice

1. Put the cucumber slices in a large bowl. Sprinkle with salt. Add the onions. Cover with ice and cold water. Let sit for 6 hours, adding ice and stirring occasionally. Drain thoroughly.

2. In a large nonreactive pot, combine the vinegar, sugar, water, mustard seeds, peppercorns, garlic, and allspice. Stir to dissolve the sugar. Bring to a boil; cook for 5 minutes. Add the cucumbers and onions; remove from heat. Stir with a wooden spoon for 1 to 2 minutes. Let cool for about 15 minutes.

3. Fill each of 8 hot sterilized pint-size preserving jars with cucumbers and onions, dividing them evenly, and enough of the liquid to come within ½ inch of the top. With a clean damp towel, wipe the rim and fit with a hot lid. Tightly screw on the metal ring. Process in a hot-water bath (see page 18) for 15 minutes.

4. Using tongs, remove the jars, place on a towel, and let cool. Test the seals. Tighten the rings. Store in a cool dry place. Let age for at least 2 weeks before using.

8 pints

Fig Preserves

ach year, around the Fourth of July, you will find people climbing up ladders to pick ripe, juicy figs. Old-timers tell me that you have to keep a keen eye on the fruit so that it is picked at just the right time, and before the birds get to it. The plump purple figs are heavenly, fresh from the trees and plunked in cold heavy cream. When there's a bumper crop, it's time to make preserves. During the winter months, the preserves are delicious on biscuits, Skillet Corn Bread (page 284), muffins, toast, Pain Perdu (page 295), and Home-Style French Bread (page 286). We used them too on our Duck with Fig Glaze (page 156).

16 cups whole figs (4 to 5 pounds)

1 tablespoon salt

1 tablespoon baking soda

8 cups sugar

1. To wash the figs, fill a bowl large enough to submerge the figs with water. Dissolve the salt and baking soda in the water. Using your hands, toss gently so as not to bruise the figs. Drain the water, rinse in clear water, and drain again.

2. Put the figs and sugar in a large pot over medium-low heat. Stir gently as they begin to cook. Raise the heat to medium when syrup forms and let it come to a gentle boil. Simmer, uncovered, for about 3 hours, or until a foam appears around the edges of the pot. Stir occasionally.

3. Spoon the hot mixture into 5 hot sterilized pint-size preserving jars, filling to within 1/2 inch of the top. With a clean damp towel, wipe the rim and fit with a hot lid. Tightly screw on the metal ring. Process in a hot-water bath (see page 18) for 15 minutes.

4. Using tongs, remove the jars, place on a towel, and let cool. Test the seals. Tighten the rings. Store in a cool dark place. Let age for at least 2 weeks before using.

5 pints

Preserved Pears

sk people about their pear tree down here and they will beam with pride. They'll tell you that it just wouldn't be fitting not to have a pear tree. After all, there was always a pear tree, if not in their family yard, in their neighbor's, and everyone shared in the harvest. To this day, you will find people picking pears all summer long. While these preserved pears are good with biscuits and Brioche (page 288), try them on a bed of shredded salad greens, dabbed with a bit of mayonnaise and sprinkled with grated cheddar cheese.

2½ pounds sugar

1 cup port wine

½ teaspoon ground cinnamon

¼ teaspoon freshly grated nutmeg

¼ teaspoon freshly ground black pepper

12 large Oriental or Bartlett pears (about 5 pounds), peeled, cut in half, and cored

1. Combine the sugar, wine, cinnamon, nutmeg, and pepper in a large nonreactive pot over medium heat. Stir to dissolve the sugar, about 2 to 3 minutes. Add the pears and bring to a boil over medium-high heat. Reduce heat to medium, and simmer for about 30 minutes or until a foam appears on the surface and the pears are fork-tender and transparent.

2. Remove the pears with a slotted spoon.

3. Continue to cook the cooking liquid until it has thickened into a syrup, about 1½ hours.

4. Return the pears to the liquid and reheat for about 5 to 8 minutes, or until they are warmed through.

5. Remove the pears and place in 3 hot sterilized quart-size preserving jars. Pour the syrup over the pears to within ½ inch of the top of each jar. With a clean damp towel, wipe the rim and fit with a hot lid. Tightly screw on the metal ring. Process in a hot-water bath (see page 18) for 20 minutes. Using tongs, remove the jars, place on a towel, and let cool. Test the seals.

6. Tighten the rings. Store in a cool dark place. Let age for at least 2 weeks.

3 quarts

CHAPTER 2

Sauces

TARTAR,

REMOULADE,

ROUX,

AND MORE

he first settlers in Louisiana were French, and the food was inspired by the haute cuisine of France. Classic sauces, such as béarnaise and hollandaise, have long been served in the finer restaurants of New Orleans. French aristocrats settled in other parts of the state as well and brought with them sophisticated palates. St. Martinville, a small town on Bayou Teche in the southern part of the state, was called Le Petit Paris with grand balls and lavish dinners the order of the day. Also residing in St. Martinville, and other areas, were the exiled Acadians who brought their own style of French cooking. Recipes, ideas, and ingredients were exchanged and in the process some sauces were redefined. A little cayenne here, some chopped tomatoes there, were added to satisfy the ever-changing tastes as Louisiana cuisine developed through the years. What I find exciting about Louisiana cooking is that there are no hard-and-fast rules. Taste is what counts. For example,

combining some pickled mirlitons with mustard, mayonnaise, herbs, and spices results in a remoulade of a different kind. But, what is a remoulade, you ask? The classical French version is a sauce of mayonnaise with mustard, anchovy paste, pickles, capers, and herbs. In Louisiana, remoulade also includes mustard, and sometimes horseradish, ketchup, chopped onions, green onions, and celery. A Louisiana bordelaise sauce is chock-full of garlic and bears little resemblance to a traditional wine-based bordelaise. In oyster bars, a ketchup-based cocktail sauce is one that I love for dipping.

Roux

he term "roux" is familiar in French cooking, but the kind of roux used in Louisiana is unique. Equal parts of flour and oil are slowly cooked and constantly stirred until the mixture is brown and has a nutlike aroma and taste. It serves as a base and thickening agent for bisques, gumbos, stews, and gravies. In the last few years, I've noticed people have become reluctant to eat anything made with a roux because of the oil. But when a roux is made, say, with half a cup of oil and half a cup of flour, for a pot of gumbo that will serve eight to twelve people, the amount of oil is negligible. Roux is easy to make as long as you follow some guidelines:

Basic Roux

1 cup vegetable oil

1 cup flour

• Use a heavy pot, preferably cast-iron or enameled cast-iron, because it retains heat and cooks the roux evenly.

• Stir the roux slowly and continuously using a metal spatula, wooden spoon, or whisk while it's cooking. Roux gets very hot while it is cooking, so take care when stirring not to burn yourself.

• Discard the roux if small brown or black bits appear. It has burned and will have a bitter taste.

• Cooking time will vary according to the type of pot used, the heat source (gas or electric), the intensity of heat, and the amount of roux that is being prepared. A range of time is given in the recipes, but the color is also indicated to give you a visual clue.

I use three different colors of roux. Blond roux, the color of sandpaper, is used in delicate soups. A medium brown roux, the color of peanut butter, is preferable for gravies and dishes made with fish and some fowl. A dark brown roux, the color of chocolate, which has an intense flavor, is used in most gumbos and stews.

Put the oil and flour in a cast-iron or enameled cast-iron pot over medium heat. Stir slowly and constantly. After 5 minutes, the mixture will begin to foam. This foaming may continue for several minutes. The roux will begin to darken as it cooks and will have a nutty aroma. For a blond roux, cook for 10 to 15 minutes. For a medium brown roux, cook for 30 to 35 minutes. For a dark brown roux, cook for 40 minutes.

When finished, roux can be cooled, then stored for 1 month in an airtight container in the refrigerator. When it cools, the roux will separate. Before using, stir to blend and bring the roux to room temperature.

2 cups

Creole Tartar Sauce

f there's one condiment sauce we can't live without in south Louisiana, it's tartar sauce. There's nothing better to spread on a fried catfish, shrimp, or oyster poor boy. The poor boy is often described as the New Orleans version of a hoagie or sub, but I find the comparison is inadequate, maybe because of the tartar sauce generously spread on the sandwich.

1 egg	1 cup olive oil
1 tablespoon minced garlic	1/4 teaspoon cayenne
2 tablespoons fresh lemon juice	1 tablespoon Creole or whole-grain mustard
1 tablespoon chopped parsley	
2 tablespoons chopped green onions	1 teaspoon salt

1. Put the egg, garlic, lemon juice, parsley, and green onions in a food processor and puree for 15 seconds. With the processor running, pour the oil through the feed tube in a steady stream. Add the cayenne, mustard, and salt and pulse once or twice to blend.

2. Cover and let sit for 1 hour in the refrigerator before using. Best if used within 24 hours.

1 1/3 cups

One-Egg Mayonnaise

 ouisianians consume a lot of mayonnaise (pronounced "MY-O-naze" down here). It's used in salads, slathered on sandwiches, dabbed on vegetables, and spread on cold meats.

1 egg

1 tablespoon fresh lemon
juice

1 cup olive oil

⅛ teaspoon freshly ground
black pepper

½ teaspoon salt

In a food processor or blender, blend the egg and lemon juice for 10 seconds. With the processor running, slowly pour in the oil through the feed tube. Mixture should thicken. Add the pepper and salt and pulse once or twice to blend. Transfer to an airtight container and refrigerate for at least 30 minutes before using. Best if used within 24 hours.

1 ¼ cups

Remoulade

raveling around the state, you will no doubt encounter many different remoulade sauces. Some are very spicy, others are tamer. Some are red, made so with ketchup, others are white, made with mayonnaise. Which is best? Which is right? If you ask a local, he'll probably tell you, the one that is best, or right, is the one *you* like. Remoulade is traditionally served over cold boiled shrimp or chilled lump crabmeat on a bed of shredded lettuce as an appetizer. But no one says you can't serve it with another kind of boiled or steamed shellfish. If you want something a little different, try Shrimp with Warm Remoulade (page 87).

¼ cup fresh lemon juice	3 tablespoons prepared yellow mustard
¾ cup vegetable oil	3 tablespoons ketchup
½ cup chopped onions	3 tablespoons chopped parsley
½ cup chopped green onions	1 teaspoon salt
¼ cup chopped celery	¼ teaspoon cayenne
2 tablespoons chopped garlic	⅛ teaspoon freshly ground black pepper
2 tablespoons prepared horseradish	
3 tablespoons Creole or whole-grain mustard	

Put all the ingredients in a food processor and process for 30 seconds. Use immediately or store. Will keep for several days in an airtight container in the refrigerator.

2 cups

Pickled Mirliton Remoulade

ickled mirlitons, along with some of the pickled carrots, onions, and garlic from the jar, are combined with mayonnaise, mustard, and seasonings to make an unusual remoulade. It's superb on Panfried Oysters (page 104).

1/2 cup chopped Pickled Mirliton (page 17)

4 tablespoons chopped pickled carrots, from the pickling jar

3 tablespoons chopped pickled onions, from the pickling jar

1 tablespoon chopped pickled garlic, from the pickling jar

2 tablespoons chopped parsley

1 tablespoon Creole or whole-grain mustard

3/4 cup One-Egg Mayonnaise (page 29)

1 tablespoon prepared yellow mustard

1/4 teaspoon salt

1/8 teaspoon cayenne

1/4 cup chopped onions

1. Combine the pickled mirliton, carrots, onions, and garlic, the parsley, Creole mustard, mayonnaise, and yellow mustard in a mixing bowl and toss. Add the salt, cayenne, and chopped onions and mix well.
2. Cover and refrigerate for 15 minutes before using. Will keep for at least 24 hours in an airtight container in the refrigerator.

1 1/2 c u p s

Cocktail Sauce, My Way

here are cocktail sauces and then there is this cocktail sauce. When you visit seafood restaurants or oyster bars in Louisiana, you'll find a tray of condiments set out in the middle of the table. It's up to each individual to mix up his or her own batch of sauce for dipping. Some like it hot, others like it hotter. Some like it tart with lots of lemon juice, others like it with only a few drops. *Cher*, I like it this way.

1 cup ketchup	½ teaspoon Tabasco sauce
1 tablespoon prepared horseradish	Pinch of salt
1 tablespoon fresh lemon juice	Pinch of freshly ground black pepper
½ teaspoon Worcestershire sauce	

In a small bowl, combine all of the ingredients and stir to blend well. It will keep, covered and refrigerated, up to 1 week.

1 cup

Hollandaise Sauce

 've included this basic recipe since I use it as the basis for so many other sauces.

2 egg yolks

1 teaspoon fresh lemon juice

1/4 teaspoon salt

1/8 teaspoon cayenne

2 teaspoons water

1 stick (1/4 pound) butter, melted and warm

In a stainless steel bowl set over a pot of simmering water over medium heat, whisk the egg yolks with the lemon juice, salt, cayenne, and water until pale yellow and slightly thick. Be careful not to let the bowl touch the water.

Remove the bowl from the pot and whisking vigorously, add the butter, 1 teaspoon at a time, until all is incorporated. Serve immediately.

3/4 cup

Béarnaise Sauce

Combine 2 tablespoons dried tarragon, 2 tablespoons finely chopped onions, 1/4 teaspoon salt, a pinch of freshly ground black pepper, and 3/4 cup distilled white vinegar in a saucepan over medium heat. Simmer for 15 minutes until almost all of the vinegar evaporates, leaving about 1 tablespoon. Let cool. Can be made ahead and stored for up to 1 day in an airtight container in the refrigerator. Fold into the hollandaise when ready to serve.

Creolaise Sauce

Add to the hollandaise 1 tablespoon Creole or whole-grain mustard and 2 teaspoons finely chopped parsley. Use on fried seafood.

Choron Sauce

omatoes and tarragon are added to this hollandaise-based sauce, which I've spiced up with cayenne and chopped garlic to satisfy the Louisiana palate. My choron goes well with both grilled fish and steaks.

½ cup chopped, peeled, and seeded tomatoes, or ½ cup chopped canned tomatoes	1 tablespoon chopped garlic
	3 tablespoons distilled white vinegar
	1 cup dry red wine
2 tablespoons dried tarragon	1 tablespoon chopped parsley
¼ teaspoon salt	1 recipe Hollandaise Sauce
⅛ teaspoon cayenne	(page 33)

1. Combine the tomatoes, tarragon, salt, cayenne, garlic, vinegar, and wine in a saucepan over medium-high heat. Bring to a boil. Reduce the heat to medium and simmer for 20 to 25 minutes, or until the mixture is dark brown and thick. Remove from the heat and add the parsley. Let cool.

2. Add the mixture to the hollandaise and whisk together until well blended.

3. Choron can be made ahead and stored in the refrigerator, covered, for up to 3 days.

1 ½ cups

Tasso Hollandaise

 **t**asso, a highly seasoned smoked ham, is often used to give a dish the added flavor that's so common to Louisiana cooking. This smoky-flavored sauce is especially good on Fried Soft-shell Crabs (page 81) or any fried seafood. Try it too on grilled steaks.

2 egg yolks

1 teaspoon fresh lemon juice

¼ teaspoon salt

⅛ teaspoon Tabasco sauce

2 teaspoons water

1 stick (¼ pound) butter, melted and warm

About ¼ cup (2 ounces) finely chopped tasso or spiced ham

1. In a stainless steel bowl set over a pot of simmering water over medium heat, whisk the egg yolks with the lemon juice, salt, Tabasco, and water until pale yellow and slightly thick. Be careful not to let the bowl touch the water.

2. Remove the bowl from the pot and whisking vigorously, add the butter, 1 teaspoon at a time, until all is incorporated. Add the tasso and continue whisking for 30 seconds. Serve immediately.

¾ c u p

Port Wine Sauce

ragrant with garlic, tomatoes, and port, this rustic but regal sauce is perfect with Quail with Forcemeat (page 143) and Panéed Quail (page 147). It's also quite compatible with roast pork or chicken.

1 tablespoon butter	¼ cup chopped parsley
½ cup chopped onions	1 tablespoon chopped garlic
½ teaspoon salt	¼ cup port wine
⅛ teaspoon cayenne	1 cup Chicken Broth (page 11)
1 cup chopped, peeled, and seeded tomatoes, or 1 cup chopped canned tomatoes	

1. Heat the butter in a skillet over medium heat and sauté the onions with the salt and cayenne, stirring often, for 4 to 5 minutes, or until soft. Add the tomatoes, parsley, and garlic and sauté, stirring often, for 4 to 5 minutes, or until tomatoes are soft. Add the wine and simmer for 1 minute. Add the broth and simmer, stirring occasionally, for 6 to 7 minutes.

2. Remove from the heat.

3. Let rest for about 5 minutes before serving. The sauce will keep, covered, in the refrigerator for up to 1 week.

1 ¾ cups

Lemon, Butter, and Tomato Sauce

fter going on many fishing trips and watching the men cook the catch, I've learned that they like to flavor their fish with lemons, butter, and, often, tomatoes. Try this on Crispy-Fried Redfish (page 123).

1/4 cup chopped onions	1 teaspoon chopped garlic
6 tablespoons fresh lemon juice	1/2 cup dry white wine
1/4 cup chopped, peeled, and seeded tomatoes, or 1/4 cup chopped canned tomatoes	1/4 cup heavy cream
	1 stick (1/4 pound) butter, cut into 1/2-inch chips
1/4 teaspoon salt	
1/8 teaspoon cayenne	2 tablespoons chopped parsley

1. In a saucepan, combine the onions, lemon juice, tomatoes, salt, cayenne, garlic, and wine over medium-high heat and bring to a boil. Reduce the heat to medium and simmer until vegetables are soft, about 12 minutes.
2. Add the cream and simmer for about 4 minutes or until the sauce thickens. Stirring constantly, add half of the butter, a little at a time. Remove from the heat and, stirring constantly, add the remaining butter. Add the parsley. Serve immediately.

1 3/4 **c u p s**

Bordelaise Sauce

his garlic-flavored sauce can be used for dipping boiled shrimp or ladling over grilled steaks.

3 tablespoons olive oil	1 tablespoon chopped garlic
1/2 stick (4 tablespoons) butter	1 tablespoon chopped parsley
1/4 teaspoon salt	1/4 cup dry red wine
1/8 teaspoon freshly ground black pepper	

In a saucepan over medium heat, warm the olive oil and butter. Add the salt and pepper and simmer for about 4 minutes. Add the garlic and parsley and cook for 30 seconds. Drizzle in the wine and simmer for 3 minutes. Remove from heat and serve immediately.

3/4 **c u p**

CHAPTER 3

Soups, Stews, and Gumbos

TURTLE SOUP,

OYSTER STEW,

SEAFOOD GUMBO,

AND MORE

t any given time, on any given day, big pots simmer on the stoves of Louisiana with the tantalizing aroma of a soup, stew, or gumbo pervading the house and wafting out the windows. It could be a pot of seafood gumbo teeming with plump shrimp and oysters, or maybe a robust beef fricassee. Then again, if the hunters were lucky, it could be a stew of rabbit and wild mushrooms. If it's springtime, a rich crawfish bisque might be in the offing. A pot of fluffy, perfectly cooked white rice stands nearby. One never knows who will drop by and *faire une veillée* (make a visit). Cousins from down the bayou and neighbors from next door may be sharing the next meal at the big kitchen table. There's no need to worry about having enough, for Louisiana cooks are always prepared for unexpected guests, because they

have learned to make do with whatever is at hand. The early settlers brought a knowledge of French cooking with them. When they couldn't find the ingredients they had in France, they used what was available. A case in point is bouillabaisse. Here they found no *rascasse*, eels, or lobsters, but they did find redfish and shrimp. When the Acadians arrived and settled in south Louisiana, they used the wild game that was plentiful in the swamps and marshes for their stews. The Indians showed them how to use sassafras. Black slaves contributed okra from their native Africa. The Spanish introduced peppers.

Courtbouillon

 used to think there were just two kinds of courtbouillon. There is the classic French *court-bouillon*, a spiced aromatic stock used for cooking fish and shellfish, and a New Orleans courtbouillon, a whole baked fish cooked in Creole sauce, a combination of onions, bell peppers, and celery flavored with a healthy helping of tomatoes. But it wasn't until I visited rural south Louisiana that I realized there is another type—a hearty, thick soup of fish, vegetables, and seasonings. This recipe is what Marcelle's papa, Mr. Blackie to all who knew him, called a perfect courtbouillon. His philosophy was that it was best to live to eat, rather than eat to live, and this fish soup proves his point. Serve the soup ladled over steamed rice in large soup bowls and be sure to have lots of crusty French bread on hand.

1½ pounds redfish fillets or other firm white fish, such as snapper, drum, or grouper

1 tablespoon plus 1 teaspoon Rustic Rub (page 9)

⅓ cup vegetable oil

⅓ cup flour

1 cup chopped celery

1 cup chopped onions

½ cup chopped bell peppers

2 mild green chilies or banana peppers, sliced lengthwise in half and seeded

2 bay leaves

1 tablespoon minced garlic

2 cups chopped, peeled, and seeded tomatoes, or 2 cups chopped canned tomatoes

1 cup water

1¾ cups Chicken Broth (page 11)

¾ teaspoon salt

¼ teaspoon cayenne

¼ cup chopped green onions

2 tablespoons chopped parsley

1. Cut the fish fillets into 3-inch pieces. Season with 1 tablespoon of the rub. Set aside in the refrigerator.

2. Make a roux by combining the oil and flour in a large cast-iron or enameled cast-iron Dutch oven over medium heat. Stir slowly with a wire whisk or wooden spoon for 15 to 20 minutes, or until the roux becomes dark brown, the color of chocolate.

3. Add the celery, onions, bell peppers, and chilies. Cook, stirring often, for 6 to 7 minutes. Add the bay leaves and garlic and cook for about 2 minutes. Add the tomatoes, water, and the remaining 1 teaspoon rub. Reduce the heat to medium-low and cook, uncovered, for about 1 hour, or until a thin oil film appears on the surface. Stir occasionally to prevent the mixture from sticking.

4. Increase the heat to medium, add the broth, salt, and cayenne and cook for about 15 minutes. Lay the fish in the mixture and cook for 10 to 15 minutes, or until the fish flakes easily with a fork. During the last 5 minutes of cooking time, add the green onions and parsley.

5. Remove the bay leaves. Serve hot.

4 main-course servings

Bouillabaisse

the early French settlers who arrived in New Orleans had a great fondness for bouillabaisse, a fish stew that originated in Marseilles, made with a variety of fish and shellfish. Without their familiar Mediterranean fish and crustaceans, they could prepare a stew with the local crabs, oysters, shrimp, red snapper, and pompano. When the Acadians passed through the port city on their way to the bayous and marshlands to the west, they more than likely picked up some ideas from their fellow countrymen as to how to contend with the local ingredients for fish soup. But, alas, they had to be even more creative when they discovered they would have to use freshwater fish and, with any luck, some shrimp from the nearby bays. I prefer this version. The flavors of the fish and shrimp meld together with the onions, bell peppers, celery, and tomatoes. A spoonful of rouille or a fiery garlicky mayonnaise gives the soup a finishing touch. Serve in large soup bowls with rice and French bread.

Rouille

1 head of garlic, cut crosswise in half

Pinch of salt

1/2 teaspoon plus 1/2 cup olive oil

1 egg

3 teaspoons fresh lemon juice

1 tablespoon chopped parsley

1/2 teaspoon salt

1/4 teaspoon cayenne

1. Preheat the oven to 375°F.

2. Place the garlic on a square of aluminum foil. Sprinkle with the salt and drizzle with 1/2 teaspoon of the olive oil. Gather the corners of the foil together to make a pouch and seal. Roast for 30 minutes, or until the garlic is soft when tested with a fork. Holding each clove between your thumb and index finger, pop out the garlic from the skin.

3. Place the garlic and egg in a food processor and blend for 10 seconds. Add the lemon juice. With the motor running, slowly add the remaining ½ cup olive oil through the feed tube. The mixture will be thick, like mayonnaise. Add the parsley, salt, and cayenne and pulse 3 or 4 times to blend. Can be stored for up to 24 hours in a covered container in the refrigerator.

Bouillabaisse

2½ pounds freshwater fish fillets, such as perch, bass, trout, or farm-raised catfish

4 teaspoons salt

¾ teaspoon cayenne

3 cups chopped onions

2 cups chopped bell peppers

1 cup chopped celery

¼ cup chopped garlic

¼ pound (1 stick) butter

4 cups chopped, peeled, and seeded fresh tomatoes, or 4 cups chopped canned tomatoes

6 bay leaves

1 pound medium shrimp, peeled and deveined

½ cup dry white wine

¼ cup chopped parsley

4. Season the fish with 2 teaspoons of the salt and ¼ teaspoon of the cayenne. Combine the onions, bell peppers, celery, and garlic in a bowl and season with the remaining 2 teaspoons salt and remaining ½ teaspoon cayenne.

5. Melt the butter in a large cast-iron or enameled cast-iron Dutch oven over medium heat. Place one third of the mixed vegetables on top of the butter, stirring to coat with the butter. Spread the vegetables evenly on the bottom of the pot. Place one third of the tomatoes and 2 of the bay leaves on the vegetables. Place one third of the fish on top of the vegetable and tomato mixture. Layer the vegetables, tomatoes, bay leaves, and fish 2 more times. Scatter the shrimp on top. Add the wine down the side of the pot. Cover and reduce the heat to medium-low. Cook for 1 hour without removing the lid. Remove the bay leaves.

6. Serve in large soup bowls and garnish with parsley. Drizzle 1 tablespoon of the rouille in each bowl. Serve immediately.

8 to 10 servings

Crawfish Bisque

n south Louisiana, crawfish is king. And understandably so. The legend of crawfish that is often told goes like this: After the Acadians were exiled from L'*Acadie* or Acadia, now Nova Scotia, the lobsters yearned for their French friends, so much so that they set out across the country to find them. The journey south was so long and treacherous that they began to shrink in size. By the time they reached Louisiana and their long-lost friends, they were only miniatures of their former selves. Ah, but the story continues... although they shrank in size, their flavor had intensified. To celebrate their reunion, the Acadians created many crawfish dishes—étouffées, stews, boulettes, pies, and this, the sublime bisque—to honor their friends. The preparation of this dish takes time, passion, and love, but the reward is great.

Crawfish and Stock

5 pounds boiled crawfish (page 94) or see Source Guide (page 342)

4 quarts water

1. Remove the tails and peel, reserving the meat and peelings. Clean the head section, using your index finger to remove cartilage and membranes. Pinch off the claws and reserve. Rinse the cleaned heads (you should have about 100) in cool water and soak in cool water for 15 minutes. Drain and pat dry. Set aside.
2. Put the tail peelings and claws in a stockpot and cover with the water. Bring to a boil. Simmer, uncovered, for 45 minutes. Drain. You should have about 3 quarts of stock. Let the stock cool.

Stuffed Crawfish Heads

1/4 pound (1 stick) butter

2 cups chopped onions

1 cup chopped bell peppers

1 cup chopped celery

1 tablespoon salt

1 teaspoon cayenne

10 to 12 ounces crawfish tails (page 44) plus about 1 1/4 pounds peeled uncooked crawfish tails, chopped

2 tablespoons chopped garlic

1/2 cup water

1 1/2 cups dried fine bread crumbs

2 tablespoons chopped parsley

100 crawfish heads

Flour, for dredging

3. Melt the butter in a large skillet over medium-high heat. Add the onions, bell peppers, celery, salt, and cayenne and sauté for 6 to 7 minutes, or until the vegetables are soft and golden. Add the crawfish tails and the garlic. Cook, stirring occasionally, for 8 to 9 minutes, or until slightly golden. Add the water and simmer for 2 minutes. Remove from the heat and put the mixture into a mixing bowl. Add the bread crumbs and parsley and mix well. Let cool.

4. Preheat the oven to 350°F.

5. Stuff each head with about 2 teaspoons of the stuffing. The amount will vary depending on the size of the heads. Reserve any remaining stuffing mixture. Dredge the heads in flour and place on a baking sheet. Bake for 30 minutes.

Bisque

1 cup vegetable oil

1 cup flour

3 cups chopped onions

1 1/2 cups chopped bell peppers

1 1/2 cups chopped celery

1 teaspoon salt

1/2 teaspoon cayenne

2 pounds peeled crawfish tails (uncooked)

3 quarts crawfish stock (page 44)

100 stuffed crawfish heads (above)

1/4 cup chopped green onions

1/4 cup chopped parsley

continued

6. Combine the oil and flour in a large cast-iron or enameled cast-iron Dutch oven over medium heat. Stirring slowly and constantly for 20 to 25 minutes, make a medium brown roux, the color of peanut butter.

7. Add the onions, bell peppers, celery, salt, and cayenne. Cook, stirring often, for 6 to 7 minutes, or until the vegetables are soft. Add the crawfish tails. Stir and cook for 3 to 4 minutes. Add the crawfish stock and bring to a boil. Simmer over medium heat, uncovered, for about 1 hour 15 minutes. Add the reserved stuffing mix, stuffed crawfish heads, and cook, stirring occasionally, for 15 minutes. Add the green onions and parsley.

8. Serve in deep soup bowls. Remove the stuffing from the heads with your fork.

10 to 12 main-course servings

Turtle Soup

n the early 1700s when the French colonists arrived in New Orleans, freshwater turtles were plentiful in the bayous and streams. By adapting their French cooking techniques to local ingredients, the colonists created a new version of an old favorite. This turtle soup is not a thin watery broth, but rather a deep brown potage, smooth and pungent with a whiff of sherry. A single spoonful will show you the magic that can be done when turtle meat is combined with onions, bell peppers, celery, tomatoes, garlic, and other seasonings. In some restaurants, this soup is offered as a first course. In rural areas, it is more often served as a main course. If turtle meat is unavailable, substitute veal or beef for a mock turtle soup. It's not quite the same, but it comes pretty close to the real thing.

1½ pounds turtle meat

2¾ teaspoons salt

¾ teaspoon cayenne

6 cups water

¼ pound (1 stick) butter

½ cup flour

1½ cups chopped onions

¼ cup chopped bell peppers

¼ cup chopped celery

3 bay leaves

½ teaspoon dried thyme

2 tablespoons chopped garlic

1 cup chopped, peeled, and seeded fresh tomatoes, or 1 cup chopped canned tomatoes

½ cup Emeril's Worcestershire Sauce (page 7) or any commercial brand

1 tablespoon lemon zest

3 tablespoons fresh lemon juice

½ cup dry sherry

¼ cup chopped parsley

½ cup chopped green onions

4 hard-boiled eggs, finely chopped

Lemon slices, for garnish

1. Put the turtle meat in a large saucepan with 1 teaspoon of the salt, ¼ teaspoon of the cayenne, and the water. Bring to a boil. Skim off any foam that rises to the surface. Reduce the heat to medium and simmer uncovered for 20 minutes. With a slotted spoon, transfer the meat to a platter. Let cool for a few minutes, then cut into ½-inch cubes. Set aside. Reserve the stock. You should have about 6 cups.

2. In a large saucepan, combine the butter and flour over medium-high heat. Stir constantly with a wooden spoon for 10 to 12 minutes to make a dark brown roux, the color of chocolate. Add the onions, bell peppers, and celery. Stir occasionally for 2 to 3 minutes until the vegetables are slightly limp. Add the bay leaves, thyme, and garlic and cook for 2 minutes. Add the tomatoes and the turtle meat. Cook, stirring occasionally, for 5 to 6 minutes. Add the Worcestershire, the remaining 1¾ teaspoons salt and remaining ½ teaspoon cayenne, the reserved turtle stock, lemon zest, lemon juice, and sherry. Bring to a boil. Reduce the heat to medium and simmer for 10 minutes. Add the parsley, green onions, and eggs and simmer uncovered, for about 45 minutes. Remove the bay leaves.

3. Serve in soup cups or bowls, garnished with lemon slices.

8 servings

Oyster and Spinach Soup

his is a soup version of oysters Rockefeller, one of my favorite dishes. And while the oysters Rockefeller created at Antoine's in New Orleans does not contain any spinach, most other recipes do. Somehow oysters and fresh spinach make a good marriage, especially when teamed with onions, garlic, and parsley and thickened with potatoes and cream. During the cold months of November, December, and January when oysters are at their peak down here, this soup is a good start to any meal.

4 dozen oysters	2 quarts Chicken Broth (page 11)
½ stick (4 tablespoons) butter	4 cups cleaned, stemmed, and shredded spinach (about 6 ounces)
1½ cups chopped onions	
1 cup chopped celery	½ cup heavy cream
2 teaspoons salt	¼ cup chopped green onions
½ teaspoon cayenne	¼ cup chopped parsley
½ teaspoon freshly ground black pepper	4 tablespoons cornstarch
	1 teaspoon Worcestershire sauce
4 bay leaves	½ teaspoon Tabasco sauce
½ cup Pernod	1 tablespoon fresh lemon juice
1 tablespoon chopped garlic	¼ cup freshly grated parmesan
1 large baking potato, peeled and diced (about 2 cups)	

1. Shuck the oysters, reserving the liquor. You should have about 1½ cups.
2. Heat the butter in a large enameled cast-iron Dutch oven over medium-high heat. Add the onions, celery, salt, cayenne, black pepper, and bay leaves. Sauté until the vegetables are wilted, 4 to 5 minutes. Add ¼ cup of the Pernod and the garlic and cook, stirring, for 2 minutes. Add the potato and broth and bring to a boil. Cook, uncovered, for about 20 minutes, or

until the potato is very tender. With the back of a spoon, mash the potato pieces against the side of the pot and stir into the mixture to thicken. Add the spinach, cream, green onions, parsley, and oyster liquor. Continue to boil for 6 minutes.

3. Dissolve the cornstarch in the remaining $1/4$ cup Pernod. Slowly add to the pot, stirring to blend well. Reduce heat to medium. Continue to cook, stirring until the mixture thickens slightly, about 8 to 10 minutes.

4. Add the Worcestershire, Tabasco, lemon juice, oysters, and cheese. Stir. Cook for 4 to 5 minutes, or until the edges of the oysters curl. Remove the bay leaves.

5. Serve hot in soup cups or bowls.

12 servings

Oyster Stew

Sunday dinner, with all the trimmings, is served in Louisiana at noon when extended families gather after church services. It is a custom, too, that a lighter meal is served for supper that evening. In many families, oyster stew, served with soda crackers or French bread, is traditionally enjoyed on Sunday evenings during the winter months when oysters are in season.

½ stick plus 2 tablespoons (6 tablespoons) butter

2 tablespoons flour

½ cup chopped onions

2 cups milk

2 dozen oysters, shucked and drained, with ¼ cup oyster liquor reserved

1 teaspoon salt

¼ teapoon cayenne

¼ teaspoon freshly ground black pepper

3 tablespoons chopped parsley

¼ cup chopped green onions

1 tablespoon chopped garlic

1. Melt ½ stick (4 tablespoons) of the butter in a skillet over medium-high heat. Add the flour and cook, stirring constantly, for 3 to 4 minutes to make a blond roux, the color of sandpaper.

2. Add the onions and cook for 2 minutes. Add the milk, oyster liquor, salt, cayenne, and black pepper and bring to a gentle boil. Stir constantly for 3 to 4 minutes, or until the mixture thickens slightly. Add the parsley, green onions, garlic, and oysters. Bring to a gentle boil and cook until the edges of the oysters curl, 3 to 4 minutes.

3. Cut the remaining 2 tablespoons of butter into chips and add to the stew.

4. Remove from the heat and serve immediately.

4 main-course servings

Creole Onion Soup

his fragrant onion soup is made with a rich chicken broth, then thickened with a creamy blond Louisiana roux and some cheese to give it a silky texture. Topped with French bread croutons tossed with Rustic Rub, it's a soup that I like to serve when it's cold and blustery.

½ cup vegetable oil	2 quarts Chicken Broth (page 11)
½ cup flour	2 cups cubed French bread, lightly toasted
6 cups thinly sliced onions	
1½ teaspoons salt	2 tablespoons olive oil
½ teaspoon cayenne	1 tablespoon Rustic Rub (page 9)
4 bay leaves	½ cup grated white medium-sharp cheddar
½ teaspoon dried thyme	
½ teaspoon dried oregano	½ cup yellow medium-sharp cheddar
½ teaspoon dried basil	½ cup freshly grated parmesan
2 tablespoons chopped garlic	

1. In a large saucepan over medium heat, combine the vegetable oil and flour. Stirring slowly and constantly for about 10 minutes, make a blond roux, the color of sandpaper.

2. Add the onions, salt, cayenne, bay leaves, thyme, oregano, and basil. Stirring often, cook for about 10 minutes, or until the onions are golden. Add the garlic and cook for 2 minutes, stirring constantly. Add the broth and stir to blend well into the roux mixture. Reduce heat to medium-low and cook, uncovered, stirring, for about 1 hour. Remove bay leaves.

3. In a bowl, toss the bread with the olive oil and rub.

4. When ready to serve, add the cheeses, ½ cup at a time, to the soup, stirring to blend until completely melted.

5. Serve in soup cups and top with the croutons.

8 servings

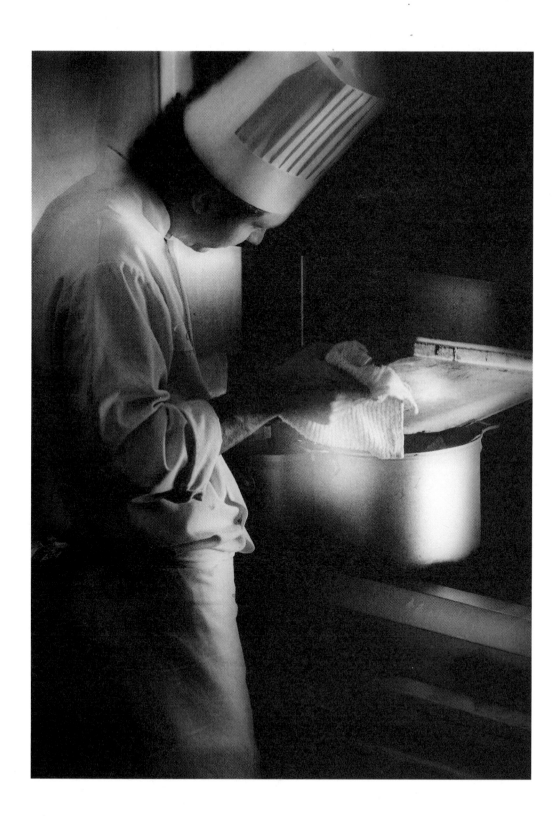

Ham Hock and Cabbage Soup

12/30/98
Really good!

simple soup made with cabbage from the garden and a ham hock from the smokehouse or the local butcher. Marcelle's mama tells me that this soup was often served for supper during the winter months.

1 tablespoon vegetable oil	2 bay leaves
½ pound bacon, chopped	½ teasoon freshly ground black pepper
1 ham hock (about 1 pound)	1½ teaspoons salt
1 cup chopped onions	¼ teaspoon cayenne
1 cup chopped carrots	4 cups Chicken Broth (page 11)
6 cups chopped cabbage (about 1½ pounds)	3 cups peeled and cubed red potatoes (about 1 pound)
3 tablespoons chopped garlic	

1. Heat the oil in a large deep pot over high heat. Add the bacon and fry until it is slightly crisp. Add the ham hock, onions, and carrots. Cook for about 2 minutes, or until the onions are slightly wilted.

2. Add the cabbage, garlic, bay leaves, black pepper, salt, and cayenne. Cook for about 4 minutes, or until the cabbage is slightly wilted. Pour in the broth and bring to a boil. Reduce the heat to a simmer and cook, uncovered, for 30 minutes. Add the potatoes. Cover and cook for 1 hour, or until the cabbage and potatoes are soft and tender.

3. Remove the ham hock from the soup. Pick off the meat and add to the pot. Skim off any fat that has risen to the surface and remove the bay leaves.

4. Serve in large soup bowls.

8 main-course servings

If ham hock already cook i.e. for stock only cook for about an hour of everything

Red Bean Soup

onday's fare is traditionally red beans and rice. In cafés, restaurants, and homes, a big cast-iron pot, filled to the brim with this creamy delight, bubbles and simmers for the better part of the day. Rarely is there any left after a meal, but when there is, it is turned into a delectable soup for the next day. Spiked with a dash of sherry, it's full-bodied and hearty. I like it as a first course with a poor boy.

2 tablespoons vegetable oil

1½ cups chopped onions

½ cup chopped celery

½ cup chopped bell peppers

1 teaspoon salt

¼ teaspoon cayenne

¼ teaspoon freshly ground
   black pepper

4 bay leaves

2 quarts Chicken Broth
   (page 11)

4 cups cooked red beans
   (page 226), pureed in a
   food processor

¼ cup dry sherry

½ cup chopped green
   onions

¼ cup chopped parsley

½ teaspoon Tabasco sauce

1. Heat the oil in a large heavy pot over medium heat. Add the onions, celery, bell peppers, salt, cayenne, black pepper, and bay leaves. Cook, stirring often, for about 5 minutes, or until the vegetables are wilted. Add the broth and beans, stirring to mix well. Reduce the heat to medium-low and simmer, uncovered, until the mixture is creamy, about 2 hours.

2. Just before serving, add the sherry, green onions, parsley, and Tabasco. Remove the bay leaves.

3. Serve hot in soup cups.

12 servings

Creole-Style Tomato Soup

s summer approaches, everyone eagerly waits for the first of the Creole tomatoes to ripen and arrive at the French Market in New Orleans or farm stands along country roads in the southeastern part of the state. The tomatoes, grown in the alluvial soil along the Mississippi River in Plaquemines Parish, south of New Orleans, are especially prized. Agriculturalists believe that the area's soil and weather conditions produce their characteristic flavor. Asked to describe the taste, some locals will say it has a hint of salt and smells like the rich soil. I can only tell you that the taste is distinctive and delicious. Any variety of tomato is considered a Creole tomato as long as it's grown in the soil of the Mississippi Delta. To confuse the matter, there is a Creole variety that is grown in home gardens all over the state; it is quite good, but lacks some of the flavor. If Creole tomatoes are unavailable, select the best plump, red, ripe tomatoes you can find. Serve this soup warm or slightly chilled.

continued

2 tablespoons vegetable oil

2 cups chopped onions

1 cup chopped celery

1 cup chopped carrots

2 teaspoons salt

1/4 teaspoon cayenne

1/4 teaspoon freshly ground black pepper

2 tablespoons chopped garlic

8 cups chopped, peeled, and seeded fresh tomatoes (about 5 1/2 pounds), or 8 cups chopped canned tomatoes

2 quarts Chicken Broth (page 11)

1/4 cup chopped parsley

1. In a large saucepan, heat the oil over medium-high heat. Add the onions, celery, and carrots. Season with the salt, cayenne, and black pepper. Sauté for 4 to 5 minutes. Add the garlic and tomatoes. Cook for 3 to 4 minutes, stirring often. Add the broth and bring to a boil. Reduce the heat to medium and simmer, uncovered, for 1 hour 15 minutes.

2. Remove half of the mixture and puree it in a blender. Return it to the pot. Add the parsley and serve. Or refrigerate and serve chilled.

8 to 10 servings

Creamy Creole-Style Tomato Soup

Add 1/2 cup heavy cream after the soup has been pureed and returned to the pot. Cook, stirring, over medium heat for 3 to 4 minutes, to heat through.

Stewed Chicken and Sausage

1 small chicken (about
2½ pounds)

1 tablespoon Rustic Rub
(page 9)

½ cup flour

¼ cup vegetable oil

1 pound smoked hot pork
sausage, cut crosswise
into ½-inch slices

2 cups chopped onions

1 cup chopped celery

½ cup chopped bell peppers

4 bay leaves

1 tablespoon minced garlic

6 cups Chicken Broth
(page 11)

½ teaspoon salt

¼ teaspoon cayenne

¼ cup chopped parsley

¼ cup chopped green
onions

Northerners don't believe we have cold weather in the South. Believe me, when it's raining and the temperature dips to about forty-two degrees, the chill seeps to the bone. One such cold night found me at a duck camp in Vermilion Parish in the southern part of the state. Unfortunately we had had no luck hunting, but luckily our host had brought along a chicken and some smoked sausage for backup. He and I conspired in the kitchen while the rest of the hunters played cards and sipped bourbon poured over chipped ice. Just when I thought our fellow campers were going to attack us out of sheer hunger, we brought out the pot of this thick hearty stew. Just goes to show what you can do with a roux, a few kitchen staples, a chicken, and some sausage. Serve this in deep bowls with steamed white rice and lots of French bread.

continued

1. Cut the chicken in half, then cut each half into 4 pieces. Season with the rub. Toss the chicken pieces with ¼ cup of the flour to coat evenly. Heat the oil in a large cast-iron or enameled cast-iron Dutch oven. When the oil is hot, add the chicken. Turn to brown on all sides. Cook until evenly browned, 5 to 6 minutes. Add the sausage, stir, and cook for 5 to 6 minutes. Add the remaining ¼ cup flour and cook, stirring constantly, for 2 to 3 minutes.

2. Add the onions, celery, and bell peppers and stir. Cook for 5 to 6 minutes, or until the vegetables are soft. Add the bay leaves and garlic and cook for 5 to 6 minutes, stirring occasionally to prevent sticking.

3. Add the broth, salt, and cayenne and bring to a boil. Reduce the heat to medium-low and cook, uncovered, for 1 hour. Remove the bay leaves.

4. Add the parsley and green onions and serve immediately.

4 main-course servings

Stewed Rabbit

When I was a youngster and Mama fixed a rabbit dish for dinner, it was a celebration. It was my idea to add wild mushrooms to this basic stew, which is flavored with tasso and port wine. I served it one night at the hunting camp with steamed rice and Black Pepper Drop Biscuits (page 294).

¼ cup vegetable oil	1 teaspoon salt
1 small rabbit, cut into serving pieces (about 2½ pounds, dressed)	¼ teaspoon cayenne
1 tablespoon Rustic Rub (page 9)	1 teaspoon coarsely ground black pepper
¼ cup flour	3 ounces tasso, finely chopped
3 cups sliced onions	1 cup port wine
3 cups sliced assorted wild mushrooms, such as shiitakes, oysters, and chanterelles	2 cups Chicken Broth (page 11)
	2 tablespoons chopped green onions

1. Heat the oil in a large heavy skillet over medium-high heat. Season the rabbit with the rub. When the oil is hot, brown the rabbit evenly, about 3 minutes on each side. Transfer the rabbit to a platter and set aside.

2. Add the flour to the skillet and, stirring constantly, make a medium brown roux, the color of peanut butter.

3. Add the onions, mushrooms, salt, cayenne, and black pepper and cook, stirring constantly, for 3 minutes. Add the tasso and cook for 2 minutes. Return the rabbit to the pan and add the wine. Cook for 2 minutes. Add the broth and bring to a boil. Reduce the heat to medium and cook, uncovered, for 30 to 35 minutes, or until the rabbit is tender. Turn the rabbit pieces over in the sauce every 10 minutes to prevent the rabbit from drying out.

4. Sprinkle with green onions and serve immediately.

4 main-course servings

Beef Fricassee

n classic French cooking, a fricassee is a stew of white meat, usually chicken or veal, cooked in a white sauce. But in Louisiana, it's a stew that begins with a dark roux, and it can be made not only with chicken but also with beef, duck, venison, or pork—whatever is at hand, particularly meats that are not very tender. The fricassee is cooked long and slow; the aroma is almost as thick as the stew. It's usually served with rice, but I've also seen it ladled over creamy grits.

3/4 cup vegetable oil

3/4 cup flour

1 pound beef stew meat, cut into 2-inch chunks

4 teaspoons salt

1/2 teaspoon cayenne

4 to 5 carrots, trimmed and cut into 2-inch chunks (about 2 cups)

2 cups chopped onions

1 cup chopped celery

1 cup dry red wine

5 cups water

6 small red potatoes, cut into 2-inch chunks (about 2 cups)

3 bay leaves

1/2 teaspoon freshly ground black pepper

1/4 teaspoon dried thyme

1. Combine the oil and flour in a large heavy saucepan over medium-high heat. Stirring constantly for 10 to 15 minutes, make a dark brown roux, the color of chocolate.

2. Season the stew meat with 2 teaspoons of the salt and the cayenne. Add the meat to the roux and brown the meat, stirring constantly, about 3 minutes. Add the carrots, onions, and celery. Cook, stirring often, for 2 minutes. Add the wine and stir for 1 to 2 minutes, until a paste forms. Add the water and stir to blend into the roux mixture. Add the potatoes, bay leaves, the remaining 2 teaspoons salt, the black pepper, and thyme. Bring to a gentle boil and cook, uncovered, stirring occasionally, for 1 hour, or until the meat is tender.

3. Remove the bay leaves, skim any fat that has risen to the surface, and serve.

4 servings

Frog Legs Sauce Piquante

Piquante means "stinging" and this sauce should be distinctly peppery. Louisiana cooks also make sauce piquante with turtle meat, rabbit, chicken, and just about anything that doesn't eat them first. Men especially like to prepare this dish; I'm told this is so because it allows them to make it distinctly their very own. One cook may add more tomatoes, another may make his gravy thicker than most. One fellow says he likes to use coarsely chopped onions and a handful of green olives. The cook who prepared my very first sauce piquante must have been a staunch pepper lover, because when I finished, beads of perspiration rolled down my face. I developed this recipe one cold afternoon while a fire roared in the fireplace. It's a bit peppery, but not so much so that you won't enjoy it. Serving it over steamed rice quiets down the piquancy. If you prefer even more heat, dribble a few drops of Tabasco on your portion.

continued

2 tablespoons vegetable oil

12 frog legs (about 1 pound)

1 tablespoon flour

1 cup chopped onions

1/4 cup chopped bell peppers

1/4 cup chopped celery

1 teaspoon salt

1/2 teaspoon cayenne

1 bay leaf

1/2 teaspoon dried thyme

2 teaspoons chopped garlic

3 cups chopped, peeled, and seeded tomatoes, or 3 cups chopped canned tomatoes

1 teaspoon Tabasco sauce

1 tablespoon fresh lemon juice

2 tablespoons chopped parsley

1. Heat the oil in a large skillet over medium-high heat. Add the frog legs and brown lightly on both sides, 2 to 3 minutes. Transfer the frog legs to a platter and set aside.

2. Add the flour to the oil. Stirring constantly for 4 to 5 minutes, make a medium brown roux, the color of peanut butter.

3. Add the onions, bell peppers, celery, salt, and cayenne. Sauté for 3 to 4 minutes, or until wilted. Add the bay leaf and thyme. Add the garlic and cook for 1 minute. Add the tomatoes and Tabasco. When the mixture begins to bubble, reduce the heat to medium. Simmer uncovered, stirring occasionally, for 25 to 30 minutes. Lay the frog legs in the sauce and cook for 3 to 4 minutes, basting with the sauce. Sprinkle with the lemon juice and add the parsley.

4. Remove the bay leaves and serve.

2 servings

Chicken or Rabbit Sauce Piquante

Substitute 1 pound boneless chicken or rabbit. Cut the meat into 2-inch cubes. Brown the meat and proceed with the recipe, cooking the meat for 15 to 20 minutes.

Shrimp and Okra Gumbo

All gumbos start with a roux. Well, most of the time. I find that a gumbo made with okra doesn't need a roux because the okra acts as a thickening agent. This one is as rich, thick, and full of flavor as a gumbo should be. Be sure not to cook gumbo made with okra in a cast-iron pot; it will turn black. It's also important to cook the okra until all of the slime disappears. In summer, when okra is young and tender and shrimp are in season, I look forward to a supper of this gumbo eaten outdoors.

2 pounds small okra	1 3/4 teaspoons salt
1/4 cup vegetable oil	1/2 teaspoon cayenne
2 cups chopped, peeled, and seeded fresh tomatoes, or 2 cups chopped canned tomatoes	5 bay leaves
	1/2 teaspoon dried thyme
1 cup chopped onions	2 quarts water
1 cup chopped celery	2 pounds medium shrimp, peeled and deveined

1. Wash the okra in cool water. Remove the caps and tips and cut into 1/4-inch rounds. Heat the oil in a large pot over medium-high heat. Fry the okra, stirring constantly, for 10 to 12 minutes, or until most of the slime disappears. Add the tomatoes, onions, and celery and cook, stirring often, for 18 to 20 minutes, or until the okra and other vegetables are soft and the slime has completely disappeared. Add the salt, cayenne, bay leaves, thyme, and water. Stir and bring to a boil. Reduce the heat to medium and simmer, uncovered, for 15 minutes. Add the shrimp and cook, stirring occasionally, for 30 minutes.

2. Remove the bay leaves and serve in deep bowls.

6 servings

Seafood Gumbo

lassically, a gumbo is a spicy, thick soup composed of fish or shellfish, poultry, game, meat, and vegetables in any of a great variety of combinations. Gumbo is thickened with okra or filé powder, never both, and served ladled over rice. It is a true melting pot dish. The French donated the roux, the basis of gumbos; the okra was introduced by African slaves; the Indians contributed the filé powder. All gumbos are different, much like fingerprints. Seafood gumbo is without a doubt one of the best gumbos offered in Louisiana. In New Orleans, tomatoes are usually added to the pot. An old fisherman prepared this one for me, without tomatoes, on a makeshift burner on his shrimp boat. He had been out all day in the Gulf and he had all of the ingredients on hand. His shrimp boat, a model known as a Lafitte skiff, was washed down, and his work was done. The gumbo simmered while we sipped cold beers and watched other shrimpers putt-putt to their moorings along Bayou Lafourche as the sun dropped below the horizon. The mingling smells of the salt marsh and the aroma from the pot heightened my appetite. By the light of an old lantern, we consumed several bowls of the gumbo before I bid him *adieu*. I've used gumbo crabs to intensify the flavor of the soup, but they are not absolutely necessary. The combination of shrimp, crabmeat, and oysters will give you taste enough.

3/4 cup vegetable oil

3/4 cup flour

2 cups chopped onions

1 cup chopped bell peppers

1 cup chopped celery

1 tablespoon salt

1 teaspoon cayenne

5 bay leaves

8 cups water

6 gumbo crabs, broken in half
   (optional)

1 pound medium shrimp, peeled and
   deveined

1 pound lump crabmeat, picked over
   for shells and cartilage

2 dozen oysters, shucked, with their
   liquor

1/4 cup chopped green onions

1/4 cup chopped parsley

Filé powder

1. Combine the oil and flour in a large cast-iron or enameled cast-iron
Dutch oven over medium heat. Stirring slowly and constantly for 20 to 25
minutes, make a dark brown roux, the color of chocolate.

2. Add the onions, bell peppers, celery, salt, cayenne, and bay leaves. Cook,
stirring occasionally, for about 10 minutes, or until very soft. Add the
water and mix to blend with the roux. Add the crabs and simmer, uncovered, stirring occasionally, for 1 1/2 hours. If you are not using the crabs,
simmer the roux mixture for the same length of time. Add the shrimp and
crabmeat and cook for 15 minutes. Add the oysters, green onions, and
parsley and cook for 2 to 3 minutes, or until the edges of the oysters curl.

3. Remove from the heat. Remove the bay leaves.

4. Serve with the filé powder passed at the table for guests to thicken the
gumbo to their personal taste.

6 servings

Chicken and Oyster Gumbo

 n Louisiana, you'll find gumbos made with crabs, oysters, shrimps, chicken, duck, and, yes, even one made with herbs and greens, Gumbo z'Herbes. Some purists don't like to mix seafood with chicken or duck. Another school says you can do anything you like. I'm with them. In and around Lafayette, the heart of Acadiana, this gumbo is a favorite. *Gumbo, c'est bon—c'est tout.* Gumbo, it's good—that's all there is to it.

3/4 cup flour

3/4 cup vegetable oil

2 cups chopped onions

1/2 cup chopped bell peppers

1/2 cup chopped celery

1 tablespoon salt

1 teaspoon cayenne

2 quarts Chicken Broth
(page 11)

3 bay leaves

1 chicken, cut into 8 pieces
(about 3 pounds)

2 dozen oysters, shucked,
with 1/4 cup of their liquor

3 teaspoons filé powder

2 tablespoons chopped
parsley

---

1. Combine the flour and oil in a large cast-iron or enameled cast-iron Dutch oven over medium heat. Stirring constantly for 20 to 25 minutes, make a dark brown roux, the color of chocolate. Season the onions, bell peppers, and celery with the salt and cayenne. Add them to the roux and cook, stirring occasionally, until soft, about 5 minutes. Add the broth, bay leaves, and chicken. Bring to a boil. Reduce the heat to medium-low and cook, uncovered, stirring occasionally, for 2 hours. Skim off any fat that rises to the surface and continue to simmer for 30 minutes.

2. Add the oysters and the oyster liquor. Cook for 2 to 3 minutes, or until the edges of the oysters curl.

3. Remove from the heat. Remove the bay leaves. Add the filé powder and parsley.

4. Serve in soup bowls with rice.

6 servings

Chicken and Smoked Sausage Gumbo

his chicken and sausage gumbo is dark and sultry. It is favored by the prairie Acadians who live in Evangeline and Acadia parishes. They celebrate Mardi Gras by gathering the ingredients on horseback. They gallop from farmhouse to farmhouse, then rendezvous back in town to cook this gumbo. Serve it with steamed rice.

1 cup vegetable oil	¼ teaspoon cayenne
1 cup flour	3 bay leaves
1½ cups chopped onions	6 cups water
1 cup chopped celery	1 pound boneless chicken meat, cut into 1-inch chunks
1 cup chopped bell peppers	1 teaspoon Rustic Rub (page 9)
1 pound smoked sausage, such as andouille or kielbasa, cut crosswise into ½-inch slices	2 tablespoons chopped parsley
1½ teaspoons salt	½ cup chopped green onions
	1 tablespoon filé powder

1. Combine the oil and flour in a large cast-iron or enameled cast-iron Dutch oven over medium heat. Stirring slowly and constantly for 20 to 25 minutes, make a dark brown roux, the color of chocolate.

2. Add the onions, celery, and bell peppers and continue to stir for 4 to 5 minutes, or until wilted. Add the sausage, salt, cayenne, and bay leaves. Continue to stir for 3 to 4 minutes. Add the water. Stir until the roux mixture and water are well combined. Bring to a boil, then reduce heat to medium-low. Cook, uncovered, stirring occasionally, for 1 hour.

3. Season the chicken with the rub and add to the pot. Simmer for 2 hours.

4. Skim off any fat that rises to the surface. Remove from the heat. Stir in the parsley, green onions, and filé powder.

5. Remove the bay leaves and serve in deep bowls.

4 servings

Turkey Bone Gumbo

friend of Marcelle's loves to make a big turkey gumbo on the day after Thanksgiving. He rises early on Friday, gathers turkey carcasses from friends around town, and spends the rest of the day making broth and putting together his gumbo. By early evening, the friends from whom he got the carcasses gather around his big table for one or two bowls, followed by a serious card game.

3/4 cup vegetable oil

3/4 cup flour

2 cups chopped onions

1/2 cup chopped bell peppers

1/2 cup chopped celery

1 teaspoon salt

1/2 teaspoon cayenne

1/2 pound smoked sausage, such as andouille or kielbasa, chopped

2 quarts Turkey Broth (page 13)

Reserved turkey meat from broth

Reserved onions and celery from broth

2 tablespoons chopped parsley

2 tablespoons chopped green onions

1. Combine the oil and flour in a large cast-iron pot or enameled cast-iron Dutch oven, over medium heat. Stirring slowly and constantly for 20 to 25 minutes, make a dark brown roux, the color of chocolate.

2. Season the onions, bell peppers, and celery with the salt and cayenne. Add this to the roux and stir until soft, about 5 minutes. Add the sausage and cook, stirring often, for 5 minutes. Add the broth and bring to a boil. Reduce the heat to medium-low and simmer, uncovered, for 45 minutes. Add the reserved turkey meat and the reserved onions and celery and cook for 15 minutes. Add the parsley and green onions.

3. Serve in soup bowls with rice. (Filé powder can be added at the table according to personal taste.)

8 servings

Duck and Wild Mushroom Gumbo

y the time winter winds blow through Louisiana, avid sportsmen have readied their hunting camps, located either in the lowlands of south Louisiana or on the lakes scattered throughout the state. When flocks of green-winged teal, mallards, and pintails fly overhead in loose V formations, passionate hunters can hardly wait to prepare the first duck gumbo of the season. A young friend of mine explained once that there are several rites of passage that every young man in south Louisiana must go through on his way to manhood. Eating raw oysters, killing a buck, and mastering the art of frogging are all part of the experience. One ritual that many consider to be the most sacred of all is cooking supper for a group of men at the camp. When I cooked my first duck dinner at a camp, I sweated it out until I was given the nod of approval from my companions. Here is my recipe. If a wild duck is unavailable, a domestic duck will do fine. I advise baking the duck a day ahead.

continued

1 large duck (4½ to 5 pounds) or 2
    smaller ducks of the same weight

2 teaspoons plus ¾ cup vegetable oil

2 teaspoons Rustic Rub (page 9)

¾ cup flour

1½ cups chopped onions

1 cup chopped bell peppers

1 cup chopped celery

2 cups sliced assorted wild
    mushrooms, such as shiitakes,
    oysters, or chanterelles

1 tablespoon chopped garlic

½ teaspoon salt

¼ teaspoon cayenne

½ teaspoon dried thyme

3 bay leaves

2 quarts Chicken Broth (page 11)

2 cups water

2 tablespoons chopped green onions

1. Preheat the oven to 400°F.

2. Rub the duck with 2 teaspoons of the oil and season with the rub. Bake in a roasting pan, uncovered, for 45 minutes, or until tender. Remove and let cool. Cut the duck into 8 serving pieces. Refrigerate until ready to use.

3. Combine the remaining ¾ cup oil and the flour in a large cast-iron or enameled cast-iron Dutch oven over medium-high heat. Stirring slowly and constantly for 12 to 15 minutes, make a medium brown roux, the color of peanut butter.

4. Add the onions, bell peppers, celery, and duck pieces. Reduce the heat to medium. Cook, stirring occasionally, for 10 minutes, or until the vegetables are wilted and golden. Add the mushrooms, garlic, salt, cayenne, thyme, and bay leaves. Cook, stirring often, for 5 minutes. Add the broth and water. Bring the mixture to a gentle boil and simmer, uncovered, for 2 hours.

5. Remove the bay leaves and add the green onions.

6. Serve in soup bowls.

4 servings

Rabbit Gumbo

 raveling around rural Louisiana, you quickly learn why the state is called a "Sportsman's Paradise." The waterways teem with fish, shrimp, and crab. Waterfowl crisscross the skies. The woods are alive with rabbits and squirrels. Whether you're a sportsman or merely a lover of good food, you'll enjoy this rich gumbo, one of my personal favorites, which I ate one day at a camp on Catahoula Lake in St. Martin Parish, which hugs the levee along the Atchafalaya River Basin. A cold front had blown in that morning, and the gumbo was cooked over a wood-burning fire on the bank of the lake.

1 small rabbit, cut into serving pieces (about 2½ pounds, dressed)

1 tablespoon Rustic Rub (page 9)

1 cup vegetable oil

1 cup flour

2 cups chopped onions

1 cup chopped celery

1 cup chopped bell peppers

1 tablespoon chopped garlic

3 teaspoons salt

¼ teaspoon cayenne

¼ teaspoon freshly ground black pepper

3 bay leaves

3 quarts water

1. Season the rabbit with the rub. Heat the oil in a cast-iron pot over medium-high heat. When the oil is hot, brown the rabbit, cooking for 3 to 4 minutes on each side. Transfer to a platter and set aside.
2. Reduce the heat to medium and add the flour. Stirring constantly for about 10 minutes, make a dark brown roux, the color of chocolate.
3. Add the onions, celery, bell peppers, and garlic. Cook, stirring constantly, for about 5 minutes, or until the vegetables are wilted. Add the salt, cayenne, black pepper, and bay leaves. Add the rabbit and cook for 1 minute. Add the water, stirring to mix well. Bring to a gentle boil and simmer, uncovered, for 1 hour, or until rabbit is tender.
4. Remove the bay leaves and serve in soup bowls.

4 servings

Gumbo z'Herbes

his gumbo, sometimes called green gumbo, is often dubbed the king of the gumbos. Sometimes made with a roux, sometimes not, it's always made with assorted greens. Traditionally served on Good Friday throughout Louisiana's predominately Catholic communities, which observed the rules of fast and abstinence, this gumbo could be made without meat. Legend has it that for every green that was put into the gumbo, a new friend would be made during the year. Thus, cooks gathered as many different kinds of greens as possible. These days, green gumbo is eaten on any day of the year, and more often than not, you'll find it made with salt meat or pickled pork. Salt meat is pork packed in coarse salt to preserve it while pickled pork is packed in a liquid brine. They impart more or less the same flavor.

1½ pounds salt meat or pickled pork (optional)

1 teaspoon salt

½ teaspoon cayenne

5 bay leaves

8½ cups water

4 pounds assorted greens, such as collards, mustard or turnip greens, spinach, chard, and kale, trimmed, washed, and dried

2 tablespoons vegetable oil

2 cups chopped onions

1 cup chopped bell peppers

1 cup chopped celery

½ teaspoon dried thyme

½ teaspoon dried oregano

½ teaspoon dried basil

¼ cup chopped fresh parsley leaves

Filé powder

1. Put the meat, if using, with the salt, cayenne, and bay leaves in a large deep pot and add the water. Bring to a boil over medium-high heat and cook for 30 minutes. With a slotted spoon, remove the meat and chop it. Set aside.

2. Reduce the heat to medium and add the greens, a handful at a time, and blanch until they are wilted. Drain, reserving the liquid. Coarsely chop the greens. Set aside.

3. In the same pot, heat the oil over medium heat and add the onions, bell peppers, and celery. Cook, stirring often, until the vegetables are wilted and golden, about 10 minutes.

4. Add the meat, greens, reserved liquid, thyme, oregano, basil, and parsley. Bring to a gentle boil and simmer for 1 1/2 hours. Remove the bay leaves. If not using meat, add 4 tablespoons butter to the pot just before removing from the heat.

5. Serve in deep soup bowls with filé powder passed at the table for guests to thicken the gumbo to their personal taste.

8 to 10 servings

CHAPTER 4

Shellfish

CRAB PIE,

CRAWFISH

PATTIES, SHRIMP

ÉTOUFFÉE,

OYSTERS CANOU,

AND MORE

long the Gulf Coast, from the Sabine River on the Texas-Louisiana border, to the east where the Pearl River marks the state line on the Mississippi border, is a vast area that is sometimes referred to as the liquid land. Millions of acres of marshland where the swaying marsh grass interlaced with water pools gives an illusion of sameness. It's neither land nor sea, but a combination of both. This seemingly desolate area, lying between the swamps and the Gulf, where an occasional whiff of sea salt blows gently from the south, teems with wildlife. Blue crabs and shrimp thrive in the brackish water of inland bays that are fed by the waters of the Gulf. Freshwater crawfish habitate the swamps of the lower Atchafalaya River Basin. When French settlers, followed by the Spanish, then the Acadians, arrived in this untamed wilderness, it did not take them long to combine their cooking techniques with the abundantly available crabs, shrimp, and crawfish. Crab Chops, Crab Pie, and Crabmeat

Ravigote have become local favorites. Fried soft-shell crabs are a delicacy, and sweet bay or Gulf shrimp are boiled, fried, sautéed, and combined with local vegetables. Crawfish, pond-raised or harvested in deep fresh water, are the quintessential crustaceans of the state. Crawfish Pie, Crawfish Étouffée, and Crawfish Bisque (page 44), dishes that for years were cooked and served only at home, because visitors were repulsed at the thought of eating "mudbugs," are found on menus in restaurants and cafés throughout the state. If you are a seafood lover, as I am, the repertoire of dishes in this section is for you. The ingredients are simple and the preparations, for the most part, take little time.

Crab Chops

 hese patties are called crab chops because of the way they are formed to resemble breaded veal or pork chops. They were probably prepared in this manner for meatless Fridays and the Lenten days of abstinence. Whatever the origin, they are popular both in the city and in the country. The crabmeat is held together with a thick white sauce and then coated with bread crumbs before being fried. I like to dab them with Creole Tartar Sauce (page 28) after they are cooked.

7 tablespoons butter	1 egg, beaten
2 tablespoons flour	1 pound lump crabmeat, picked over for shells and cartilage
½ cup chopped green onions	
1 teaspoon salt	20 saltine crackers, finely crushed in a blender or food processor
¼ teaspoon cayenne	
¼ teaspoon freshly ground black pepper	1 cup dried fine bread crumbs
	1 tablespoon Rustic Rub (page 9)
1 cup milk	¼ cup vegetable oil

1. Melt 3 tablespoons of the butter in a large skillet over medium heat. Add the flour and whisk for 2 to 3 minutes, or until well blended.

2. Add the green onions, salt, cayenne, and black pepper. Stir for 2 to 3 minutes. Slowly add the milk and stir constantly until mixture thickens, about 4 minutes. Remove from the heat.

3. In a mixing bowl, combine the egg with the crabmeat and cracker crumbs. Mix gently so as not to break up the crabmeat. Fold in the milk mixture and let cool. Divide the mixture into 6 equal portions and shape into patties, in the shape of chops if you wish. In a shallow bowl, combine the bread crumbs and the rub.

4. Heat the remaining 4 tablespoons butter and the oil in a nonstick skillet over medium-high heat. Dredge the patties, coating evenly, in the bread crumb mixture. Fry the patties for 3 to 4 minutes on each side, or until golden brown.

5. Drain on paper towels and serve hot.

6 servings

Crab Pie

uring the warm months, when we have a windfall of fresh crab, everyone is looking for different ways to prepare the delicate sweet meat, like this gratin. It's really more like a crustless pie or casserole. I like to serve it as a first course or for Sunday supper with hot French bread and a Fried Okra Salad (page 269).

1 tablespoon butter	1 pound lump crabmeat, picked over for shells and cartilage
1 tablespoon flour	
½ cup chopped onions	3 tablespoons chopped parsley
¼ cup chopped celery	3 tablespoons chopped green onions
1 teaspoon salt	½ cup dried fine bread crumbs
¼ teaspoon cayenne	2 teaspoons Rustic Rub (page 9)
1½ cups milk	4 ounces grated white cheddar (about 1 cup)

1. Preheat the oven to 400°F.

2. Combine the butter and flour in a skillet over medium heat. Stir for 3 to 4 minutes, or until well blended.

3. Add the onions, celery, salt, and cayenne. Cook, stirring for 3 to 4 minutes, or until slightly soft. Add the milk. Stir for 3 to 4 minutes, or until the sauce thickens slightly. Add the crabmeat, parsley, and green onions. Stir and cook for about 1 minute. Remove from the heat.

4. Pour the mixture into a 9-inch glass pie dish or 6 small ramekins.

5. Combine the bread crumbs and the rub. Sprinkle over the top of the crabmeat mixture. Sprinkle the cheese over the bread crumbs. Bake for about 20 minutes or until bubbly and brown.

6. Remove from the oven and let stand for 2 minutes before serving.

6 first-course servings

Crabmeat Ravigote

avigote is a classic French sauce that is traditionally served with calf's head and brains in France. I prefer it on seafood, hot or cold, shrimp or crabmeat. The word "ravigote" comes from the French word *ravigoter*, which means to invigorate. I'll buy that. Ravigote livens up my palate quite a bit. I also like the sauce chilled on thick slices of tomato.

2 teaspoons chopped garlic

2 tablespoons chopped parsley

6 tablespoons minced onions

2 tablespoons chopped capers

1 teaspoon salt

¼ teaspoon cayenne

2 tablespoons fresh lemon juice

¼ teaspoon Rustic Rub (page 9)

1 pound lump crabmeat, picked over for shells and cartilage

¼ cup Creole or whole-grain mustard

¼ cup One-Egg Mayonnaise (page 29)

1 tablespoon ketchup

1. In a mixing bowl, combine the garlic, parsley, onions, capers, salt, cayenne, and lemon juice and rub. Using a fork, mash and stir the ingredients in the bottom of the bowl to extract all of the flavors. Let sit for about 2 minutes. Add the crabmeat, mustard, mayonnaise, and ketchup. Toss gently but thoroughly. Refrigerate for at least 1 hour.
2. Serve chilled.

4 first-course servings

Soft-shell Crabs

The term "soft-shell" refers not to a kind of crab, but to a specific time in the crab life cycle. All crabs periodically outgrow their shells and live for a few hours in a soft-shell state before the new shell begins to harden. Farming these soft-shells is tricky. Hard-shell crabs are put in underwater boxes and are checked sometimes three or four times a day when they are molting. When the shells split, the crabs creep out with their new paper-thin shells, at which point they are almost entirely edible. To clean soft-shell crabs, use a pair of kitchen shears to cut them across the face. Remove the eye sockets and the lower mouth. Carefully lift up the apron and remove the gills. Cut off the taillike part of the apron. The crabs are then ready to cook.

Fried Soft-shell Crabs

North of New Orleans lies Lake Pontchartrain. On the lake's west end are several casual seafood restaurants, some of which are on piers and jut out over the water. For years, people in and around the city have gathered there for relaxing meals on picnic tables. Amid the din of lively conversation and the lapping of the water, diners dig into trays of boiled crabs and shrimp and platters of fried seafood. It was at one of these places that I enjoyed the best-ever fried soft-shell crabs shortly after moving to Louisiana. I've become a real fan of these crunchy, fried delicacies.

¼ cup flour

5 teaspoons Rustic Rub (page 9)

1 cup dried fine bread crumbs

2 eggs, beaten

2 tablespoons water

4 large soft-shell crabs, cleaned and rinsed gently in cool water

Solid vegetable shortening for deep-frying

1 recipe Spinach Cakes (page 261)

1 recipe Tasso Hollandaise (page 35)

1. Combine the flour with 1 teaspoon of the rub in a shallow bowl. In another shallow bowl, combine the bread crumbs with the remaining 4 teaspoons of rub. In a third bowl, mix together the eggs with the water.

2. Dredge the crabs in the flour, dip into the egg mixture, then dredge in the bread crumb mixture, coating evenly.

3. Heat the shortening to 360°F. Hold the body of the crab with the claws and legs hanging down over the hot fat and carefully drop it in. Repeat with the remaining crabs. Fry until golden brown, flipping the crabs with tongs 2 to 3 times to brown evenly. The crabs will float to the surface of the oil when they are cooked. Drain on paper towels.

4. To serve, place a spinach cake in the center of each dinner plate. Put a crab on each cake, then top with the hollandaise.

4 servings

Soft-shell Crabs with Almonds and Brown Butter

his preparation is simple but elegant. The crabs are panfried, then topped with a brown butter and toasted almonds. Serve the crabs on slices of toasted French bread accompanied with Brabant Potatoes (page 252).

¼ cup flour	1 tablespoon Worcestershire sauce
1 teaspoon Rustic Rub (page 9)	1 tablespoon fresh lemon juice
2 large soft-shell crabs, cleaned and rinsed gently in cool water	1 tablespoon chopped parsley
	2 tablespoons chopped green onions
3 tablespoons vegetable oil	¼ teaspoon salt
½ stick (4 tablespoons) butter	⅛ teaspoon freshly ground black pepper
¼ cup (about 2¼ ounces) sliced almonds	¼ cup heavy cream

1. Season the flour with the rub. Dredge the crabs in the flour, coating evenly.

2. Heat the oil in a nonstick skillet over medium-high heat. Add the crabs, top side down. Cook for about 2 minutes, then turn them over and cook about 2 minutes more, or until golden. Remove from the heat. Transfer the crabs to a warm platter.

3. In another nonstick skillet, melt the butter over medium heat. Add the almonds and, shaking the pan back and forth, lightly toast them. Add the Worcestershire, lemon juice, parsley, and green onions. Stir for about 1 minute. Remove from the heat. Add the salt, black pepper, and cream. Stir to mix.

4. Spoon the sauce over the crabs and serve.

2 servings

Perfect Spiced Boiled Shrimp

ears ago, before the price of shrimp sky-rocketed, it was traditional for families to gather for shrimp boils on Friday evening. Picnic tables were spread with old newspapers and it was nothing for a family of six to eight to eat twenty to twenty-five pounds of shrimp, fresh from the bays. These days, shrimp boils are still held, but only when the prices are reasonable. The shrimp are boiled with the heads and shells on. The trick is to cook them for a very short time, or they become soggy and difficult to peel. Then it's up to each individual to pinch off the heads and deftly peel off the shells. Children learn this method at a young age, else they would starve. At these occasions, it's every man for himself. Sometimes boiled corn and boiled potatoes are served along with the shrimp and, of course, loaves of buttered French bread are always handy. Bowls of Remoulade (page 30) or Cocktail Sauce, My Way (page 32) are placed on the tables for dipping. Down here, people can consume at least a pound (usually more) of shrimp per person. Elsewhere, they might eat less. If you can, buy the shrimp with the heads on. It makes for a more flavorful boil.

continued

2 lemons, halved

4 quarts water

4 bay leaves

3 teaspoons salt

1/2 teaspoon cayenne

2 tablespoons Zatarain's Concentrated Crab & Shrimp Boil

3 pounds large shrimp with heads or 2 1/2 pounds headless shrimp

1. Squeeze the juice from the lemons into a large pot. Add the halves. Add the water, bay leaves, salt, cayenne, and Zatarain's liquid boil. Bring to a boil and cook for 5 minutes.

2. Add the shrimp. Return to a boil. Remove from the heat, cover, and let stand for 4 to 5 minutes. Drain.

3. Cool for about 5 minutes before serving.

4 to 6 servings

Corn-Battered Shrimp

 n the summertime, when the shrimp boats come into port with hauls of fresh Gulf shrimp and the corn is as high as the proverbial elephant's eye, these shrimp are a sure bet for appetizers for a leisurely meal. Golden, crispy, and dipped in Creole Tartar Sauce (page 28), they can be served with Corn Maque Choux (page 234).

1 egg, beaten	¼ cup flour
1 cup milk	¼ teaspoon salt
2 teaspoons Rustic Rub (page 9),	¼ teaspoon freshly ground black pepper
½ heaping cup of corn kernels and the milk scraped from 1 ear of corn	18 large shrimps, peeled, deveined, and butterflied
½ teaspoon baking soda	Sold vegetable shortening for deep-frying
2 teaspoons baking powder	
¾ cup yellow cornmeal	

1. Combine the egg, milk, 1 teaspoon of the rub, and the corn and corn milk in a bowl and whisk for about 1 minute. Add the baking soda, baking powder, cornmeal, flour, salt, and black pepper. Mix well to make a thick batter.

2. Season the shrimps with the remaining 1 teaspoon rub. Roll each shrimp in the batter and coat evenly. Heat the shortening to 360°F. Fry about 3 shrimps at a time, until golden brown.

3. Drain on paper towels and serve immediately.

6 first-course servings

Shrimp Pernod

I like to visit the ports of Morgan City, Grand Isle, or Delcambre along the south Louisiana coast or any of the small fishing communities along the Mississippi River south of New Orleans in Plaquemines Parish. There, one can usually strike a bargain with the fishermen as they unload the shrimp, packed in crushed ice, from the hold of their boats. I can hardly wait to get home to throw them into a pan. The fresh salty-sweet shrimp are spiked with a little Pernod to give them a gentle anise flavor.

24 large shrimps, peeled, deveined, and butterflied	½ cup Pernod
1 teaspoon Rustic Rub (page 9)	2 tablespoons chopped parsley
1 tablespoon olive oil	1 cup heavy cream
½ cup chopped onions	½ teaspoon salt
½ cup chopped celery	¼ teaspoon cayenne
2 tablespoons chopped garlic	1 egg yolk
	1 recipe Spinach Cakes (page 261)

1. Rub the shrimps with the rub. Heat the olive oil in a skillet over medium heat. Sauté the shrimps for 2 to 3 minutes. Add the onions, celery, and garlic and sauté for 2 to 3 minutes. Add the Pernod and cook for 1 minute. Add the parsley and cream and bring to a boil. Add the salt and cayenne and cook for about 1½ minutes, stirring.

2. Push the shrimps to the side of the skillet and add the egg yolk. Whisk for about 30 seconds, then pull the shrimps into the mixture, stirring for about 1 minute.

3. Place a hot spinach cake in the center of each dinner plate. Spoon equal portions of the shrimp mixture over and around the cakes.

4 servings

Shrimp with Warm Remoulade

raditionally, remoulade sauce is served chilled with a variety of cold seafood in Louisiana. At NOLA, my restaurant in the French Quarter, we serve this full-bodied sauce warmed with shrimp over pasta, and the locals and visitors love it. You can substitute scallops if you wish.

1 pound medium shrimp, peeled with tails on and deveined

2 teaspoons Rustic Rub (page 9)

2 tablespoons vegetable oil

¼ cup dry white wine

1 cup Remoulade (page 30)

¼ cup chopped green onions

6 ounces angel hair pasta, cooked and drained

1. Rub the shrimp with the rub. Heat the oil in a skillet over medium heat. Sauté the shrimp for 3 to 4 minutes. Add the wine and cook for 1 minute. Add the remoulade sauce and simmer for about 2 minutes. Add the green onions.

2. Spoon the sauce over cooked pasta and serve immediately.

4 first-course servings

Shrimp Étouffée

*É*touffee simply means "smothered." "Smothering" is a term used in the South, and especially in Creole and Acadian cuisine, for cooking anything in its own juices, and sometimes water or other liquid; because evaporation is kept to a minimum, the flavor is enhanced and intense. You'll find the word "étouffée" spelled many different ways: with two f's, two *e*'s, then again with one f, one *e*, sometimes with accents on the first *e* and on the second to last *e*. It really doesn't matter, it's always pronounced the same— "ay-too-FAY." Traditionalists will tell you étouffée is not made with a roux. Once you add a roux, they say, you have a stew or fricassee. There are those who say you must add tomatoes. But then again, those who know, say no to tomatoes. No roux and no tomatoes. In New Orleans, however, you'll find étouffées made with both a roux and tomatoes. They're good, but they're not a true étouffée. After having tasted many renditions of this dish in New Orleans, I tasted one in St. Martinville and realized what a simple, delicious dish it is. Serve it with steamed rice.

1½ sticks (6 ounces) butter

4 cups chopped onions

2 cups chopped bell peppers

2 cups chopped celery

2 teaspoons chopped garlic

2 pounds medium shrimp, peeled and deveined

2 teaspoons salt

½ teaspoon cayenne

2 tablespoons flour

2 cups water

6 tablespoons chopped parsley

½ cup chopped green onions

1. Melt the butter in a large skillet over medium heat. Add the onions, bell peppers, and celery and sauté until soft and golden, about 10 minutes. Add the garlic and cook for 2 minutes. Add the shrimp, salt, and cayenne and cook for about 4 minutes, or until the shrimp turn pink.

2. Dissolve the flour in the water and add to the shrimp mixture. Stir until the mixture thickens slightly. Reduce heat to medium-low and simmer for 6 to 8 minutes, stirring occasionally. Add the parsley and green onions. Stir and cook for about 2 minutes more.

3. Serve right away.

4 to 6 servings

Eggplant and Shrimp Bake

delicate eggplant perks up when baked with shrimp. In the country towns around Lafayette, in the southern part of the state, you'll find a similar mixture stuffed into eggplant shells, bell peppers, and tomatoes. I like it plunked on top of a thick, grilled pork chop. Or serve this as a side dish with Panfried Catfish with Lemon and Garlic (page 120).

¼ cup olive oil

1 medium eggplant peeled and cut into 1-inch cubes (about 1 pound)

1½ teaspoons salt

½ teaspoon cayenne

¼ teaspoon freshly ground black pepper

1 cup chopped onions

¼ cup chopped bell peppers

¼ cup chopped celery

½ pound medium shrimp, peeled, deveined, and cut into 1-inch pieces

½ teaspoon dried thyme

½ teaspoon dried oregano

2 tablespoons minced garlic

2 cups water

2 tablespoons chopped parsley

1 cup dried fine bread crumbs

½ cup grated parmesan

1. Preheat the oven to 375°F.

2. Heat the oil in a large skillet over medium-high heat. Add the eggplant, salt, cayenne, and black pepper. Sauté for 2 to 3 minutes, or until slightly soft. Add the onions, bell peppers, and celery and sauté for 2 to 3 minutes, or until slightly wilted. Add the shrimp, thyme, oregano, and garlic. Stir and cook for about 1 minute, or until the shrimp turns pink. Add the water and parsley and cook for about 3 minutes, stirring. Remove from heat and add the bread crumbs and cheese. Mix well.

3. Spoon into a casserole dish and bake for about 45 minutes, or until bubbly and golden brown.

4. Serve hot.

4 servings

Eggplant-Shrimp Beignets

beignet makes most people think of the sweet doughnuts or fritters served in the French Quarter with café au lait, but there are all kinds of beignets in Louisiana. When shrimp season opens and gardens yield plump, purple eggplants, I crave anything cooked with these two favorites of mine. These crunchy tidbits are addictive when dipped in Creole Tartar Sauce (page 28).

1 medium eggplant, peeled and chopped (about 1 pound)	3 eggs, beaten
1½ teaspoons salt	1½ cups milk
½ teaspoon cayenne	2 teaspoons baking powder
2 tablespoons vegetable oil	3¼ cups flour
½ cup chopped onions	Solid vegetable shortening for deep-frying
½ pound large shrimp, peeled, deveined, and cut into ½-inch pieces	1 teaspoon Rustic Rub (page 9)

1. Season the eggplant with ½ teaspoon of the salt and ¼ teaspoon of the cayenne. Heat the oil in a skillet over medium-high heat. Sauté the eggplant until slightly soft, 2 to 3 minutes. Add the onions and sauté for about 3 minutes, or until slightly wilted. Add the shrimp and sauté until the shrimp turn pink, 2 to 3 minutes. Remove and set aside to cool.

2. Make a batter of the eggs, milk, baking powder, and the remaining 1 teaspoon salt, and ¼ teaspoon cayenne. Add the flour, ¼ cup at a time, beating and incorporating until the batter is smooth. Add the eggplant-shrimp mixture and fold to mix. Heat the shortening to 360°F. Drop in the batter, a heaping tablespoon at a time. When the beignets pop to the surface, roll them around in the oil with a slotted spoon to brown them evenly. Remove and drain on paper towels.

3. Sprinkle the beignets with the rub and serve.

About 2 dozen

Crawfish

Back in the 1950s, local fishermen brought crawfish from the swampy waters primarily for consumption by their own families. If there was more than enough for even the largest Acadian family, the fishermen peddled the crawfish to friends and neighbors. The Atchafalaya River, which flows south for about seventy-five miles through the Atchafalaya Basin, the largest river swamp in North America, is home to alligators, wild turkeys, many species of fish, waterfowl, mink and muskrat, and zillions of crawfish. Water levels and food supplies in the Basin determine how much crawfish can be harvested in any given year, at any given time. The Basin was once the only source of crawfish, and there was plenty to keep up with the demand. But once crawfish was discovered, about thirty years ago, for the sweet tasty meat, the world began clamoring for more. To meet the demand, crawfish farming has developed into a science. And the mudbug market has soared—and continues to soar. In 1991, over sixty million pounds were harvested in the crawfish farming ponds alone. In 1992, an estimated 125,000 acres of ponds brought in six to eight hundred pounds per acre. That's a lot of crawfish, my friends. Some rice farmers are also crawfish farmers. Once the rice is harvested, the watery fields are turned into crawfish ponds. The fields, or ponds, are then flooded around October for the year's crop of crawfish. As in any farming industry, production depends on weather conditions. Heavy rains and freezes definitely have an effect on the crop. Crawfish season runs roughly from January to June, but again, sometimes weather conditions will allow crawfish to be harvested almost year round. The farmer must maintain a certain water level in the ponds by pumping water in or out and hope that nature provides the food supply. The farmers also have to be innovative to keep production costs down and get the best price they can on the market. Some farmers, for example, are using a new aeration and recirculating system to save money because the old water pumping system has become too costly. When the Basin and the ponds produce a bountiful supply of crawfish, then everyone hopes that demand stays high so that prices won't fall. Customers have become choosy, too. For instance, large live crawfish are in great demand, so the industry has to find ways to grow larger crawfish in the ponds. Purging is done in a couple of instances. In the past, when crawfish were not sold commercially on a large scale, families would catch their crawfish in muddy roadside ditches or in other accessible shallow water. The crawfish were then purged, or cleaned, by placing them in large metal tubs filled with salted water. The crawfish were then removed from the tubs of water, ready for the pot. Nowadays, most commercial fishermen and especially those who farm the ponds, take care of this procedure for the consumer. They place the crawfish in purging tanks, in which aerated water flushes them clean. Purged crawfish also stay alive longer, which is a benefit when they go to market. The crawfish industry has been a boon to south Louisiana. Besides the farmers, there are businesses that peel and boil crawfish for fresh or frozen tails that are shipped all over the country.

Crawfish or Crab Boil

A favorite get-together in Louisiana is a seafood boil. During crawfish season, you'll find anywhere from forty pounds (a sack) to a couple hundred pounds being boiled up for a party. It's a sight to see hundreds of people at company picnics or scores at family reunions standing elbow to elbow, peeling, sucking, and eating mounds of these bright-red bugs. The secret is seasoning the seafood just right. Here are instructions for boiling ten pounds of seafood, which can be done in your kitchen. Serve it with French bread.

2 recipes Seafood Boil
Seasoning Mix (page 10)

8 quarts water

1 dozen small red potatoes,
scrubbed

2 large onions, unpeeled, cut
in half crosswise

2 lemons, halved

1¼ cups plus
1 tablespoon salt

¼ cup plus 1 tablespoon
cayenne

1 large head garlic, cut in
half crosswise

½ pound andouille or
kielbasa sausage

4 ears fresh corn, shucked
and cut in half

10 pounds crawfish or crabs

1. Put the bags of seasoning mix, the water, potatoes, onions, lemons, 1¼ cups of the salt, ¼ cup of the cayenne, and the garlic in a large stockpot. Bring to a boil, cover, and boil for 15 minutes.
2. Add the sausage, corn, and crawfish or crabs. Using a long-handled spoon, stir around and press the contents of the pot down well into the water. Cover the pot and return to a boil. Boil for 2 minutes.
3. Turn off the heat. Add the remaining 1 tablespoon salt and 1 tablespoon cayenne.
4. Using the long-handled spoon, push down the contents in the pot. Cover and let stand for 15 minutes. Drain.
5. Divide the potatoes, onions, corn, and sausage into equal portions and serve with the seafood on large platters or trays.

4 to 6 servings

Crawfish Pie

ou've probably heard the refrain from the song "Jambalaya." It goes: "Jambalaya, crawfish pie, and filé gumbo, for tonight I'm gonna see my cher-a-meeo ..." That song is like the state's national anthem. Crawfish pie has to be experienced to understand the feeling from the heart that these cooks have. The crust is flaky and moist and the filling, well, it's a gastronomic delight. Serve it for supper or lunch, with a salad of crisp greens tossed with Green Onion Dressing (page 280) and some cold beer.

½ stick (4 tablespoons) butter

1 cup chopped onions

½ cup chopped bell peppers

½ cup chopped celery

1½ teaspoons salt

½ teaspoon cayenne

¼ teaspoon freshly ground black pepper

½ cup chopped, seeded, and peeled tomatoes, or ½ cup chopped canned tomatoes

1 pound crawfish tails

2 tablespoons chopped parsley

2 tablespoons flour

1 cup water

½ recipe Basic Savory Pie Crust (page 314)

1. Preheat the oven to 400°F.

2. Melt the butter in a large skillet over medium-high heat. Add the onions, bell peppers, celery, salt, cayenne, and black pepper. Sauté for about 8 minutes, or until golden and wilted. Add the tomatoes and cook for about 6 minutes, stirring occasionally. Add the crawfish tails and parsley. Cook, stirring occasionally, for about 4 minutes. Dissolve the flour in the water and add to the pan. Stir for about 2 minutes, or until the mixture thickens. Remove from the heat. Let cool for at least 30 minutes.

3. Place the crust in the bottom of a 9-inch pie pan and crimp the edges. Pour the crawfish mixture into the pie crust. Place the pie on a baking sheet and bake for about 45 minutes, or until the edges of the pie crust are golden. Cool for several minutes.

4. Cut into wedges to serve.

One 9-inch pie, 6 servings

Crawfish Patties

ne day, at the height of crawfish season, Marcelle, Rock, Tari (my wife), and I joined a group of friends who had just come home with a couple of sacks of crawfish, caught in a pond near Catahoula, a small community in St. Martin Parish within a stone's throwing distance of the Atchafayala River Basin. Everyone squealed with delight when the crawfish were dumped into large metal tubs to be purged. "Y'all, these are as big as some lobsters!" exclaimed the hostess, a tall, brunette Acadian beauty. Her husband, a former LSU football player and as big as the brown bears that roam around Avery Island (where Tabasco sauce comes from), eyed the tub of reddish-brown crustaceans and announced, "I don't know what y'all are going to eat. This looks like just enough for me—all fifty pounds of them." Then, from somewhere in the crowd, came a commanding voice. "Everybody calm down. We're going to boil a few pounds just to get our taste buds warmed up. Then Marcelle is going to make a pot of bisque, Rock is going to peel some tails and fry them up. Some we can use for étouffée and I'll make some of my mama's famous crawfish patties." In the wink of an eye, everyone found himself a corner of the kitchen and went to work. Onions were peeled and chopped. A fragrant roux was stirred in an old black iron pot. I helped the fellow make his patties. These little beauties can be slapped on buns, onion rolls, French bread, or even corn bread. But that night, we made small ones (about two inches in diameter), fried them up, spiked them with Tabasco sauce, and ate them like popcorn. The mixture can also be used as stuffing as for Catfish Roulade (page 122).

½ stick (4 tablespoons) butter	1 pound peeled crawfish tails
1 cup chopped onions	1 tablespoon flour
½ cup chopped bell peppers	1 cup water
½ cup chopped celery	20 saltine crackers
½ teaspoon salt	1 cup dried fine bread crumbs
¼ teaspoon cayenne	1 tablespoon Rustic Rub (page 9)
2 ounces chopped tasso	¼ cup vegetable oil

1. Heat the butter in a skillet over medium-high heat. Add the onions, bell peppers, celery, salt, and cayenne. Cook for 7 to 8 minutes, stirring often, or until lightly browned and soft. Add the tasso and cook for about 2 minutes. Add the crawfish tails and, stirring occasionally, cook for 3 to 4 minutes. Dissolve the flour in the water and add to the crawfish mixture. Stir for about 2 minutes, or until the mixture thickens slightly. Remove from heat and let cool.

2. Put the mixture in a food processor and pulse 2 to 3 times to chop. Add the crackers and pulse several times to combine thoroughly. Shape into 3-inch patties. Season the bread crumbs with the rub. Dredge the patties in the bread crumbs. Heat the oil in a large nonstick skillet and panfry the patties, about 2 minutes on each side.

3. Drain on paper towels and serve hot.

About 10 patties

Crawfish Imperial

hen I first arrived in New Orleans to head up the kitchen at Commander's Palace, I tasted their Crabmeat Imperial, and it is, without a doubt, one of the richest dishes I've ever put in my mouth. The crabmeat was bound together with a rich piquant mayonnaise and served in scallop shells. One day during crawfish season, when I had a heap of crawfish tails, I experimented and came up with this imperial dish of crawfish. I like to serve it as an appetizer prior to a meal of Skillet Snapper (page 125) for a celebratory seafood dinner.

1 tablespoon vegetable oil

3/4 cup chopped onions

1/4 cup chopped bell peppers

1/4 cup chopped celery

3/4 teaspoon salt

1/4 teaspoon cayenne

1 pound peeled crawfish tails

1 tablespoon chopped garlic

2 tablespoons chopped parsley

1/4 cup chopped green onions

1 cup One-Egg Mayonnaise (page 29)

2 tablespoons Creole or whole-grain mustard

1/4 teaspoon Tabasco sauce

1/4 cup dried fine bread crumbs

1/2 teaspoon Rustic Rub (page 9)

1. Preheat the oven to 400°F.

2. Heat the oil in a large skillet over high heat. Add the onions, bell peppers, celery, salt, and cayenne. Sauté for about 5 minutes, or until wilted. Add the crawfish tails and cook for about 5 minutes, stirring occasionally. Remove from the heat. Let cool for about 30 minutes.

3. In a mixing bowl, combine the crawfish mixture with the garlic, parsley, green onions, 3/4 cup mayonnaise, mustard, and Tabasco. Mix well. Spoon the mixture into a 1-quart casserole or into 4 individual gratin dishes or scallop shells. Mix together the bread crumbs, the remaining mayonnaise, and the rub. Spread the top of the crawfish mixture with this mixture. Bake for about 20 minutes, or until bubbly and brown.

4. Remove from the oven and let stand for 2 to 3 minutes before serving.

4 first-course servings

Crawfish Boulettes

boulettes are meat, seafood, or poultry that's been minced, chopped, or pureed and formed into bite-size balls. They are usually coated with flour or bread crumbs and may be fried, poached, or baked. The locals often munch 'em before meals to tease the appetite. Children gobble them up. Adults love them dipped in Creole Tartar Sauce (page 28). They are often served at weddings and large family gatherings.

1/2 cup chopped onions	2 tablespoons chopped parsley
1/4 cup chopped bell peppers	1 teaspoon salt
1/4 cup chopped celery	1/4 teaspoon cayenne
1 pound peeled crawfish tails or 1 pound cooked and peeled shrimp	1/8 teaspoon freshly ground black pepper
4 slices stale bread, broken into small pieces	1 1/2 cups dried fine bread crumbs
1 egg, beaten	1 teaspoon Rustic Rub (page 9)
3 tablespoons chopped green onions	Solid Vegetable shortening, for deep-frying

1. Combine the onions, bell peppers, celery, crawfish, and bread in a bowl and toss thoroughly. Finely chop this mixture in a food processor by pulsing the motor on and off several times. Do not puree. Transfer the mixture to a bowl and add the egg, green onions, parsley, salt, cayenne, and black pepper. Mix well and shape into balls the size of walnuts.

2. Season the bread crumbs with the rub. Roll the balls in the bread crumbs. Heat the oil to 360°F. and deep-fry the boulettes until golden brown. Or bake them in a preheated 350°F. oven for 15 to 20 minutes, or until golden brown.

3. Serve hot, warm, or at room temperature.

About 2 1/2 dozen

Crawfish Turnovers

 first discovered crawfish turnovers at one of the many festivals held throughout the state. A husband and wife team was frying them up in a booth on a street corner. The lines were long, but the reward was great. The hot pastries, filled with perfectly seasoned crawfish, were wrapped in paper napkins, and I sat down right on the curb and ate several. Serve the turnovers for Sunday lunch or supper anytime. Nothing more than a tart green salad is needed to go along with them. Prepare the dough ahead of time since it has to chill.

Turnover Dough

3 cups flour

1 teaspoon salt

1½ cups solid vegetable shortening

3/4 cup ice water

Combine the flour and salt in a mixing bowl. Add the shortening and work it in with your hands until the mixture resembles coarse meal. Using the tines of a fork, stir as much of the water as you need to bring the dough together, 1 tablespoon at a time. Work it with your hands until you have a smooth ball of dough. Don't overhandle the dough. Wrap it in plastic wrap and refrigerate for at least 1 hour.

Crawfish Filling

1 cup chopped onions	1 pound peeled crawfish tails
1/2 cup chopped bell peppers	2 tablespoons flour
1/2 cup chopped celery	1/2 cup water
1 1/2 teaspoons salt	3 tablespoons chopped parsley
1/4 teaspoon cayenne	3 tablespoons chopped green onions
3/4 teaspoon paprika	1 egg, beaten
1/2 stick (4 tablespoons) butter	

1. Combine the onions, bell peppers, and celery in a bowl and season with the salt, cayenne, and paprika.

2. Melt the butter in a skillet over medium-high heat. When the foam subsides, add the seasoned vegetables and sauté until soft and brown, 6 to 7 minutes. Add the crawfish tails and cook for 5 to 6 minutes, stirring occasionally. Dissolve the flour in the water and add to the crawfish mixture. Stir for 1 to 2 minutes, or until the mixture thickens. Remove from the heat and add the parsley and green onions. Cool to room temperature.

3. Preheat the oven to 375°F. and lightly oil a baking sheet.

4. Remove the dough from the refrigerator and place it on a lightly floured surface. With a knife, cut the dough into 8 equal portions. Lightly flour each piece. Using your fingers, flatten each piece into a 6-inch round, about 1/4 inch thick. Fill the center of each one with a heaping 1/3 cup of the crawfish mixture. Brush the edges of each round with some of the beaten egg. Fold the rounds in half and crimp the edges with the tines of a fork. Brush the tops of the turnovers with the remaining beaten egg.

5. Place the turnovers on the baking sheet about 1 inch apart. Bake for 45 minutes, or until golden brown.

6. Serve hot.

8 turnovers

Crawfish Étouffée

elieve it or not, this now-familiar crawfish dish was not known beyond Louisiana until the late 1940s or early 1950s when the oil boom brought an influx of outsiders to Acadiana, and in particular to Breaux Bridge, in St. Martin Parish, now home of the world-famous crawfish festival. It was in this small town on Bayou Teche, or so some food historians tell us, that crawfish étouffée originated. At the time it was unfashionable, except for Acadians, to eat mud-bugs. Now just about the whole world flocks to Breaux Bridge for the rich, full flavors of étouffée. Serve it with steamed rice.

1 stick (¼ pound) butter	1 tablespoon flour
2 cups chopped onions	1 cup water
1 cup chopped celery	1 teaspoon salt
½ cup chopped bell peppers	¼ teaspoon cayenne
1 pound peeled crawfish tails	2 tablespoons chopped parsley
2 bay leaves	3 tablespoons chopped green onions

1. Melt the butter in a large skillet over medium-high heat. Add the onions, celery, and bell peppers and sauté until soft and golden, 10 to 12 minutes. Add the crawfish and bay leaves. Reduce the heat to medium. Stirring occasionally, cook until the crawfish begin throwing off a little liquid, 10 to 12 minutes.

2. Dissolve the flour in the water. Add to the crawfish mixture and season with salt and cayenne. Stir until the mixture thickens, about 4 minutes. Add the parsley and green onions and cook for about 2 minutes.

3. Remove the bay leaves and serve.

4 servings

Oysters

Shortly after moving to New Orleans, I spied a bumper sticker on a beat-up pickup truck at the Acme Oyster House that read "Eat Louisiana oysters and love longer." People strongly believe in the aphrodisiac legends surrounding these plump mollusks; they belly up to oyster bars and eat huge quantities on a daily basis. It's nothing to eat a dozen or two, raw and served on the half shell, then take a breather and have another dozen of them golden fried and piled high on a plate with hot french fries. One of my customers once told me that he sometimes eats oysters seven days a week—oysters Rockefeller, oysters Bienville, oysters en brochette, fried oysters on a poor boy, oyster soup, oyster pie, and, of course, raw oysters, right off the half shell. The oyster fishermen's work is year-round and arduous. The oyster beds along the Gulf Coast must be seeded and reseeded year after year with oyster shells. When the oysters have grown and matured, they are harvested for the market. I've gone out on oyster luggers and watched these men work, hauling up heavy nets and baskets, sorting oysters, icing them down, and racing to the docks to meet up with the refrigerated trucks that will take them to market. Everyone here has a favorite recipe. Marcelle introduced me to Oyster-Bacon Pie. Mr. "Canou" Toups, who welcomed photographer Brian Smale aboard his lugger, was the inspiration for Oysters Canou, and a fun-loving cook in the town of Cut Off on Bayou Lafourche showed me his version of Skillet Oysters.

4 servings

Panfried Oysters

rispy fried oysters are popular for Friday night suppers in the predominantly Catholic communities of south Louisiana. Families, often with children and toddlers in tow, flock to the many seafood restaurants, and are willing to stand in line waiting for their turn at the tables. Everyone can then get caught up on the local gossip, football tales, and hunting forecasts. It's not uncommon to find yourselves seated with the people you met while waiting in line. But what better way to make new friends? Serve these oysters with Real Potato Salad (page 267), the way they do down here. Sometimes I give them a little dazzle by topping them with Pickled Mirliton Remoulade (page 31). Or, you might find it necessary to make a Peacemaker (page 105). Down here, a dozen oysters serve one. That may be a bit much elsewhere, so six oysters per serving will probably suffice. If you need more, simply double the recipe. After frying a dozen, wipe the pan clean, add fresh oil, and start again.

---

1 dozen shucked oysters, drained well

1 tablespoon Rustic Rub (page 9)

½ cup yellow cornmeal

¼ cup vegetable oil

---

1. Season the oysters with ½ tablespoon of the rub. Season the cornmeal with the rest of the rub.
2. Heat the oil in a nonstick skillet over medium-high heat. Dredge the oysters in the cornmeal, a few at a time, coating evenly. When the oil is hot, but not smoking, lay the oysters, four or five at a time, in the skillet. Do not crowd the pan. Cook for about 1 minute on each side, or until golden brown.
3. Drain on paper towels and serve hot.

2 servings

Peacemaker

 n the nineteenth century, according to legend, a New Orleans husband who had spent the night in the French Quarter saloons brought this fried oyster sandwich home to his wife as a *médiatrice*, or peacemaker. Today, the same holds true for husbands or wives who work late or are detained downtown, for whatever reason. Crusty loaves of French bread are cut lengthwise and the soft centers are pulled out to make room for a cargo of fried oysters. Traditionally, the inside of the bread is generously buttered, then layered with the oysters. But if and when a great peace must be made, you'll find them dressed with sliced tomatoes, shredded lettuce, and a goodly amount of tartar sauce.

1 French bread loaf, about 15 inches long, cut lengthwise in half	4 tablespoons Creole Tartar Sauce (page 28) (optional)
½ stick (4 tablespoons) butter, melted	1 cup shredded lettuce (optional)
2 recipes Panfried Oysters (page 104)	2 medium tomatoes, thinly sliced (optional)

1. Pull out the soft centers of each half of the bread. Generously brush the inside of each half with the melted butter and lightly toast the bread in an oven. Arrange the fried oysters on the bottom half of the bread, then set the top half over them.

2. Or, after toasting the bread, spread the tartar sauce on the bottom half of the loaf. Arrange the lettuce on top of the tartar sauce. Arrange the tomatoes on top of the lettuce. Layer the oysters over the tomatoes and set the top half of the bread over them.

3. Cut across into 2 or 4 pieces to serve.

2 servings

Oysters Canou

n a chilly, fall afternoon with an electric-blue sky overhead, Marcelle, Brian Smale, and I boarded a weather-beaten oyster lugger owned and operated by Dallas "Canou" Toups. The boat slowly circled over his oyster beds in Barataria Bay. The brisk sea air tingled our noses as we slurped oysters fresh from the water. We listened to Canou, his tanned face crinkling in a smile, as he went about his work, hauling up his basket, sorting and sacking the mollusks. He talked about the oysters as though they were his children, and indeed in a way they were. Over the years, he had nurtured them, watched them grow and mature, and sent them off to be enjoyed by people all over the state. When we chugged to shore in the waning sun at dusk, he bid us *adieu* and presented us with a bucket of freshly shucked oysters. We couldn't wait to get to the kitchen to cook our treasure. This dish was inspired by Canou because I knew the oysters he gave us were the best of his beds. Serve on toasted French bread or on top of pasta.

2 dozen shucked oysters, with their liquor

1 tablespoon vegetable oil

½ cup chopped onions

½ teaspoon plus a pinch of salt

½ teaspoon coarsely ground black pepper

2 teaspoons chopped garlic

2 tablespoons chopped parsley

½ cup Brown Chicken Broth (page 12)

2 tablespoons Worcestershire sauce

2 tablespoons fresh lemon juice

3 tablespoons heavy cream

2 tablespoons butter

3 tablespoons chopped green onions

1. Drain the oysters, reserving ¼ cup of the liquor. Set aside.

2. Heat the oil in a large skillet over medium-high heat. Add the onions, ½ teaspoon of the salt, and black pepper. Sauté for 4 to 5 minutes, or until wilted. Add the garlic and 1 tablespoon of the parsley. Cook for about 2 minutes. Add the broth, Worcestershire, and lemon juice. Stir until the mixture becomes slightly thick, 4 to 5 minutes. Add the oyster liquor and cream and bring to a boil, stirring occasionally, and cook until the mixture thickens. Blend in the butter. Add the oysters and the pinch of salt. Simmer for about 2 minutes, or until the edges curl. Add the green onions and the remaining parsley. Remove from the heat.

3. Serve right away.

4 first-course servings

Skillet Oysters

hen north winds blow across Barataria Bay, south of New Orleans, oyster luggers cut through the rough, choppy water to the reefs where the oysters are plumped up by the cold water, making them perfect for harvesting. Once shucked, the oysters are quickly cooked with onions, lemon juice, lemon zest, and herbs and spices. With hot French bread and ice cold beer, I can make a meal of these oysters, but you can serve them as a first course.

½ stick (4 tablespoons) butter

1 tablespoon flour

2 cups thinly sliced onions

¾ teaspoon salt

¾ teaspoon freshly ground black pepper

2 tablespoons chopped garlic

3 tablespoons plus 2 teaspoons chopped parsley

¼ cup chopped green onions

1 cup Brown Chicken Broth (page 12)

1 teaspoon Worcestershire sauce

¼ teaspoon Tabasco sauce

1 teaspoon lemon zest

2 tablespoons fresh lemon juice

2 dozen shucked oysters, with their liquor

¾ cup dried fine bread crumbs

½ cup freshly grated parmesan

1 teaspoon Rustic Rub (page 9)

1 teaspoon dried oregano

½ teaspoon dried thyme

1 teaspoon dried basil

2 tablespoons olive oil

1. Preheat the oven to 450°F.

2. Melt the butter over medium-high heat in a large skillet with an oven-proof handle. Add the flour and blend. Cook for 2 to 3 minutes, stirring constantly, until the roux is light brown, the color of sandpaper.

3. Add the onions, salt, and black pepper. Cook, stirring often, for 6 to 8 minutes, or until the onions are golden. Add the garlic, 3 tablespoons of the parsley and the green onions. Cook for about 2 minutes, stirring constantly. Add the broth, Worcestershire, and Tabasco. Stir and bring to a boil. Reduce the heat to medium and cook for 4 to 5 minutes. Add the lemon zest and 1 tablespoon of the lemon juice. Remove from the heat and add the oysters. Mix well and set aside.

4. In a mixing bowl, combine the bread crumbs, cheese, the remaining 2 teaspoons parsley, the rub, oregano, thyme, basil, olive oil, and the remaining 1 tablespoon lemon juice. Mix well. Spread this mixture over the oyster mixture in the skillet. Bake for 15 minutes, or until the mixture is bubbly.

5. Serve hot.

4 first-course servings

Oyster-Bacon Pie

omething like a pot pie with a soft, moist filling, but the similarities stop there. The combination of bacon, onions, peppers, milk, and oysters makes this a full-bodied, lusty dish, best enjoyed on a cold winter's night. Marcelle's Aunt Grace made these during the Christmas holidays when the house was busy with friends and relatives dropping by for a visit or a quick nip. Always gracious and always ready to put something on the big kitchen table, no matter what time of day, she often offered big slices of this thick pie.

½ pound bacon, chopped	2 bay leaves
¼ cup flour	¼ cup chopped parsley
1 cup chopped onions	½ cup chopped green onions
½ cup chopped bell peppers	1 tablespoon chopped garlic
½ cup chopped celery	2 cups milk
2 teaspoons salt	2 dozen shucked oysters, drained well
¼ teaspoon cayenne	
½ teaspoon freshly ground black pepper	1 recipe Basic Savory Pie Crust (page 314)

1. Preheat the oven to 400°F.

2. Fry the bacon in a large skillet over medium-high heat until crisp. With a slotted spoon, transfer the bacon to a platter and drain on paper towels. Set aside.

3. Reduce the heat to medium and add the flour. Stirring constantly for 5 minutes, make a medium brown roux, the color of peanut butter.

4. Add the onions, bell peppers, celery, salt, cayenne, and black pepper. Stirring constantly, cook for about 8 minutes, or until wilted and brown. Add the bay leaves, parsley, green onions, garlic, and milk. Blend into the

roux and vegetable mixture and cook, stirring often, for 8 to 10 minutes, or until the mixture is thick and creamy. Add the oysters and the reserved bacon. Fold into the mixture and cook until the edges of the oysters curl, 2 to 3 minutes. Remove from the heat. Remove the bay leaves.

5. Arrange a pie crust in the bottom of a 9-inch pie plate. Pour the oyster mixture into the crust. Rub the edges of the pie crust with a little water. Place the other crust on top, trim the edges, then crimp together the top and bottom crusts. Make several slashes in the top of the pie crust with a sharp, pointed knife. Place the pie on a baking sheet. Bake for 45 minutes, or until golden brown.

6. Cool for a few minutes. Cut into wedges to serve.

One 9-inch pie, 6 servings

Baked Oyster Dressing

uring the Christmas holidays, when oysters are at their peak, they are often added to a stuffing for chicken, quail, or fish. Baked separately as a side dish, the stuffing goes well with pork. Bruce, Marcelle's baby brother, tells me he sometimes snitches some dressing from the pot and tucks it in hot French bread for a quick snack.

2 dozen shucked oysters, with their liquor

2 tablespoons vegetable oil

2 cups chopped onions

1 cup chopped bell peppers

1 cup chopped celery

1½ teaspoons salt

½ teaspoon cayenne

3 bay leaves

1 tablespoon chopped garlic

¼ cup chopped parsley

1 cup water

¼ cup chopped green onions

4 cups cubed white bread

⅓ cup freshly grated parmesan

1. Preheat the oven to 375°F.

2. Drain the oysters, reserving 1 cup of the liquor. Set aside.

3. Heat the oil in a skillet over medium-high heat. Add the onions, bell peppers, celery, salt, and cayenne. Sauté for about 5 minutes, or until wilted. Add the bay leaves, garlic, and parsley. Sauté for about 1 minute. Add the water and cook for 2 to 3 minutes, stirring constantly. Add the green onions, the oyster liquor, and the bread. Stir. Remove from the heat.

4. In a mixing bowl, combine the bread mixture with the oysters and the cheese. Mix thoroughly. Butter a 9 × 11-inch baking pan and pour in the mixture. Bake for about 1 hour, or until bubbly and golden brown.

5. Remove the bay leaves and serve hot.

4 to 6 servings (about 5 cups)

CHAPTER 5

Fish

ne day while fishing along the banks of a languid bayou near U.S. Highway 90 between Raceland and New Orleans, I visited with an old-timer who had made himself comfortable on a ragged folding stool that was propped next to a wind-twisted water oak. We spoke in hushed whispers while we popped our lines in and out of the dark black-green water. He directed me to throw my line near a half-sunken log and I quickly hooked a silvery catfish. Another cast brought in a perch. Before long, we each had a mess of fish in our ice chests. Before calling it a day, we sipped cold beers while we discussed various methods of preparation for our catches. While explaining the art of frying trout, he proudly told me that he had learned to bait a hook before he could talk and knew the way around the family's kitchen by the time he was six. "*Mon cher*," he drawled, "fresh fish is so good, they can probably be eaten raw. But, oh, when they're batter-fried or pan-fried, baked, or cooked in a sauce, I'm real happy,

GREEN REDFISH,

TROUT

FRICASSEE,

FRIED CATFISH,

AND MORE

moi." Avid fisherman that I am, I have come to be charmed and fascinated with the beauty of the stately oaks that cast shadows on the slow-moving bayous of south Louisiana and the sound of the lapping waters of the coastal bays. I have listened to the sound of silence of the early morning broken only by the putt-putt of a fishing boat in the distance or watched fishermen glide noiselessly by in a pirogue, a light boat made from a hollowed-out cypress log. After a day spent on the water, nothing makes me happier than to dine on my catch of the day, be it delicate catfish, batter-fried or panfried, Skillet Snapper, Smothered Trout, or Cedar Plank Trout.

Rustic Rub for Seasoning Fish Dishes

've spent a lot of time observing Louisiana cooks, especially the men, preparing fish dishes. They are heavy-handed when it comes to seasoning, and their philosophy is that fish can seldom be overseasoned. I have come to agree. While many people feel that fresh-from-the-water fish need nothing more than a dash of salt and a squeeze of lemon, the methods used here bring out the flavor without overpowering it; it's this spiciness that makes the cuisine what it is. The use of my special seasoning mix, Rustic Rub, in several of the fish recipes makes them sound similar, but the cooking techniques are varied and produce different flavors. Don't be apprehensive about the amount of seasoning. This is not a subtle cuisine.

Catfish Pecan Meunière

he French à la meunière technique is a method of preparing any type of fish by lightly dredging it in flour, sautéing it in butter, and serving it with melted butter and sliced lemon. *À la meunière* means in the style of the miller's wife. This technique has long been a favorite in New Orleans, and indeed all over the state, since it works well with both freshwater and saltwater fish. Louisianians will often use an egg wash, which gives it a better crust. In this dish, our very own Louisiana pecans are used in the sauce to give the smooth fish a slight crunch. Marrying nuts with fish is not a new idea here. One of the more popular traditional dishes in New Orleans is trout amandine which is prepared à la meunière and garnished amandine style, meaning with toasted almonds. When Paul Prudhomme headed the kitchen at Commander's Palace in New Orleans, he created a dish using trout with pecans. Have the seasoned flour and the egg wash for dredging close at hand. Bread the fish just before putting it in the pan.

1 cup flour

4 teaspoons Rustic Rub (page 9)

2 eggs, beaten

1/2 cup milk

4 catfish or trout fillets
   (6 to 6 1/2 ounces each)

1/2 cup vegetable oil

1 stick (1/4 pound) butter

1 cup pecan pieces

4 tablespoons chopped parsley

2 tablespoons minced garlic

2 tablespoons fresh lemon juice

1/4 cup Worcestershire sauce

1/4 cup heavy cream

1 teaspoon salt

1/4 teaspoon cayenne

1. Combine the flour with 2 teaspoons of the rub in a shallow bowl. In another shallow bowl, blend the eggs and milk together. Season the fish with the remaining 2 teaspoons rub.

2. Heat the oil in a large nonstick skillet over medium-high heat. Dredge the fillets in the flour, coating evenly. Dip the fillets in the egg mixture. Dredge again in the flour. When the oil is hot, but not smoking, lay the fillets in the skillet. Panfry for 3 to 4 minutes on each side, or until golden. Transfer to a warm platter.

3. Discard any oil remaining in the skillet and wipe clean with paper towels. Return the skillet to the stove. Over medium-high heat, melt 2 tablespoons of the butter. When the butter foams, add the pecans and stir constantly for about 1 1/2 minutes, or until lightly toasted. Add the parsley, garlic, lemon juice, Worcestershire, and cream. Stir with a whisk for about 15 seconds and remove from heat. Add the salt, cayenne, and remaining 6 tablespoons butter, broken into small chips, and stir until the butter melts completely.

4. Spoon the sauce over the fillets to serve.

4 servings

Panfried Catfish with Lemon and Garlic

efore dawn when the mist floats heavily above the black-green water of the Atchafalaya River Basin, fishermen strike out to try their luck. By mid-morning, when the sun begins beating down on their backs, a mess of silver-gray catfish will be snapped on stringers trailing in the cool water. If the fish are small, the fisherman may simply skin, gut, and dredge them before panfrying. Larger fish are cut into fillets. These panfried catfish fillets are golden and crisp on the outside, smooth and hot within. Real Potato Salad (page 267) is all that is needed to go along with them. My friend Mr. Thibodeaux prefers his catfish on a poor boy. He hollows out a loaf of crisp French bread, lathers both sides with Creole Tartar Sauce (page 28) and fills the loaf with fried fish, then washes it down with cold Dixie beer. *Mon cher, c'est bon, oui.*

4 catfish fillets (6 to 6½ ounces each)

¾ cup fresh lemon juice

¼ cup minced parsley

¼ cup minced garlic

1 tablespoon plus 2 teaspoons Rustic Rub (page 9)

½ cup yellow cornmeal

2 tablespoons flour

½ cup vegetable oil

1. Put the catfish in a shallow bowl. Add the lemon juice, parsley, garlic, and 1 tablespoon plus 1 teaspoon of the rub. Toss to coat the catfish evenly. Cover and refrigerate for 1 hour.
2. Combine the cornmeal, flour, and the remaining rub in another shallow bowl. Remove the catfish from the marinade and dredge in the cornmeal mixture, coating evenly.
3. Heat the oil in a nonstick skillet and fry for about 3 to 4 minutes on each side, or until golden brown.
4. Serve immediately.

4 servings

Batter-Fried Catfish

raveling along U.S. Highway 90 between Houma and New Orleans, you pass through the small fishing village of Des Allemands, home of the best catfish you'll ever put in your mouth. Whether it's early in the morning, midday, or late in the afternoon, fishermen armed with cane poles drop their lines into the dark, green water and bring up plenty of fish. In this part of Louisiana, they like their catfish fried and served with White Beans (page 228) and rice. Prepare the beans the day before since they take a couple of hours to cook.

1 cup milk	4 teaspoons Rustic Rub (page 9)
½ cup Creole or whole-grain mustard	2 catfish fillets (6 to 6½ ounces each)
1 teaspoon Tabasco sauce	
1 teaspoon salt	¾ cup flour
¼ teaspoon cayenne	½ cup yellow cornmeal
⅛ teaspoon freshly ground black pepper	Solid vegetable shortening for deep-frying

1. Combine the milk, mustard, Tabasco, salt, cayenne, black pepper, and 2 teaspoons of the rub in a bowl and mix well. Add the catfish and submerge. Cover and refrigerate for 1 hour.

2. Mix together the flour, cornmeal, and the remaining 2 teaspoons rub in another bowl. Remove the catfish from the milk mixture and dredge in the flour mixture, coating evenly.

3. Heat the shortening to 360°F. Deep-fry the catfish for 5 to 6 minutes, or until golden brown. The fish will float to the surface of the hot oil when done.

4. Drain on paper towels and serve immediately.

2 servings

Catfish Roulade

roulade is a thin piece of meat or fish filled with a savory stuffing, then rolled up and baked. Catfish is used here, but any firm whitefish, such as bass or trout, will work. The filling is the same mixture used for our Crawfish Patties. To finish it off, drizzle with Lemon, Butter, and Tomato Sauce.

½ recipe Crawfish Patties (page 96)

¼ pound peeled crawfish tails

2 tablespoons chopped parsley

3 tablespoons chopped green onions

4 catfish fillets (6 to 6½ ounces each)

1 tablespoon plus 1 teaspoon Rustic Rub (page 9)

2 cups thinly sliced onions

1 tablespoon vegetable oil

1 recipe Lemon, Butter, and Tomato Sauce (page 36)

1. Preheat the oven to 400°F.

2. Combine the patty mixture with the crawfish tails, parsley, and green onions in a bowl and mix well. Divide into 4 equal portions. Season the fillets with 1 tablespoon of the rub. Spread the crawfish mixture evenly on 1 side of each fillet. Starting at the tail end of the fillet, roll each up, jelly-roll fashion, into a roulade. Lightly oil a shallow baking pan and place the roulades so that they are not touching each other.

3. Toss the onions with the remaining 1 teaspoon rub and the vegetable oil. Spread the onions on top of the roulades. Bake for about 30 minutes, or until the fish flakes easily with a fork.

4. Top with the sauce and serve.

4 servings

Crispy-Fried Redfish

One evening found Marcelle, her husband, Rock, and me watching a late-afternoon thunderstorm roll through from the shelter of their covered patio overlooking Bayou Teche. We watched the bending and swaying of the willows and young cypress trees at the water's edge and thought we were socked in for the evening. But luckily, the sky cleared just in time for us to watch a neon sunset. We were discussing the possibilities of what we would have for supper, when a neighbor walked through the yard offering us a bag of redfish fillets, fresh from an early-morning fishing expedition in Vermilion Bay. Rock pulled out his Coleman stove and we were in business. The crispy fish, dabbed with a little Creole Tartar Sauce (page 28) and accompanied by thick slices of vine-ripened tomatoes, was perfect.

4 redfish, snapper, trout, or grouper fillets (6 to 8 ounces each)

2 tablespoons Rustic Rub (page 9)

½ cup flour

1 egg, beaten

¼ cup water

⅓ cup vegetable oil

1. Season the fish with 1 tablespoon of the rub. Combine the flour with 2 teaspoons of the rub in a shallow bowl. Mix together the egg, water, and the remaining 1 teaspoon rub in another bowl. Dredge the fish, first in the seasoned flour, then in the egg mixture, then again in the flour, shaking off any excess.

2. Heat the oil over medium heat in a large nonstick skillet. Panfry the fish for 4 to 5 minutes on each side.

3. Drain on paper towels and serve immediately.

4 servings

123

Green Redfish

n Louisiana, everyone, and I mean everyone, young and old, male and female, owns a fishing pole or rod and reel for there is always a body of water nearby to sink a line into, be it a slow-moving bayou, a pristine lake, an inland bay, or the great Gulf of Mexico. They never tire of fishing and preparing their catch, especially when it slept in the water the night before. Here, the fish is marinated in jalapeño sauce and onions, which you might think would make it too hot, but some of the heat burns off during the grilling. In fact, I like to dab more sauce on the fish after it's cooked. Serve it with Corn Maque Choux (page 234).

4 redfish, snapper, or trout fillets (about 8 ounces each)

1/2 teaspoon salt

1/4 teaspoon Green Jalapeño Sauce (page 8) or Tabasco Jalapeño Sauce

2 medium onions, thinly sliced

1 tablespoon vegetable oil

1. Prepare a grill and light the fire.
2. With a sharp knife, make 2 diagonal slits on the skin side of each fillet. Season the fish with the salt and jalapeño sauce. Put the fish in a shallow bowl and cover with the onions. Cover and refrigerate for 30 minutes.
3. Remove from the refrigerator and drizzle with the oil on the skinless side of the fillets. Place the fillets, skinless side down, on the hot grill. Cook for 5 to 6 minutes, then turn the fillets over and cook for 5 to 6 minutes more. Place the onions in a wire basket and grill alongside the fish, turning several times to prevent burning.
4. Transfer the fish to a warm platter, garnish with the onions, and serve.

4 servings

Skillet Snapper

Bright red snapper from the Gulf of Mexico is not only pretty to look at but it is also especially flavorful. To snag these beauties, you have to bottom-fish, which is hard work because you have to sink that line thirty to forty feet, then reel up the catch. But it's all worth it when you come home with the limit. I consider red snapper a special gem of the sea and nothing much has to be done to it to make it absolutely delicious. It can be served on a bed of Brabant Potatoes (page 252).

4 red snapper fillets (6 to 6½ ounces each)

4 teaspoons Rustic Rub (page 9)

½ cup flour

6 tablespoons vegetable oil

1. Season the fish with 2 teaspoons of the rub. Season the flour with the remaining 2 teaspoons rub.
2. Heat the oil in a large nonstick skillet over medium-high heat. Dredge the fish in the seasoned flour. Panfry the fish, about 3 minutes on each side, or until golden brown.
3. Drain on paper towels and serve immediately.

4 servings

Cedar Plank Trout

everal years ago, when I was creating the very first menu for NOLA, my restaurant in the French Quarter, sous chefs David McCelvey and Michael Jordan and I were reminiscing about meals we had enjoyed by the campfire at fishing camps. I was staring at this gigantic wood oven at the restaurant, when—bingo!—I remembered a dish prepared by the late James Beard. Together we developed what has become one of NOLA's signature dishes. Serve it with Maw-Maw's Slaw (page 265). Untreated cedar shingles are available at home-improvement centers and lumberyards.

2 untreated cedar shingles, about 5½ × 10 inches each

1 teaspoon vegetable oil

2 trout fillets (8 to 10 ounces each)

1 teaspoon Rustic Rub (page 9)

½ cup peeled and grated fresh horseradish root or drained bottled white horseradish

2 teaspoons grated orange zest

2 teaspoons grated lemon zest

½ teaspoon salt

¼ teaspoon cayenne

2 teaspoons sugar

1. Prepare a grill and light the fire. Rub 1 side of each shingle with ½ teaspoon oil.
2. Season the fish on both sides with the rub. Place a fillet on each oiled shingle. Combine the horseradish, orange zest, lemon zest, salt, cayenne, and sugar in a small bowl. Divide the mixture into 2 equal portions and place on top of the fish.
3. Place the shingles in the center of a hot barbecue grill. Close the lid and cook for about 10 minutes, or until the fish flakes easily with a fork. Remove the shingles from the grill using a long-handled spatula. If the shingles catch fire, sprinkle with a little water.
4. Put the shingles in the center of large platters to serve.

2 servings

Trout Fricassee

 fricassee is usually made with meat or poultry, but who says it can't be made with fish? When I showed Marcelle this recipe, she kept mumbling about having seen fish prepared many ways, but this was a new one for her. When she tasted it, her eyes widened and I waited for the verdict. Looking up to heaven, she announced, "Papa, you were a mighty fine cook who always experimented in the kitchen and always said to keep an open mind about cooking. Well, here's one you would have loved."

4 trout fillets (7 to 8 ounces each)

1 tablespoon plus 1 teaspoon Rustic Rub (page 9)

½ stick (4 tablespoons) butter

¼ cup flour

6 cups thinly sliced onions

¼ cup chopped celery

¼ cup chopped bell peppers

1 teaspoon salt

½ teaspoon cayenne

1 teaspoon freshly ground black pepper

3 cups water

2 tablespoons fresh lemon juice

2 tablespoons chopped parsley

1. Season the fish with the rub.

2. Heat the butter in a large skillet over medium-high heat. Add the flour and, stirring constantly for 5 to 6 minutes, make a medium brown roux, the color of peanut butter.

3. Add the onions, celery, bell peppers, salt, cayenne, and black pepper. Stir briskly, coating the vegetables with the roux mixture and separating the onion rings. Continue stirring for 6 to 7 minutes, or until the vegetables are wilted. Add the water and stir until the mixture thickens, 6 to 7 minutes. Add the lemon juice and lay the trout in the pan and baste with the sauce. Cover and cook for 6 to 7 minutes, or until the fish flakes easily with a fork. Add the parsley and remove from heat.

4. Serve right away.

4 servings

CHAPTER 6

Chicken, Duck, Quail, and Goose

SUNDAY ROAST

CHICKEN, DUCKS

WITH FIG GLAZE,

PANÉED QUAIL,

AND MORE

ne of Marcelle's first memories of visiting her Grandfather Broussard's farm goes back to when she was four years old. Her Aunt Cina and her kitchen helpers, Yola and *La Vieille* (the Old One), taught Marcelle how to feed the chickens, ducks, and geese that had the run of the fenced-in backyard. The feed was kept in a large barrel with a heavy wooden lid near the kitchen door. Nearby, a tin pan hung on a hook. The women showed Marcelle how to dip the pan in the barrel and fill it with grain, then how to scatter the feed around the dusty yard near the hog pen. All was well and good until a large goose decided it wanted the whole pan of feed. Marcelle ran squealing inside the screen porch and henceforth

adamantly refused to be in charge of feeding the birds. She did, however, spend many days watching the cooks select plump hens, wring their necks, and prepare them for Sunday dinner. She gathered goose eggs which made grand omelets. And each year a turkey was penned and fattened for Thanksgiving dinner. Marcelle brags about her Aunt Git Broussard, who was taught by her mother to know the anatomy of a turkey, chicken, and duck as well as a surgeon knows the human body. These birds were stuffed, fried, stewed, and sometimes deboned and filled with herbs and spices for festive celebrations. Fowl has been and still is indispensable to the cuisine of Louisiana. Since colonial days, fowl, both wild and domestic, have been baked, roasted, or fricasseed. Wild mallard and teals, plump yard hens, farm-raised quail—small but succulent—turkeys, and geese are a welcome dish at any meal. Chicken and Dumplings, a dish favored by north Louisianians, is the quintessential comfort food. Duck, Hunter's Style, a hearty stewlike dish composed of onions, garlic, celery, mushrooms, and tomatoes, is loved by hunters and nonhunters alike. Tiny quail, wrapped around forcemeat, panéed, or cooked with mushrooms, are a treat. The Pepper-Stuffed Turkey, one of Aunt Git's creations, is packed with peppers, onions, and garlic.

Sunday Roast Chicken

At Marcelle's Grandfather Broussard's farm, Sunday dinner usually included a huge pork roast, a pot of seafood gumbo, and a slab of smoked ribs along with such garden vegetables as smothered okra and butter beans and, of course, rice dressing. A golden brown, juicy chicken was always on the sideboard for those who wanted "just a little chunk." Sunday dinner was incomplete without a roasted chicken. Before going any further, let's discuss chickens. Broilers are the youngest. Then come the fryers. Following the fryers are the roasting hens. While the younger chickens are more tender, they just don't have the flavor of the older ones. A young roasting hen is the best choice for this preparation. The chicken is stuffed with onions and garlic under the breast skin and along the shoulders to enhance the flavor. The skin is rubbed with lemon to make it a little tart and crispy. Before serving, the chicken is put in the pan juices to absorb all the buttery flavor. That's how it's done down South.

½ stick (4 tablespoons) butter, cut into ⅛-inch slices

1½ teaspoons salt

½ teaspoon cayenne

1 cup chopped onions

½ cup chopped celery

½ cup chopped bell peppers

1 tablespoon chopped garlic

½ teaspoon dried thyme

1 lemon, halved

1 roasting hen (about 4 pounds)

3 sprigs of thyme

¼ teaspoon freshly ground black pepper

1. Preheat the oven to 400°F.

2. Sprinkle the butter slices with ½ teaspoon of the salt and ¼ teaspoon of the cayenne. Freeze the butter for about 15 minutes, or until firm.

3. Season the onions, celery, bell peppers, and garlic with ½ teaspoon of the salt, the remaining ¼ teaspoon cayenne, the dried thyme, and the juice of the lemon (about 2 tablespoons). Reserve the lemon halves.

4. With the chicken breast side up, and the neck opening facing you, lift the skin flap and make a slit, about 1 inch long, down the wing from the shoulder following the bone line, on each side of the neck, using a sharp pointed knife. Fill each slit with 2 slices of butter and 1 to 2 teaspoons of the vegetables. Press the butter and vegetables into the slit with your fingers.

5. Fold the neck flap down and turn the chicken, breast side up, with the cavity facing you. Make several slits, each about 1 inch long, inside the cavity along the breastbone and rib bones. Do not pierce through to the skin. Insert butter slices and vegetables in each slit. Again push in the butter and vegetables with your fingers. Put any remaining butter and vegetables in the cavity. Rub the chicken with the lemon halves, then put them and the sprigs of thyme inside the cavity. Season the outside of the chicken with the remaining salt and the black pepper.

6. Place the chicken, breast side up, in a roasting pan and roast, uncovered, for about 45 minutes, or until golden brown. Place a sheet of aluminum foil loosely over the chicken to cover the drumsticks and breast. Roast for 45 minutes to 1 hour more, or until the chicken is tender and the drumsticks and thighs are easy to move. Baste occasionally with pan juices during the last 30 minutes of roasting. Remove foil.

7. Remove the thyme sprigs and lemon halves. Allow the chicken to sit for 15 minutes and then carve. Lay the cut-up pieces in the pan juices for a few minutes and serve.

4 to 6 servings

Chicken and Dumplings

 t's not a gumbo; it's not a stew; but people in north Louisiana adore it. At cafés and restaurants in and around Shreveport, chicken and dumplings are usually a daily special. The baking powder dumplings are light and fluffy. And I'm told it's important that each dumpling land in a different spot in the cooking pot, or a gooey globby mess will result. Southerners are very particular about their chicken and dumplings, and you'll find several different versions around the state. Some cooks prefer a stewing hen, but I think a large fryer works quite well in this recipe.

Chicken and Broth

1 large fryer (about 3½ pounds)	3 bay leaves
2 cups coarsely chopped onions	4 quarts water
1½ cups coarsely chopped celery	1 tablespoon salt
1½ cups coarsely chopped carrots	3/4 teaspoon freshly ground black pepper
8 garlic cloves	1/4 teaspoon cayenne
	1/2 teaspoon dried thyme

1. Put the chicken, onions, celery, carrots, garlic, and bay leaves in a large kettle. Cover with the water. Add the salt, black pepper, cayenne, and thyme and bring to a boil over high heat. Reduce the heat to medium and simmer for about 2 hours, or until the chicken is very tender. Remove from the heat.

2. Remove the chicken from the pot. With a slotted spoon, remove 1 cup of the vegetables from the pot. Set aside. When the chicken has cooled, skin and debone it. Set aside.

Baking Powder Dumplings

1 egg

1 cup milk

1/2 teaspoon salt

1/4 teaspoon white pepper

2 tablespoons baking powder

3 tablespoons chopped parsley

1 1/4 cups flour

1 cup reserved vegetables

3 tablespoons cornstarch

3/4 cup milk

3. Beat together the egg and milk in a mixing bowl. Add the salt, pepper, baking powder, and parsley. Mix well. Add the flour and mix to make a thick batter. Fold the reserved vegetables into the batter. Set aside.

4. Remove any fat that has risen to the surface of the broth. Return the chicken meat to the pot and bring to a boil over medium-high heat. Dissolve the cornstarch in the milk and add to the pot. Stir and bring back to a boil. Reduce heat to medium.

5. Drop heaping tablespoons of the dumpling batter into the hot mixture, distributing the dumplings evenly, until all is used. When the dumplings rise to the surface, simmer and cook for 4 minutes, stirring gently, being careful not to break up the dumplings.

6. Remove the bay leaves and serve immediately in soup bowls.

8 servings

Chicken Smothered in Onions

ommonly called chicken *aux gros oignons* in south Louisiana, it's a dish you won't find anywhere but in a home kitchen. The chicken is browned, then the onions are added and cooked to a golden color. Everything is "smothered," cooked in its own juices and, in this case, a bit of added water. According to Marcelle, this dish is often prepared when aunts, uncles, and cousins drop by unannounced. Mushrooms, young peas, and tender sweet corn are added to the pot "to make it stretch."

1 large fryer, cut into serving pieces (about 3½ pounds)

2 teaspoons salt

½ teaspoon cayenne

1 tablespoon flour

¼ cup vegetable oil

8 cups thinly sliced onions (about 2½ pounds)

1 cup thinly sliced bell peppers

1 bay leaf

¼ cup water

1 cup whole kernel corn

1 cup young sweet green peas

2 cups sliced mushrooms

3 tablespoons chopped parsley

1. In a mixing bowl, toss the chicken with 1½ teaspoons salt, ¼ teaspoon cayenne, and flour.

2. In a large cast-iron or enameled cast-iron Dutch oven, heat the oil over medium-high heat. When the oil is hot, but not smoking, add the chicken and brown, cooking for about 6 to 8 minutes on each side. Add the onions and the remaining ½ teaspoon salt and remaining ¼ teaspoon cayenne. Stirring constantly, wilt and brown the onions, scraping the bottom of the pan to loosen any browned particles, about 10 minutes. Add the bell peppers and bay leaf. Continue stirring, again scraping the bottom of the pot to loosen any browned particles, for about 15 minutes. Add the water, cover, and reduce the heat to medium. Stir occasionally and cook for about 30 minutes, or until the chicken is tender.

3. Add the corn, peas, and mushrooms, cover, and cook for 15 minutes more, stirring occasionally. Add the parsley.

4. Remove the bay leaf and serve immediately.

4 to 6 servings

Panroasted Chicken with Oyster Dressing

his is one of those fancy chicken dishes that are reserved for holidays or a special Sunday dinner. It's a natural when oysters are in season during the cooler months from September to March. Louisianians living along the Gulf have a penchant for combining oysters with chicken, and when they do, it's always good.

1 tablespoon butter

½ teaspoon freshly ground black pepper

1½ teaspoons salt

4 chicken breasts, halved, breastbone removed, wings attached (about 8 ounces each)

4 garlic cloves, sliced

1 cup Baked Oyster Dressing (page 113)

1 tablespoon fresh lemon juice

1 tablespoon fresh rosemary leaves

1. Preheat the oven to 400°F.
2. Butter an 8 × 11½ × 2-inch (or 2-quart) baking dish.
3. Mix together the pepper and salt and season the chicken breasts. Divide the garlic slices into 4 equal portions. Lay the breasts, skin side down, in the pan and place the garlic in the center of each breast. Put ¼ cup of the oyster dressing on each breast, then carefully fold together, bringing the bottom end of the breast up to the wing section. Drizzle with the lemon juice and sprinkle with the rosemary leaves. Bake for 45 minutes.
4. To serve, spoon the pan drippings over the breasts.

4 servings

Batter-Fried Chicken

n Louisiana, a lot of cooking and eating is done outdoors. As my friend Mr. Thibodeaux says, everything "just plain tastes better" when it's cooked outside. Frying outdoors also doesn't mess up the kitchen. He also impressed upon me that the chicken must be deep-fried and not panfried, and heaven forbid, not oven-fried. In the old days, lard was used for frying and that was good, oui. Nowadays, solid vegetable shortening does a good job. One final tip from Mr. Thibodeaux: fry just three or four pieces at a time.

1 large fryer, cut into 10 servings pieces (about 3½ pounds)

1½ teaspoons salt

½ teaspoon cayenne

½ teaspoon freshly ground black pepper

¼ cup Rustic Rub (page 9)

Solid vegetable shortening for deep-frying

2 eggs

½ cup buttermilk

2½ cups flour

1. In a mixing bowl, toss the chicken with the salt, cayenne, black pepper, and 1 tablespoon of the rub. Cover and refrigerate for 2 hours.

2. Heat the shortening to 360°F. in an electric deep-fryer or deep cast-iron pot. There should be enough shortening for the chicken pieces to immerse.

3. Whisk together the eggs, buttermilk, and 1 tablespoon of the rub in another shallow bowl.

4. Combine the flour and the remaining 2 table-spoons rub in another shallow bowl. Roll the chicken in the flour mixture, then in the milk-egg mixture, then again in the flour. Shake off excess batter. Fry 2 to 4 pieces (the number will depend on the size of your frying pot) at a time, 10 to 12 minutes for thighs and drumsticks, 8 to 10 minutes for wings and breasts. When they pop to the surface of the oil and are golden brown, remove and drain on paper towels.

5. Serve hot or at room temperature.

4 servings

Chicken Loaf

n Louisiana, chicken is baked, stewed, fried, and roasted; put in casseroles and stuffings; and when ground chicken is available, it is used in a loaf, much like a meatloaf. Serve it with Smothered Green Beans and Potatoes (page 241). If there are any leftovers, tuck a slice or two between two pieces of French bread and dress the sandwich with tomatoes and Creole mustard. Substitute ground turkey if you wish.

2½ pounds white and dark chicken meat, coarsely ground	2 teaspoons salt
1 cup chopped onions	½ teaspoon freshly ground black pepper
2 tablespoons chopped garlic	¾ teaspoon cayenne
½ cup chopped celery	½ teaspoon Worcestershire sauce
¼ cup chopped bell peppers	¼ teaspoon Tabasco sauce
2 tablespoons chopped parsley	1 cup dried fine bread crumbs
1 egg	

1. Preheat the oven to 350°F.
2. Combine the chicken, onions, garlic, celery, bell peppers, and parsley together in a mixing bowl. If you have a meat grinder, you can grind this mixture through a ½-inch die for a smoother texture, but it's not necessary for flavor.
3. Add the egg, salt, black pepper, cayenne, Worcestershire, Tabasco, and bread crumbs. Using your hands, mix thoroughly. Mold the mixture into a 5 × 10-inch loaf and place on a baking sheet lined with aluminum foil. Bake for 1 hour, or until juices run clear.
4. Remove from the oven and let stand for 10 minutes before slicing to serve.

6 to 8 servings

Pepper-Stuffed Turkey

arcelle's Aunt Git makes this amazing roast turkey for every family occasion—funerals, weddings, christenings— and sometimes for no special occasion at all. Onions, garlic, bell peppers, and butter, seasoned with salt and cayenne, along with hot sport or lady finger peppers are stuffed into slits all over the turkey. The end result is a flavorful, moist turkey like no other I've ever eaten. Finding a gravy at the end will surprise you since the bird is placed in a dry pot. Aunt Git usually carves the bird and places the meat in this gravy before serving. She recommends using Cajun Chef Brand Sport Peppers, but Pickled Banana Peppers (page 19) can also be used for a less hot version. If your hands are sensitive to hot peppers, you might want to wear surgical gloves; they can be purchased at most pharmacies.

2 sticks (½ pound) butter, cut into ¼-inch slices

8 teaspoons salt

4 teaspoons cayenne

1 cup chopped onions

½ cup chopped bell peppers

2 tablespoons chopped garlic

8 to 10 Cajun Chef Brand Sport Peppers

3 tablespoons pickle juice from the pepper jars

1 small turkey (10 to 12 pounds)

1. Preheat the oven to 400°F.
2. Put the butter slices in a bowl and season with 2 teaspoons of the salt and 1 teaspoon of the cayenne. Freeze for 30 minutes.
3. Combine 4 teaspoons of the salt and 2 teaspoons of the cayenne in a small bowl. In another bowl, combine the onions, bell peppers, garlic,

sport peppers, the remaining 2 teaspoons salt, and the remaining 1 teaspoon cayenne with the pickle juice.

4. Prepare a work surface, either a large tray or cutting board, topped with a large clean towel to prevent the turkey from sliding around while you work. Remove the neck, gizzards, and livers from the cavity of the turkey. Rinse the turkey under cool water and pat dry with paper towels. Place the turkey, breast side up, on the work surface with the cavity facing you. Lift the skin flap and make 2 to 3 slits on either side of the breastbone, inside the cavity, with a sharp pointed knife, without piercing through to the skin.

5. Insert 2 to 3 slices of the frozen butter into each slit. Next, spoon about $\frac{1}{4}$ teaspoon of the salt and cayenne mixture into the slits. Insert about 1 teaspoon, more if you can, of the vegetable mixture into each hole, pushing with your fingers.

6. Gently pull the drumstick forward and outward to expose the inner thigh. Pull the skin away from the meat. Make a slit following the bone lines from the top of each leg. Use your index finger to make a path and repeat the stuffing procedure described above.

7. Where the skin has been loosened on the inner thigh, spoon in about $\frac{1}{4}$ teaspoon of the salt and cayenne mixture.

8. Turn the turkey breast side up, with the neck opening facing you. Lift the skin flap and make a slit down each wing from the shoulder, again following the bone lines. Repeat the stuffing process on both wings.

9. Season the outside of the turkey with any remaining salt and cayenne mixture. Place any leftover butter or vegetable mixture inside the cavity. Secure the wings by folding the lower half back over the top of the wing. Tie the legs together with kitchen twine. Place the turkey in a large deep roasting pan. No fat or cooking liquid is required.

10. Roast at 400°F. for 15 to 20 minutes to get the browning process going. Lower the temperature to 350°F. Cover with a lid and bake for 3 to $3\frac{1}{2}$ hours, or until juices run clear.

11. Remove from the oven and let cool for 10 minutes. Lift the turkey out of the pan and carve. Serve warm with pan juices.

8 to 10 servings

Chicken-Andouille Hash

lthough hash is usually prepared from leftovers, in Louisiana, cooks make this heavenly hash with spicy andouille and potatoes and topped with eggs, it is traditionally served at breakfast or brunch, but it makes a fine supper, too.

1 pound chicken meat, both white and dark, cut into ½-inch cubes

1 teaspoon salt

¼ teaspoon cayenne

1 cup chopped onions

½ cup chopped bell peppers

2 tablespoons vegetable oil

4 ounces andouille, chopped

2 tablespoons Creole or whole-grain mustard

2 cups peeled and grated Idaho potatoes

4 eggs

1. Preheat the oven to 475°F.

2. Season the chicken with ½ teaspoon of the salt and ⅛ teaspoon of the cayenne. Season the onions and bell peppers with the remaining ½ teaspoon salt and the remaining ⅛ teaspoon cayenne.

3. Heat the oil in a large skillet with an ovenproof handle, over medium-high heat. Brown the chicken, stirring constantly, 3 to 4 minutes. Add the andouille and cook, stirring constantly, for about 3 minutes. Add the onions and bell peppers. Cook for about 6 minutes, stirring constantly, or until the vegetables are soft and golden. Add the mustard and mix well. Add the potatoes. Brown and fold. With the back of a spoon, pat down the mixture into the bottom of the skillet. Cook for about 1 minute. Brown and fold and pat down the mixture again. Cook for 2 to 3 minutes, or until the potatoes are tender. Crack the eggs on top of the hash and bake, in the skillet, for 2 to 3 minutes, or until the eggs set.

4. Serve immediately.

4 servings

Quail with Forcemeat

orcemeat is a seasoned mixture of ingredients often used to stuff game. I've thickened this one up with some bread crumbs and stuffed chunks of it into quail for a delicious old-time French dish. Serve it with Port Wine Sauce (page 36).

Forcemeat

½ pound beef stew meat, cut into 1-inch pieces

1 tablespoon plus 2 teaspoons Rustic Rub (page 9)

1 teaspoon salt

1 teaspoon cayenne

½ cup chopped onions

¼ cup chopped celery

½ cup chopped carrots

⅓ cup chopped, peeled, and seeded tomatoes, or ⅓ cup chopped canned tomatoes

3 bay leaves

2½ cups water

1 tablespoon chopped parsley

¼ cup dried fine bread crumbs

4 quail, breastbone removed and split down the back (about 3½ ounces each)

1. Season the beef with 1 tablespoon of the rub.

2. Combine the beef, salt, cayenne, onions, celery, carrots, tomatoes, bay leaves, and water in a saucepan over medium-high heat. Bring to a boil, then reduce the heat to medium and simmer for about 30 minutes. Remove from the heat and let cool. Remove the bay leaves.

3. When the mixture is cool, put it in a food processor and process until it forms a thick paste. Scrape down the sides of the processor bowl with a rubber spatula. Add the parsley and bread crumbs and pulse 2 or 3 times to mix well. Store in an airtight container for 8 hours in the refrigerator.

4. Preheat the oven to 375°F.

5. Lay the quail, skin side down, on a work surface. Season with the remaining 2 teaspoons rub. Divide the forcemeat into 4 equal portions and form into balls. Place a ball in the center of each quail and bring the sides of the bird together to overlap. Put the quail, breast side up, in a shallow baking pan and bake for 25 to 30 minutes, or until lightly brown.

6. Spoon the sauce over the quail and serve immediately.

2 servings

143

LOUISIANA REAL AND RUSTIC

n the early 1980s, when I was Executive Chef at Commander's Palace in New Orleans, I wanted to include quail dishes on the menu. While searching for good-quality birds, I found Tom LaPay, in our neighboring state of Mississippi, who agreed to raise some for the restaurant. When I opened Emeril's and NOLA in New Orleans, he continued to supply me with top-notch quail. I've prepared the birds in any number of ways, and this one is quite simple. Simmered with onions, mushrooms, a bit of sherry, and chicken broth, they become tender and succulent. They can be served on toasted slices of Home-Style French Bread (page 286) or atop a pile of Smashing Smashed Potatoes (page 251).

144

6 slices (about 4 ounces) bacon, cut into 1-inch pieces

¼ cup flour

1 cup chopped onions

2 cups sliced mushrooms, such as shiitakes, oysters, or hedgehogs

1 tablespoon chopped garlic

½ cup dry sherry

1 cup chopped, peeled, and seeded tomatoes, or 1 cup chopped canned tomatoes

1½ cups Chicken Broth (page 11)

8 quail, breastbone removed and split down the back (3½ to 4 ounces each)

1 teaspoon salt

¼ teaspoon cayenne

⅛ teaspoon freshly ground black pepper

1 tablespoon fresh lemon juice

2 tablespoons chopped parsley

1. Fry the bacon in a large skillet over medium heat until crisp. Using a slotted spoon, remove the bacon, drain, and set aside.

2. Add the flour to the fat in the skillet and make a medium brown roux, the color of peanut butter, by stirring constantly for 8 to 10 minutes.

3. Add the onions and stir constantly for about 3 minutes, or until slightly wilted. Add the mushrooms and cook for 2 minutes. Add the garlic and the sherry and cook for 2 minutes. Add the tomatoes and broth and bring to a boil. Add the quail, salt, cayenne, and black pepper and simmer for about 30 minutes, basting and turning the quail every 10 minutes. Stir in the lemon juice and parsley.

4. Serve garnished with the reserved bacon pieces.

4 servings

Quail Stuffed with Corn Bread and Andouille Dressing

orn bread, smoky andouille, and tender quail—three of my favorite things make a down-home dish that is wonderful served with Smothered Green Beans and Potatoes (page 241). Quail usually can be found in large supermarkets or specialty meat markets. Most of the time, the breastbone has been removed and the birds are split down the back. If not, the butcher can usually do this for you.

8 quail, breastbone removed, and split down the back (about 3½ ounces each)

2 teaspoons Rustic Rub (page 9)

2 cups Corn Bread and Andouille Dressing (page 231)

1. Preheat the oven to 400°F.
2. Lay the quail, skin side down, on a work surface. Season with the rub. Divide the corn bread dressing into 8 equal portions and shape into balls. Place a ball in the center of each quail and bring the sides of the birds together to overlap.
3. Place the quail, breast side up, in a lightly buttered baking pan and bake for 25 to 30 minutes, or until crispy and brown.
4. Serve immediately.

4 servings

Panéed Quail

n French *pané* means coated with bread crumbs. In Louisiana, cooks use this method on beef or veal and, in this instance, quail. After the quail is breaded, it is pan-fried to make it crunchy and delicious. I serve these with Brabant Potatoes (page 252) and drizzle them with my own Worcestershire sauce (page 7) or with Port Wine Sauce (page 36). Prepare the flour mix, egg wash, and bread crumb mixture ahead so that you can work fast at the stove.

½ cup flour	¼ cup chopped parsley
2 tablespoons plus 1 teaspoon Rustic Rub (page 9)	2 tablespoons olive oil
2 eggs	8 quail, breastbone removed, and split down the back (about 3½ ounces each)
½ cup water	
1½ cups dried fine bread crumbs	¼ cup vegetable oil
4 ounces (½ cup) grated parmesan	

1. Preheat the oven to 400°F.
2. Mix the flour and 1 teaspoon of the rub in a small bowl. Beat the eggs and water together in another bowl. Combine the bread crumbs, cheese, parsley, 4 teaspoons of the rub, and olive oil in a third bowl. Mix thoroughly. Season the quail with the remaining 2 teaspoons rub. Dredge the quail first in the flour, then in the egg wash, and finally in the bread crumb mixture.
3. Heat the oil in a large skillet over medium-high heat. When the oil is hot, but not smoking, panfry the quail, 3 to 4 at a time, about 3 minutes on each side. Place the quail in a shallow baking pan and bake for 5 minutes.
4. Serve immediately.

4 servings

Two-way Duck with Sweet Potatoes

hen the first cool front of the autumn comes in from the west, hunters rush to their duck camps to check the blinds, oil their shotguns, and prepare their decoys. In south Louisiana, millions of acres of marshland teem with wildlife and hunters are eager for the season to open. But alas, we have to confine our hunting to the supermarket, making our selection from neatly dressed and packaged domestic ducklings. Not to worry, this dish was created for domestic birds. I call it Two-way Duck because you can serve it for dinner à deux or you can stretch it to serve four.

1 domestic duck, rinsed in cool water (5½ to 6 pounds)	1 teaspoon coarsely ground black pepper
½ cup stemmed and sliced jalapeños, with seeds	1 tablespoon salt
12 garlic cloves plus 1 medium head garlic, cut in half crosswise	½ teaspoon cayenne
	½ cup sugar
2 medium lemons, halved	2 medium sweet potatoes, scrubbed (about 14 ounces)

1. Remove any excess fat pieces from the cavity of the duck. Remove the neck flap. With the duck breast side up and the cavity facing you, make a 1-inch slit on each side of the breastbone inside the cavity. Insert 1 slice of jalapeño and 1 clove garlic in each hole. With your fingers, separate the skin from the breast meat and insert 5 pieces of jalapeño and 5 garlic cloves under the skin and push them well along the breast. Turn the duck around so that the neck is facing you. Slice the remaining 2 cloves garlic and put these and the remaining jalapeño slices in the neck cavity. Put the

duck in a deep glass or plastic container. Squeeze the lemons and pour the juice over the duck and inside the cavity. Rub the duck with the lemon skins. Combine the black pepper, salt, cayenne, and sugar in a small mixing bowl. Rub the duck, inside and out, with this mixture. Cover and refrigerate for 8 hours.

2. Preheat the oven to 450°F.

3. Remove the duck from the container and place it on a rack in a roasting pan. Stuff the cavity with the sweet potatoes and head of garlic. Bake for 30 minutes. Reduce the heat to 350°F. and continue to bake for 1 hour, or until the duck legs pull easily away from the body.

4. To serve two, remove the sweet potatoes and garlic from the cavity. Cut the duck in half. Using your thumb and index finger, squeeze out the garlic from the skin and place on top of the duck halves, skin side up. Cut the sweet potatoes in half and serve with the duck.

2 to 4 servings

Variation

1. To serve four, carve the duck into 4 pieces. Peel and chop the sweet potatoes. Squeeze the garlic from the skin and set aside. Pour the oil (about ½ cup) from the roasting pan into a large skillet and heat over medium-high heat for about 2 minutes. Add 1 tablespoon flour and blend with a wire whisk for 5 to 6 minutes to make a medium brown roux, the color of peanut butter. Add 1 cup each chopped onions and celery and cook, stirring often, for 5 to 6 minutes. Add the chopped sweet potatoes and roasted garlic. Cook, stirring occasionally, for about 3 minutes.

2. Add 3 cups Chicken Broth (page 11) and bring to a boil. Reduce the heat to medium-low and cook, stirring occasionally, until mixture thickens, 6 to 7 minutes. Add 1 teaspoon salt, ¼ teaspoon cayenne, and 2 tablespoons Steen's 100% Pure Cane Syrup. Simmer for about 3 minutes. Add 3 tablespoons chopped green onions and 1 tablespoon chopped parsley. Lay the duck pieces in the sauce and spoon it over. Increase the heat to medium, cover, and cook for about 20 minutes. Remove the lid and cook for 5 minutes more.

3. To serve, place a piece of duck in the center of each dinner plate and spoon sauce over it.

Duck, Hunter's Style

After several hours spent shivering in duck blinds, cold hunters find their way back to camp eagerly looking forward to a hot meal. Hunters pride themselves on being not only good sportsmen but also good cooks and good hosts. A well-stocked kitchen is the most important part of any hunting camp, for that is where the sportsmen gather in the evening to recount their day and cook their game. Hunters are always experimenting with new ideas, but this preparation is a classic one. It is served with steamed white rice (see page 220). On the average, mallards weigh 1¼ to 1¾ pounds each; teals weigh about ½ pound. Most people consider that one large duck will serve two people. The smaller ducks will serve one. Don't hesitate to substitute a domestic duckling.

2 mallards, or 4 teals, or 1 domestic
  duckling (3 to 4 pounds total
  weight)

1 teaspoon salt

1/4 teaspoon freshly ground black
  pepper

2 tablespoons vegetable oil

3 tablespoons flour

2 cups chopped onions

1/2 cup chopped celery

1/2 cup chopped bell peppers

2 cups chopped mushrooms, such as
  shiitakes, oysters, or portobellos

1 tablespoon chopped garlic

2 cups chopped, peeled, and seeded
  tomatoes or 2 cups chopped
  canned tomatoes

2 bay leaves

2 cups dry red wine

2 cups Veal Stock (page 14)

1. Cut the duck into serving pieces. Season with 1/2 teaspoon of the salt and the black pepper. Heat the oil in a large skillet over medium-high heat. When the oil is hot, add the duck and brown evenly on both sides, about 10 minutes. Sprinkle with the flour and continue to cook, stirring, for 4 to 5 minutes.

2. Add the onions, celery, bell peppers, and mushrooms. Stir, scraping the bottom of the pan to loosen any browned particles, and cook for 4 to 5 minutes. Add the garlic and tomatoes. Cook for about 2 minutes. Add the remaining 1/2 teaspoon salt, bay leaves, and wine. Continue to cook, stirring, until the sauce thickens slightly, about 5 minutes. Add the stock and reduce the heat to medium. Cook, stirring occasionally, for about 2 hours, or until the duck is tender.

3. Remove the bay leaves and serve.

4 servings

Roasted Duck with Topinambours

opinambours (Jerusalem artichokes or sun-chokes) are often cooked along with wild ducks. If they're unavailable, substitute turnips. The pan gravy is delicious and hunters argue over who's going to sop it up with bread before the pot is dunked in the dishwater. I like to serve this duck with Wild Pecan Rice Dressing (page 223).

2 mallards, or 4 teals, or 1 domestic duckling (4 to 4½ pounds total weight)	½ teaspoon freshly ground black pepper
8 garlic cloves	1 teaspoon cayenne
1 medium onion, quartered, plus 2 cups coarsely chopped onions	¼ cup flour
1 large rib celery, cut into 1-inch pieces	8 Jerusalem artichokes, peeled and quartered (about 1 pound)
3 tablespoons vegetable oil	1 cup coarsely chopped celery
3 teaspoons salt	1 cup coarsely chopped carrots
	2 cups water
	½ cup dry red wine (or dry white wine if using domestic duckling)

1. Preheat the oven to 350°F.

2. If using a domestic duck, remove the neck flap. With the duck breast side up and the cavity facing you, make ½-inch slits on each side of the rib cage inside the cavity with a sharp pointed knife. The number of slits will vary according to the size of the duck. Insert a garlic clove in each slit. Turn the duck around and insert any remaining garlic cloves in the neck cavity. Insert the quartered onion and celery pieces in the breast cavity. Rub the duck with some of the oil. Combine 2 teaspoons of the salt, the pepper, and ½ teaspoon cayenne. Season the outside of the duck with half of this mixture. Add the remaining half to the vegetables inside the cavity. Dust the duck with the flour.

3. Heat the remaining 1 tablespoon vegetable oil in a roasting pan over medium-high heat. Place the duck, breast side down, in the hot oil and brown for 2 to 3 minutes. Using a long-handled fork, turn the duck over and brown on the back and sides, 2 to 3 minutes on each side, until evenly browned.

4. Arrange the Jerusalem artichokes and chopped onions, celery, and carrots around the duck or ducks in the roasting pan. Sprinkle the vegetables with the remaining 1 teaspoon salt and remaining $^1/_2$ teaspoon cayenne. Continue to cook for 3 to 4 minutes to slightly wilt the vegetables. Add the water and wine and cook for 5 to 6 minutes more. Cover and roast for about 1 hour 15 minutes, basting occasionally with the pan juices.

5. Remove from the oven. With a large spoon, mash the vegetables against the sides of the roasting pan.

6. Return the pan to the oven and roast, uncovered, for about 45 minutes, or until the duck is tender when pierced with the tip of a pointed knife. Let stand for about 10 minutes before carving.

7. To serve, carve the ducks into serving pieces and spoon vegetables and gravy over.

4 servings

Duck with Root Vegetables

ne winter's day, while browsing through the produce stands at the French Market in New Orleans, I picked up an assortment of root vegetables—carrots, parsnips, turnips, potatoes, beets—to take home. Although the sky was bright blue, a chilly wind blew in out of the north from Lake Pontchartrain and dry leaves crackled beneath my feet. I picked up a duck on my way home and scanned my brain for some ideas. Let's see, some crunchy vegetables, perfectly seasoned and roasted, and crisp baked duck sounded like a winner. It was. And is. The key here is not to overcook the vegetables.

1 domestic duckling, quartered (3½ to 4 pounds)

1 tablespoon plus 1 teaspoon Rustic Rub (page 9)

2 tablespoons Steen's 100% Pure Cane Syrup

1 tablespoon vegetable oil

4 ribs celery, sliced lengthwise in half

1 large head garlic, cut in half crosswise

2 large carrots, sliced lengthwise in half, then cut into 3-inch pieces

2 parsnips, sliced lengthwise in half, then cut into 3-inch pieces

1 large onion, halved, then cut into wedges

1 medium turnip, halved, then cut into wedges

1 medium beet, halved, then cut into wedges

4 small red potatoes, quartered

2 tablespoons olive oil

3/4 teaspoon salt

1/4 teaspoon freshly ground black pepper

1/8 teaspoon cayenne

1 teaspoon dried rosemary

1/2 teaspoon dried basil

1/2 teaspoon dried oregano

1½ cups water

1/2 cup dry sherry

1. Preheat the oven to 450°F.

2. Rub the duck with 1 tablespoon of the rub and the syrup. Heat the vegetable oil in a large skillet over high heat and brown the duck, skin side down, for about 5 minutes. Remove from skillet.

3. Place the celery and garlic on a wire rack fitted over a roasting pan. In a large bowl, toss the carrots, parsnips, onion, turnip, beet, and potatoes with the olive oil, ½ teaspoon of the salt, ⅛ teaspoon of the black pepper, the cayenne, the rosemary, basil, oregano, and the remaining 1 teaspoon rub to coat. Spread the vegetables evenly over the celery and garlic. Place the duck pieces, skin side down, on top of the vegetables. Sprinkle the duck with the remaining ¼ teaspoon salt and remaining ⅛ teaspoon black pepper. Pour the water and sherry into the bottom of the roasting pan. Roast for about 45 minutes, or until the duck is tender.

4. To serve, mound the root vegetables in the center of dinner plates and top with the duck.

4 servings

Ducks with Fig Glaze

 he sweetness of preserved figs and the richness of duck make this a special Sunday dinner; it's ideal for a holiday dinner, too.

Fig Glaze

1 cup Fig Preserves (page 22)

½ cup water

3 tablespoons Steen's 100% Pure Cane Syrup

1 teaspoon salt

¼ teaspoon cayenne

¼ teaspoon freshly ground black pepper

1 tablespoon Dijon-style mustard

2 tablespoons plus 1 teaspoon fresh lemon juice

1. Combine all of the ingredients in a food processor and process until coarsely pureed. Set aside.

2. Preheat the oven to 450°F.

Ducks

2 domestic ducklings (about 5 pounds each)

2 tablespoons Rustic Rub (page 9)

4 Granny Smith apples, cored and quartered

6 ribs celery, cut into 2-inch pieces

8 garlic cloves

2 teaspoons salt

½ teaspoon freshly ground black pepper

3. Line a roasting pan with aluminum foil.

4. Season the ducks with the rub. Toss the apples, celery, and garlic with the salt and pepper in a mixing bowl to coat evenly. Stuff the cavities of the ducks with the apple mixture. Place the ducks on a rack in the roasting pan and roast for 45 minutes. Remove from the oven.

5. Using a pastry brush, coat the ducks evenly with the fig glaze. Reduce the heat to 350°F. and roast for about 45 minutes, or until the drumsticks are easy to move. Remove from oven; let rest 15 minutes.

6. To serve, cut the duck into quarters.

8 servings

Roast Goose with Wild Pecan Rice Dressing

From time to time in Louisiana, roast goose, instead of the traditional turkey, is served for holiday feasts. But no matter what bird has the place of honor at the celebration table, some kind of rice dressing is most certainly offered. I use one made with wild pecan rice grown near New Iberia in Iberia Parish. Make the port gravy while the goose is roasting.

½ cup chopped onions

¼ cup chopped celery

¼ cup chopped bell peppers

3 teaspoons salt

¼ teaspoon cayenne

1 stick (¼ pound) butter, cut into ⅛-inch slices

1 domestic goose, neck and giblets reserved (about 8 pounds)

½ teaspoon freshly ground black pepper

1 recipe Wild Pecan Rice Dressing (page 223)

1. Combine the onions, celery, bell peppers, 1 teaspoon of the salt, and ¼ teaspoon of the cayenne in a mixing bowl. Let sit for 1 hour at room temperature.

2. Sprinkle the butter slices evenly with 1 teaspoon of the salt and ¼ teaspoon of the cayenne. Freeze for 30 minutes. Toss the butter with the vegetables.

3. Preheat the oven to 400°F.

4. Remove any extra fat around the opening of the cavity of the goose. Prick other fatty areas of the goose with a fork at intervals. Do not prick the breast. With the goose breast side up and the cavity facing you, make slits, using a sharp pointed knife, inside the cavity between the rib bones and the breastbone. Do not puncture the breast skin. Using your fingers or the handle of a small spoon, insert 2 to 3 slices of butter and about 1 tablespoon of the vegetables into each hole. Season the outside of the goose with the remaining 1 teaspoon salt, the remaining ¼ teaspoon cayenne, and the black pepper.

5. Place the goose in a large roasting pan and roast for about 1 hour. Remove the goose from the pan and stuff it with the dressing. Reserve any

CHICKEN, DUCK, QUAIL, AND GOOSE

excess dressing to garnish the serving platter. Return the goose to the oven and roast for about 45 minutes, or until drumsticks and thighs are easy to move.

Port Gravy

2 teaspoons vegetable oil

Giblets and neck from the goose

½ cup chopped onions

¼ cup chopped celery

½ cup chopped carrots

1 teaspoon salt

½ teaspoon freshly ground black pepper

5 bay leaves

½ teaspoon dried thyme

2 tablespoons flour

2 cups port wine

2 cups water

6. Heat the oil in a saucepan over medium-high heat and brown the giblets and neck, 3 to 4 minutes. Add the onions, celery, carrots, salt, pepper, bay leaves, and thyme and cook, stirring often, for 3 to 4 minutes. Add the flour and stir to combine. Cook for about 5 minutes. Add the wine, bring to a boil, and cook, stirring occasionally, for 5 to 6 minutes. Add the water and bring to a boil. Reduce the heat to medium and simmer for about 1 hour. Strain.

7. To serve, carve the goose and serve with rice dressing and the port gravy.

6 servings

CHAPTER 7

Meat

NATCHITOCHES

MEAT PIES, PORK

BOULETTES,

GRILLADES, AND

MORE

n the rural areas of the state there are vast, lush flatlands ideal for raising cattle. In addition, most farms, small and large, have pens where hogs and pigs are fattened for a boucherie, or pig killing, and the slaughterhouse. Since the choicest cuts were, and still are, sent to market, Louisianians developed many ways to make appealing the leftover parts they did keep for their families. What has evolved is a repertoire of exquisitely seasoned, simple dishes. Hearty Round Steak and Onions is often served for supper. People from far and wide travel to Natchitoches for the famous meat pies, which are served daily for lunch and holiday feasts. Grillades, usually served with baked grits, is a favorite brunch dish. Daube Glacée, a beef and vegetable mold with aspic, takes hours to prepare, but it's like no other dish I've ever tasted. Pork, used to make tasso, andouille, and boudin, is also sent to the table in the form of chops, ribs, and boulettes, or meatballs. Lamb is usually reserved for special occasions.

Campfire Steaks

ne cold morning I was sitting in a duck blind with a fellow I had met for the first time the night before. While we shivered and waited for the ducks to fly overhead, he told me in great detail how he cooked not only duck, but also fish, shrimp, and steak. He struck a chord when he talked about steak. I admitted to being a big beef eater and promised to prepare one of my all-time favorite recipes for him. The aroma, texture, and presentation of a rib steak grilled on cedar shingles made his eyes pop when I produced the steaks for the group that evening. Untreated cedar shingles are available at home-improvement centers and lumberyards.

4 untreated cedar shingles, about 5½ × 10 inches each

2 teaspoons vegetable oil

4 rib eye steaks, about 1 inch thick (about 10 ounces each)

2 teaspoons Rustic Rub (page 9)

4 teaspoons Green Jalapeño Sauce (page 8) or Tabasco Brand Jalapeño Sauce

1 large bell pepper, thinly sliced

1 large onion, thinly sliced

1 teaspoon salt

¼ teaspoon cayenne

1. Prepare a grill and light the fire.
2. Rub 1 side of each shingle with ½ teaspoon oil. Place the steaks on the planks and flatten them out with the heel of your hand. Season each steak with ½ teaspoon rub. Spread each steak with 1 teaspoon jalapeño sauce. Combine the bell pepper and onion in a bowl and season with the salt and cayenne.
3. Divide the mixture into 4 equal portions and top each steak with a portion.
4. When the grill is hot, place the planks in the center. Close the lid and cook for about 10 minutes for rare, 14 to 16 minutes for medium-rare. Remove the planks from the grill using a long-handled spatula. If the plank catches fire, douse it with a little water.
5. Serve the steaks on the planks in the center of large plates.

4 servings

Steak in Creole Mustard Sauce

round Pecan Island and Cow Island, in the vast area of Vermilion Parish on the coast of south Louisiana, there are ridges made of mud, silt, and shells. They are called *chênières*, from the French *chêne*, meaning oak, because live oaks flourish there. The *chênières* keep the live oaks safe from the salt water; they cannot grow in salt water. During the spring and summer months, herds of cattle graze on grass that grows safe from the salt water. In the winter months, the animals forage in the dense marshland. Most of these cattle are sent to market, but now and then, one is held back by a cattleman for his family. After the slaughter, the meat is cut, packed, and frozen for use throughout the year, but a couple of rib eyes may be cooked right away in celebration. Prepared like this, with the inevitable onions, bell peppers, and celery and seasoned with cayenne and a bit of Creole mustard, they make an uncommonly good meal. Serve with Smashing Smashed Potatoes (page 251).

2 rib eye steaks, about 10 ounces each

2 teaspoons Rustic Rub (page 9)

2 tablespoons vegetable oil

2 tablespoons flour

1 cup chopped onions

1/2 cup chopped bell peppers

1/4 cup chopped celery

1/2 teaspoon salt

1/8 teaspoon cayenne

1/4 teaspoon coarsely ground black pepper

1 1/2 cups Veal Stock (page 14)

2 tablespoons Creole or whole-grain mustard

continued

1. Season the steaks on both sides with the rub. Heat the oil in a large skillet over medium-high heat. Sear each steak for about 3 minutes on each side for medium-rare, 4 minutes for medium. Transfer to a warm platter.

2. Add the flour to the skillet, and reduce the heat to medium. Stirring constantly for about 3 to 4 minutes, make a dark brown roux, the color of chocolate.

3. Add the onions, bell peppers, celery, salt, cayenne, and black pepper. Cook, stirring constantly, for 4 to 5 minutes, or until the vegetables are wilted. Add the stock and raise the heat to medium-high. Bring to a boil, add the steaks, and continue stirring the sauce until the mixture thickens, about 6 minutes. Turn the steaks several times during this cooking time, basting them with the sauce. Add the mustard, blend, and simmer for about 2 minutes.

4. Serve immediately.

2 servings

Fillet Steaks and Ratatouille

 n the heat of the summer, when gardens flourish, a thick vegetable stew is often made with tomatoes, eggplant, bell peppers, zucchini, and yellow squash. I like to pile the vegetables on top of pangrilled steaks and finish them off in the oven.

2 fillet steaks (5 to 6 ounces each)

1/2 tablespoon Rustic Rub (page 9)

1 tablespoon vegetable oil

1/4 recipe Ratatouille (page 243)

1/4 cup chopped green onions

1/4 cup freshly grated parmesan

3 tablespoons chopped parsley

Emeril's Worcestershire Sauce (page 7), for serving

1. Preheat the oven to 400°F.
2. Season the steaks with the rub. Heat the oil in a skillet over medium-high heat and sear the steaks for about 1 minute on each side. Put the steaks in a shallow baking pan. Combine the ratatouille, green onions, cheese, and parsley in a mixing bowl. Spoon this mixture on top of the steaks.
3. Bake for 6 minutes for rare, about 10 minutes for medium-rare, and 14 to 15 minutes for medium.
4. Drizzle with Worcestershire and serve.

2 servings

Round Steak and Onions

kin to Grillades, this preparation makes an inexpensive cut of meat tender, juicy, and decidedly delicious. Thin pieces of round steak are browned, then cooked with onions and bell peppers. Ask anyone in south Louisiana about this dish and they'll tell you they were raised on it. A big strapping fellow I know says he ate so much as a child, he's sure his right leg is made of it. Serve it with rice and Corn Maque Choux (page 234).

1½ pounds top round steak, about ¼ inch thick

2 teaspoons Rustic Rub (page 9)

1 tablespoon flour

2 tablespoons vegetable oil

2 cups water

4 cups sliced onions

1½ cups sliced bell peppers

1¼ teaspoons salt

¼ teaspoon cayenne

¼ teaspoon freshly ground black pepper

1. Cut the steak into 4-inch squares. Season the meat with the rub. Toss the meat with the flour to coat evenly.

2. Heat the oil in a large cast-iron skillet over medium-high heat and brown the meat, cooking on each side for 4 to 5 minutes. Add 1 cup of the water and stir, scraping the bottom and sides of the pan to loosen any browned particles. Add the onions, bell peppers, salt, cayenne, and black pepper. Stir for 6 to 8 minutes, or until the vegetables are wilted. Reduce the heat to medium. Cover and cook, stirring occasionally, for 15 minutes. Add the remaining 1 cup water and cook, uncovered, for 15 to 20 minutes, stirring occasionally and scraping the bottom and sides of the pan to loosen any browned particles.

3. Serve immediately.

4 servings

Grillades

t's pronounced "gree-YAHDS" with no l sound whatsoever. I just had to get that out of the way first. This dish uses pounded beef, veal, or both, and sometimes pork, first seared in hot oil, then braised in a sauce with onions, bell peppers, tomatoes, herbs, and just the right amount of spices. Some recipes call for tomatoes, others not. I personally like just a bit of tomatoes so that the gravy is a dark, rich color. Grillades are often served for brunch with Baked Cheese Grits (page 230), but they make a fine supper.

1½ pounds beef top round	¼ teaspoon dried thyme
1 pound veal top round	¼ teaspoon dried oregano
2 tablespoons Rustic Rub (page 9)	¼ teaspoon dried basil
½ cup flour	1 teaspoon salt
¼ cup vegetable oil	¼ teaspoon cayenne
2 cups chopped onions	⅛ teaspoon freshly ground black pepper
1 cup chopped bell peppers	
1 cup chopped celery	2 cups beef broth, homemade or canned
1½ cups chopped, peeled, and seeded tomatoes, or 1½ cups canned chopped tomatoes	½ cup dry red wine
1 tablespoon chopped garlic	3 tablespoons chopped green onions
5 bay leaves	2 tablespoons chopped parsley

1. Cut the beef and veal into 2-inch pieces. Combine the rub and flour in a small bowl. Lay the pieces of meat on a work surface or large cutting board and lightly coat with the seasoned flour. Lightly pound the meat with a meat mallet. Turn the meat pieces over and repeat the process.

continued

2. Heat the oil in a large cast-iron pot or enameled cast-iron Dutch oven over medium-high heat. Add the meat and, stirring constantly, brown evenly on both sides for 5 to 6 minutes. Add the onions, bell peppers, and celery and continue to stir, scraping the bottom and sides of the pot to loosen any browned particles. Cook for 5 to 6 minutes, or until the vegetables are wilted. Add the tomatoes and garlic. Cook, stirring often and scraping the bottom and sides of the pot for 3 to 4 minutes. Add the bay leaves, thyme, oregano, basil, salt, cayenne, black pepper, broth, and wine. Reduce heat to medium and cook, partially covered, stirring occasionally, for about 1½ hours, or until the meat is very tender.

3. Remove the bay leaves, add the green onions and parsley, and serve immediately.

6 servings

Braised Brisket of Beef with Horseradish Sauce

ne day while visiting a butcher shop in Lafayette, I overheard an old gentleman ask for a brisket, "une grande tranche, s'il vous plaît," a big one, please. When asked how many people he planned to feed, he laughed, "As many as I can find!" The Acadian philosophy is that if you're going to cook, you might as well cook a lot and share it. This brisket is cooked long and slow with tender and juicy results. When slicing, cut the meat against the grain.

Brisket and Gravy

1 brisket, 8 to 9 pounds, cut into 2 equal parts

4 garlic cloves, sliced

2 teaspoons salt

3/4 teaspoon cayenne

2 tablespoons Rustic Rub (page 9)

2 tablespoons vegetable oil

4 cups thinly sliced onions

1/4 teaspoon freshly ground black pepper

2 cans (12 ounces each) beer

1 cup water

1. Preheat the oven to 400°F.

2. With a sharp pointed knife, make about 10 slits in each of the brisket pieces. Stuff each hole with 2 to 3 slices of the garlic. Season the meat with 1 teaspoon of the salt, 1/2 teaspoon of the cayenne, and the rub. Heat the oil in a large skillet over high heat and sear the meat evenly, 2 to 3 minutes on all sides. Transfer the meat to a large lidded Dutch oven. The meat can overlap. Bake, uncovered, for about 45 minutes. Remove the pot from the oven.

3. In a mixing bowl, toss the onions with the remaining 1 teaspoon salt, remaining 1/4 teaspoon cayenne, and the black pepper. Arrange the onions around the meat in the roasting pot. Add the beer and water. Cover. Return the pot to the oven and reduce the heat to 350°F. Bake for about 2 1/2 hours, or until tender. Turn the meat over twice during the baking time.

4. Remove from the oven and let cool for about 15 minutes. Transfer the meat to a cutting board and keep warm. Reserve the pan gravy.

Horseradish Sauce

2 cups pan gravy

2 tablespoons prepared horseradish

1/4 cup heavy cream

5. Mix together the gravy, horseradish, and cream in a saucepan over medium heat. Cook, stirring occasionally, for 4 to 5 minutes.

6. To serve, thinly slice the meat and return to the gravy in the pot. Pour the horseradish sauce over the top of the meat and serve from the pot.

12 servings

Daube Glacée

At holiday parties and during Carnival season, you may find Daube Glacée the centerpiece of a buffet table. The meat is set in a stock that is rich with gelatin, chilled overnight, and unmolded. The daube is sliced and served with toasted French bread. Without a doubt, Daube Glacée is French inspired. When royalists fled the mother country during the French Revolution and found a haven in the Louisiana town of St. Martinville, le petit Paris de l'Amérique, this was one of the many dishes they brought with them. Marcelle's paternal grandmother, Léoncia Tertrou Bienvenu, was known far and wide for her daubes. She would set aside a day to make an icebox full of them for family and friends. Jenny, Léoncia's daughter, is now the keeper of the family recipe. Don't be put off by the length of the recipe. Most of the time the roasts and stocks simmer unattended. Traditionally, Daube Glacée was, and in some homes still is, served sliced for a luncheon or supper. Today, cooks find it more manageable to coarsely chop the beef roast before adding it to the gelatin so that it is easier to cut off small portions of the mold to put on crackers or toast points at cocktail-buffet parties. And instead of making one large round mold, the molds are made in loaf pans or smaller molds to make for easier serving.

1/4 pound bacon, cut into
1/2-inch pieces

3 1/2 teaspoons salt

1 3/4 teaspoons cayenne

1 1/2 teaspoons freshly ground black
pepper

1/2 teaspoon dried thyme

1 tablespoon chopped garlic

4 bay leaves

1 beef bottom round, 2 to 3 inches
thick (about 3 pounds)

1 tablespoon vegetable oil

3 cups coarsely chopped onions

2 cups coarsely chopped carrots

2 cups coarsely chopped turnips

6 quarts water

1/2 cup dry sherry

1 veal rump roast, with bone (about
3 pounds)

4 garlic cloves

3 envelopes (1/4 ounce each)
unflavored gelatin

1. Put the bacon in a small bowl and toss with 1/2 teaspoon of the salt, 1/2 teaspoon of the cayenne, 1/2 teaspoon of the black pepper, thyme, garlic, and 2 of the bay leaves, crumbled. With a sharp, pointed knife, make slits in the beef round, about 1 inch apart, being careful not to cut all the way through. Insert 2 to 3 pieces of the seasoned bacon into each hole. Season the beef with 1/2 teaspoon of the salt, 1/2 teaspoon of the cayenne, and 1/2 teaspoon of the black pepper.

2. Heat the oil in a large heavy pot over medium-high heat and brown the beef for 4 to 5 minutes on each side. Remove the beef from the pot. Add 2 cups of the onions, the carrots, and turnips. Make a bed of the vegetables on the bottom of the pot. Lay the beef on top of the vegetables and cook for 5 to 6 minutes, or until the vegetables are slightly wilted. Add 2 quarts of the water, or enough to cover the beef. Add 1/4 cup of the sherry and bring to a boil. Reduce the heat to medium, cover, and simmer, turning the beef several times, for about 3 hours, or until the meat is tender.

3. Season the veal rump with 1 teaspoon of the salt, 1/4 teaspoon of the cayenne, and 1/4 teaspoon of the black pepper. Put the veal in a large pot and add about 4 quarts of the water, or enough to cover the veal. Add the remaining 2 bay leaves, the garlic cloves, the remaining 1 cup onions, and the remaining 1/4 cup sherry and bring to a boil over medium-high heat. Reduce heat, cover, and simmer turning the veal several times, for about 3

hours, or until tender. Remove the veal from the pot and skim off any fat that has risen to the surface. Remove the bay leaves. Pour off 1 cup of the broth and cool in the refrigerator for about 1 hour. Remove any fat or gristle from the veal. Shred the meat.

4. Remove the beef from the pot. With a slotted spoon, remove the vegetables from the beef broth. Set aside. Discard the bay leaves. Skim off any fat that has risen to the surface.

5. Combine 8 cups of the beef broth with the shredded veal and season with the remaining 1 1/2 teaspoons salt, remaining 1/2 teaspoon cayenne, and remaining 1/2 teaspoon black pepper.

6. Add the gelatin to the cool veal stock. Whisk to dissolve the gelatin and let stand for 1 minute. Add this mixture to the beef stock and veal mixture and stir to combine.

7. Lay 3 cups of the cooked vegetables in the bottom of a bowl large enough to accommodate the beef. Place the beef on top of the vegetables. Pour the beef broth and veal mixture over the beef. Cover and refrigerate for 8 hours, or until the gelatin sets.

8. To serve, invert the bowl very carefully onto a large serving platter and unmold. The mold can then be sliced.

8 to 10 servings as a main course; or 50 or more as hors d'oeuvres

Variation

The beef can be coarsely chopped before adding the beef broth and veal mixture. Also, the mixture can be divided into two equal portions and poured into two smaller molds or loaf pans. Once the gelatin sets, unmold and cut into small pieces, or allow party guests to cut them and eat on crackers or toast points.

Natchitoches Meat Pies

atchitoches is known for two things. Every year on the first Saturday of December, thousands of visitors flock to this quaint town, located on the beautiful Cane River. They come to celebrate the annual Christmas Festival of Lights, when, at dusk, a switch is pulled that lights up the intricate decorations along the banks on both sides of the river. Natchitoches is also known for its meat pies, fried turnovers filled with ground meat and seasonings. The original version is believed to have been developed by the Natchitoches Indians and improved upon by Spanish settlers. For years, the meat pies were sold from carts by peddlers who roamed the streets of the town; the pies have been a staple in most kitchens in the Cane River area as well. Now you don't have to come to Natchitoches to enjoy these flavorful little turnovers. Make them for the Christmas holidays or any other time.

Filling

1 teaspoon vegetable oil

1 pound lean ground beef

½ pound ground pork

1 cup chopped onions

½ cup chopped bell peppers

½ cup chopped celery

1½ teaspoons salt

1 teaspoon Rustic Rub (page 9)

¼ teaspoon cayenne

½ teaspoon freshly ground black pepper

2 tablespoons chopped garlic

1 tablespoon flour

1 cup water

¼ cup chopped green onions

continued

1. Heat the vegetable oil over medium-high heat in a large skillet and brown the beef and pork, for 5 to 6 minutes. Add the onions, bell peppers, celery, salt, rub, cayenne, and black pepper. Cook, stirring often, until the vegetables are wilted, 10 to 12 minutes. Add the garlic and cook for 2 to 3 minutes.

2. Dissolve the flour in the water and add to the meat mixture. Stir until the mixture thickens slightly, about 3 minutes. Remove from the heat and add the green onions. Mix well and let cool.

Pastry

3 cups flour

1½ teaspoons salt

¾ teaspoon baking powder

6 tablespoons solid
   vegetable shortening

1 egg

¾ cup milk

Solid vegetable shortening
   for deep-frying

3. Sift the flour, salt, and baking powder into a mixing bowl. Cut in the shortening until it resembles coarse meal. In a small bowl, beat the egg with the milk. Gradually add the egg mixture to the flour mixture, working it to make a thick dough.

4. Break the dough into 12 equal portions. On a lightly floured surface, roll the dough pieces into thin rounds, about 5 inches in diameter. Put about ¼ cup of the meat mixture in the center of each round, fold over and crimp the edges with a fork.

5. Heat the shortening in a deep pot or an electric deep-fryer to 360°F. Fry the pies, two to three at a time, until golden brown.

6. Drain on paper towels and serve immediately.

12 hand pies

Beef Boulettes with Garlic

arcelle had a great-aunt whom she lovingly called Nannan. Nannan lived next door, and from the time Marcelle was six until she was about ten, they shared Wednesday-night supper. Right at first dark (dusk), Marcelle would go down the pathway that led to Nannan's little white cottage. Sometimes supper was fried chicken, other times it was sausage and grits. But Marcelle's favorite was beef boulettes, or meatballs, each with a clove of garlic in the center, in a pungent gravy and served over mashed potatoes or rice. Nannan and Marcelle didn't move from the table until every last one was consumed. I tried them with Corn Maque Choux (page 234) and Smothered Green Beans and Potatoes (page 241), and I ate them all, all by myself.

2 pounds ground beef	12 garlic cloves
2½ teaspoons salt	½ cup flour
¾ teaspoon freshly ground black pepper	2 teaspoons Rustic Rub (page 9)
½ teaspoon cayenne	3 tablespoons vegetable oil
½ cup finely chopped onions plus 3 cups thinly sliced onions	4 bay leaves
	2 cups water
	3 tablespoons chopped parsley

1. Put the beef in a mixing bowl and add 1½ teaspoons of the salt, ½ teaspoon of the black pepper, the cayenne, and the chopped onions. Mix well with your hands. Make 12 meatballs. Insert a clove of garlic in the center of each and pinch the beef around it. Combine the flour with the rub in a shallow plate. Roll the meatballs evenly in the flour mixture. Reserve any excess flour.

continued

2. Heat the oil in a large saucepan over high heat. Add the meatballs and brown evenly, using a spoon to turn them. With a slotted spoon, remove the meatballs and set aside.

3. Reduce the heat to medium and add the reserved flour mixture. Stirring constantly for 3 to 4 minutes, make a dark brown roux, the color of chocolate.

4. Add the sliced onions, the remaining 1 teaspoon salt, remaining ¼ teaspoon black pepper, and the bay leaves. Cook, stirring occasionally, for about 10 minutes, or until the onions are very soft. Add the water and mix well to combine. Bring to a boil and return the meatballs to the pot. Reduce the heat and simmer, uncovered, for about 1 hour. Skim off any fat that has risen to the surface. Remove the bay leaves.

5. Add the parsley and serve immediately.

6 servings

Panéed Veal

 t has to be coated with cracker meal or crumbled cracker crumbs—not anything else!" That's what Marcelle's mama told me when I was cooking a batch of these veal cutlets. Panéed, or breaded, veal is a dish that found its way from the country kitchens to the dining rooms of fine New Orleans restaurants in recent years. There is no need to dredge the cutlets in flour first. The egg wash and cracker crumb coat work just fine. Crunchy and spiced up with Rustic Rub, it's perfect with mashed potatoes, but it also goes well with fettuccine bathed in cream and romano cheese.

4 veal cutlets (about 2½ ounces each)

3 teaspoons Rustic Rub (page 9)

1 egg

1 tablespoon water

26 saltine crackers, finely crumbled in a blender or food processor

¼ cup vegetable oil

1. Wrap each cutlet in plastic wrap and pound with a meat mallet until very thin. Season the cutlets with 1 teaspoon of the rub. Mix together the egg and water in a shallow bowl. Combine the cracker crumbs with the remaining 2 teaspoons rub in a shallow platter. Dip the cutlets in the egg mixture, then in the cracker crumb mixture.

2. Heat the oil in a skillet over medium-high heat and fry the cutlets for about 30 seconds on each side, or until golden brown.

3. Serve immediately.

2 servings

Veal Sausage with Creamy Grits

ince we do a lot of our own butchering at Emeril's, my restaurant in New Orleans, we make veal sausage from the trimmings so nothing goes to waste. When I go to a fishing camp, I always pack a few links so my friends and I can have a hearty breakfast before we take to the water for the day. These can be served any time of the day though, not just for breakfast. If veal sausage is not available, substitute a fresh, not smoked, chicken or turkey sausage.

1 tablespoon olive oil

1/2 cup chopped onions

1 cup sliced shiitake mushrooms

1/2 pound veal sausage links

2 cups milk

1/4 cup chopped green onions

1 tablespoon chopped garlic

1/2 teaspoon salt

1/4 teaspoon cayenne

3 ounces white cheddar, grated (about 3/4 cup)

1/2 cup quick white grits

1. Heat the oil in a large skillet over medium heat.
2. Add the onions and mushrooms and sauté for about 1 minute. Add the sausage and brown the sausage on all sides for 2 to 3 minutes. Add the milk, green onions, garlic, salt, and cayenne and bring to a boil. Reduce the heat to medium-low and cook, stirring occasionally, for about 10 minutes. Add the cheese and stir to melt, 1 to 2 minutes.
3. Add the grits and raise the heat to medium. Cook, stirring, for about 3 minutes, basting the sausage with the creamy mixture. Continue to cook and stir for 7 to 8 minutes, or until the grits are cooked through and tender.
4. Serve immediately.

2 servings

Pork Chops and Sweet Potato Gravy

n the fall and winter, when yams, pecans, and sugarcane are being harvested, this dish, with subtle variations, is often served around the state. The deep orange flesh of the potato makes a smooth and syrupy gravy in which to bathe thick pork chops.

4 thick pork chops (6 to 8 ounces each)	1 teaspoon salt
2 teaspoons Rustic Rub (page 9)	¼ teaspoon cayenne
2 tablespoons vegetable oil	1 pound sweet potatoes, baked (see page 255), peeled, and mashed (about 1½ cups)
2 tablespoons flour	
1½ cups thinly sliced onions	3 tablespoons Steen's 100% Pure Cane Syrup
½ cup pecan pieces	
2 cups water	¼ chopped green onions

1. Season the pork chops with the rub. Heat the oil in a large skillet over medium-high heat and brown the chops, about 5 minutes on each side. Transfer the chops to a warm platter and set aside.

2. Reduce the heat to medium. Add the flour and, stirring constantly, cook for 2 to 3 minutes, or until the roux is dark brown, the color of chocolate. Add the onions and cook, stirring occasionally, for 5 to 6 minutes, or until wilted. Add the pecans, water, salt, and cayenne and mix well. Bring to a boil. Add the sweet potatoes and blend to make a smooth mixture. Stir in the syrup and green onions. Return the pork chops to the pan, reduce the heat, and simmer for 4 to 5 minutes, basting the chops with the gravy.

3. Serve immediately.

4 servings

Braised Pork Ribs and Andouille

efore electric refrigeration, farmers, with their families, friends, and field workers, would gather in the winter for a boucherie. A day was set aside to slaughter and butcher a fattened hog. Everyone worked throughout the day, making boudin, andouille, tasso, fromage de tête de cochon (headcheese), and grattons (cracklings). Pig's feet were pickled and the ponce, or stomach, was stuffed with vegetables and trimmings. Slabs of bacon, hams, and pork chops and ribs were divided among those who helped. But it was not a day of all work and no play. Often a fiddler provided toe-tapping music while a stew made with the backbone of the hog simmered over a wood fire for a late-afternoon meal, and everyone caught up on the local gossip. These days you have to go deep into the back bayous to find a real boucherie, and it may be held at any time of the year, with refrigeration making the weather irrelevant. And at butcher shops scattered around the southern part of the state, you can still find plenty of sausages, headcheese, and cracklings. It was at one of these markets that I learned about this dish of pork ribs cooked with andouille. Serve it over rice accompanied by French bread or Skillet Corn Bread (page 284).

1 rack pork ribs (3 to 4 pounds)

1 tablespoon Rustic Rub (page 9)

¼ cup vegetable oil

¼ cup flour

1 cup chopped onions

½ cup chopped bell peppers

2 teaspoons salt

½ teaspoon cayenne

½ pound Andouille Sausage
(page 205), coarsely chopped

1 cup chopped, peeled, and seeded
tomatoes, or 1 cup chopped canned
tomatoes

4 bay leaves

6 cups water

1. Cut the ribs into 1-rib pieces. Season with the rub. Heat the oil in a large heavy pot over medium-high heat. Sear the ribs, several at a time, until well browned, about 2 minutes on each side. Transfer to a platter and set aside.

2. Add the flour to the oil in the pot and stirring constantly, make a dark brown roux, the color of chocolate.

3. Scrape the bottom and sides of the pot to loosen any browned particles. Add the onions, bell peppers, salt, and cayenne. Cook, stirring constantly, for 3 to 4 minutes, or until the vegetables are wilted.

4. Add the andouille. Stir, scraping the bottom and sides of the pot to loosen any browned particles, and cook for about 3 minutes. Add the tomatoes and bay leaves. Cook, stirring constantly, for about 5 minutes. Add the water and stir to mix well. Bring to a boil. Add the ribs and reduce the heat to medium. Simmer, stirring occasionally, for about 2 hours, or until the ribs are tender.

5. Remove the bay leaves and serve.

4 to 6 servings

Pork Ribs in Red Gravy

n Louisiana, tomato sauce is called red gravy. And instead of meatballs swimming around in it, you might find pork ribs. This is a dish that typifies the Acadian philosophy that while food is prepared for nourishment, it is also a form of pleasure. Many a Saturday afternoon is spent in the kitchen, cooking, stirring, and smelling, then eating. Be sure to have lots of French bread to sop up the gravy.

2 racks pork ribs (6 to 7 pounds)	5 bay leaves
2 tablespoons Rustic Rub (page 9)	1½ cups dry red wine
½ cup flour	2 cups chopped, peeled, and seeded tomatoes, or 2 cups chopped canned tomatoes
¼ cup vegetable oil	
2 cups chopped onions	1 can (6 ounces) tomato paste
½ cup chopped bell peppers	2 cups thick tomato sauce
1 cup chopped carrots	2 quarts water
1 tablespoon salt	½ teaspoon dried thyme
1 teaspoon cayenne	½ teaspoon dried basil
3 tablespoons chopped garlic	½ teaspoon dried oregano

1. Cut the ribs into 2-rib pieces. Season with 1 tablespoon of the rub. Season the flour with the remaining 1 tablespoon rub. Dredge the ribs in the seasoned flour. Heat the oil in a large enameled cast-iron Dutch oven over medium-high heat. Brown the ribs, three to four at a time, 4 to 5 minutes. As they brown, transfer to a platter and set aside. Using a metal spatula, remove and discard any browned particles on the bottom of the pot.

2. Add the onions and bell peppers to the pot and cook, stirring constantly, for 4 to 5 minutes. Add the carrots, salt, cayenne, garlic, and bay leaves. Cook, stirring, for 2 to 3 minutes. Add the wine and simmer for 3 minutes.

Add the tomatoes, tomato paste, tomato sauce, and water. Stir to mix well.
3. Add the ribs and submerge in the mixture. Add the thyme, basil, and oregano. Reduce the heat to medium and simmer for about $2\frac{1}{2}$ hours, or until the ribs are very tender with the meat falling off the bones. Skim off any fat that has risen to the surface. Remove the bay leaves.
4. To serve, remove the meat from the bones and put the meat in the gravy. Reheat if necessary.

6 servings

Fricassee of Pork and Turnips

ussell Leger, a butcher in Lafayette in south Louisiana, makes the finest boudin I've ever tasted. When I'm in his part of the state, I make a point of visiting him to stock up on some of his meats as well. He once showed me the marinated pork pieces in his shop that his customers buy for stew. I liked the idea and concocted this pork fricassee with turnips. Serve it over rice.

3/4 pound boneless pork loin, cut into
   1-inch cubes

1 tablespoon Rustic Rub (page 9)

2 tablespoons vegetable oil

1/2 cup chopped onions

1/4 cup chopped bell peppers

1/4 cup chopped celery

1 teaspoon salt

1/4 teaspoon cayenne

2 tablespoons flour

1 pound turnips, peeled and cubed
   (about 2 cups)

2 cups Chicken Broth (page 11)

1. Toss the pork with the rub in a bowl and refrigerate for at least 1 hour.

2. Heat the oil in a large skillet over medium-high heat. Add the pork and brown evenly. Season the onions, bell peppers, and celery with the salt and cayenne. When the pork is brown, remove from the skillet with a slotted spoon. Set aside.

3. Add the flour to the oil in the skillet. Stirring constantly for 4 to 5 minutes, make a medium brown roux, the color of peanut butter.

4. Add the onions, bell peppers, and celery and cook for 2 to 3 minutes, or until slightly wilted. Return the pork to the skillet and cook, stirring constantly, for 3 to 4 minutes. Add the turnips and broth. Stir to mix well. Bring to a boil, reduce heat to medium-low, and cook stirring occasionally, for 40 to 45 minutes.

5. Serve immediately.

4 servings

Pork Burgers

ne of the specialties at Hebert's, an old-fashioned meat market near Abbeville in Vermilion Parish, is a pork patty encased in caul fat. Marcelle's papa used to bring home a paper sack full of them on the return trip from his hunting camp in Gueydan. They're good and spicy and can be grilled or panfried. Here's my version —without the caul fat. When I want to be decadent, I tuck them in between two chunks of French bread that has been slathered with One-Egg Mayonnaise (page 29).

1 pound coarsely ground lean pork

1 tablespoon chopped garlic

2 tablespoons chopped parsley

¼ cup chopped green onions

½ teaspoon salt

⅛ teaspoon cayenne

1 teaspoon Worcestershire sauce

2 teaspoons prepared horseradish

½ teaspoon Tabasco sauce

1. Combine all of the ingredients in a bowl and mix well. Divide the mixture into 4 equal portions and form into patties. On a grill or in a skillet, cook for 5 to 6 minutes on each side, or until all the pink disappears.

2. Serve immediately.

4 patties

185

Pork Boulettes

lmost every small-town grocery store or meat market in the state offers Boudin (page 202) and grattons, crunchy fried pork skins. And if you're lucky, you'll find deep-fried pork boulettes, bite-size morsels made with ground pork and rice. They're great served as an hors d'oeuvre.

½ pound ground pork	¼ cup chopped green onions
½ stick (4 tablespoons) butter	¼ teaspoon Tabasco sauce
3 tablespoons plus ¾ cup flour	2 cups dried fine bread crumbs
½ cup chopped onions	3 teaspoons Rustic Rub (page 9)
¼ cup chopped bell peppers	1 egg
1½ cups water	¼ cup milk
1 teaspoon salt	Solid vegetable shortening for deep-frying
½ teaspoon cayenne	
2 cups cooked medium-grain rice	

1. Brown the pork in a small skillet over medium-high heat. When browned, remove from the skillet with a slotted spoon and drain on paper towels. Melt the butter in a large skillet over medium-high heat. Add 3 tablespoons of the flour and, stirring constantly for 4 to 5 minutes, make a dark brown roux, the color of chocolate.

2. Add the onions and bell peppers. Stir constantly for 3 to 4 minutes until wilted. Add the pork and cook stirring constantly, for 2 to 3 minutes. Add the water, salt, and cayenne. Reduce the heat to medium-low. Simmer for 45 to 50 minutes, stirring occasionally. Add the rice, green onions, Tabasco, and ½ cup of the bread crumbs. Mix well. Remove from the heat and let cool for about 20 minutes.

3. Put the remaining ¾ cup flour and remaining 1½ cups bread crumbs in separate shallow bowls. Season each with 1½ teaspoons of the rub. Beat the egg and milk in a small bowl.

4. Shape the pork and rice mixture into balls the size of walnuts. Dredge them in the flour, dip in the egg mixture, then dredge in the bread crumbs.

5. Heat the shortening to 360°F. in a deep-fryer or deep cast-iron pot. Deep-fry the balls, five to six at a time, until golden brown. Drain on paper towels. Or bake the balls on a baking sheet for about 35 minutes at 400°F.

6. Serve hot.

About 2 dozen

Andouille Pudding

eople of Acadian descent have an innate sense of taste and style. Present them with a handful of simple ingredients—sausage, onions, eggs, cream, milk, bread, and, of course, salt and cayenne—and without so much as a moment's hesitation, they can create a dish like this. It's fluffy and moist and packed with flavor. Serve it warm as a side dish to just about anything in this book.

1 tablespoon vegetable oil

1 pound Andouille Sausage (page 205), coarsely chopped

1 cup chopped onions

1/2 cup chopped celery

2 tablespoons chopped garlic

5 eggs

1 cup heavy cream

3 cups milk

1 tablespoon salt

1/2 teaspoon cayenne

1/4 teaspoon freshly ground black pepper

8 cups 1-inch cubed white bread

8 ounces white cheddar, grated (2 cups)

1. Heat the oil in a skillet over medium-high heat and sauté the andouille for 3 to 4 minutes. Add the onions and celery. Cook, stirring often, for 4 to 5 minutes, or until slightly wilted. Add the garlic and cook for 1 minute. Remove from the heat and set aside.

2. Combine the eggs, cream, milk, salt, cayenne, and black pepper and mix well. Add the bread, the andouille mixture, and half of the cheese. Fold to mix thoroughly. Cover and refrigerate for 30 minutes.

3. Preheat the oven to 375°F.

4. Transfer the mixture to a 2 1/2- to 3-quart baking dish. Sprinkle with the remaining cheese. Bake for 45 minutes, or until golden brown on top.

5. Remove from the oven and let stand for 5 minutes.

6. Serve warm directly from the baking dish.

8 to 10 servings

Cassoulet

his casserole of white beans and assorted meats is very popular throughout southwestern France with as many versions as there are provinces—something like the infinite versions of gumbo in Louisiana. In a Louisiana cassoulet, anything goes. Use whatever you have—rabbit, duck, chicken, and most any kind of sausage. This one has pork chops, sausage, and chicken. Fragrant, intoxicating, and pungent, it's a meal to be enjoyed on a cold winter's night with a bottle of red wine and crusty French bread. You might want to prepare the beans a day ahead of time since they take a while to cook.

Beans

1 tablespoon butter

¼ cup chopped onions

¼ cup chopped celery

1 pound white navy beans, soaked overnight and drained

¼ teaspoon salt

⅛ teaspoon cayenne

2 quarts water

1 bay leaf

1. Melt the butter in a large saucepan over high heat and sauté the onions and celery for 3 to 4 minutes, or until slightly wilted. Add the beans, salt, cayenne, water, and bay leaf and bring to a boil. Reduce the heat to medium-low and cook until the beans are tender and most of the water is absorbed, about 2 hours. Remove the bay leaf.

2. If the beans are prepared ahead of time, refrigerate until ready to use.

continued

Meats

1/4 cup flour

1/4 cup oil

1 cup chopped onions

1/2 cup chopped celery

1/2 cup chopped bell peppers

1/2 cup chopped carrots

1/2 teaspoon salt

1/8 teaspoon cayenne

4 thin pork chops, cut in half (4 to 5 ounces each)

1 pound smoked sausage, such as andouille or kielbasa, cut into 6 to 8 equal portions

2 cups Chicken Broth (page 11)

1 pound roasted duck or chicken meat, cut into 2-inch pieces

1 teaspoon Rustic Rub (page 9)

3. Combine the flour and oil in a large ovenproof skillet over medium-high heat. Stirring constantly and slowly, make a medium brown roux, the color of peanut butter.

4. Add the onions, celery, bell peppers, carrots, salt, and cayenne. Cook, stirring constantly, for 3 to 4 minutes, or until the vegetables are slightly wilted. Lay the pork chops on top of the roux and vegetable mixture and cook for 2 minutes on each side. Add the sausage and cook for 2 more minutes, turning several times. Add the broth and stir until the roux and broth are combined and the mixture thickens. Scrape the bottom and sides of the pot to loosen any browned particles. Bring to a boil.

Gratin

3/4 cup dried fine bread crumbs

1/2 cup freshly grated parmesan

3 tablespoons chopped parsley

1 teaspoon Rustic Rub (page 9)

2 tablespoons olive oil

5. Season the duck pieces with the rub. Add the duck and the cooked beans to the vegetable and meat mixture. Reduce the heat to medium-low and cook for about 30 minutes.

6. Preheat the oven to 450°F. Make the gratin. Combine the bread crumbs, cheese, parsley, rub, and olive oil in a mixing bowl. Mix well.

7. When the bean and meat mixture is cooked, spoon the mixture evenly over the top and bake for about 10 minutes, or until the top has browned lightly.

8. Serve immediately.

6 to 8 servings

Baked Ham

irst, let me explain something about a ham. The best buy, and the one used most often in cooking in the South, is a whole ham—the whole hind leg of the pig, shank and butt and bone and all—cured and ready to eat. Most people pass up this large cut because it's more than they can handle, or so they think. In Louisiana, probably because baked ham is served at festive occasions, such as the Christmas holidays, weddings, and large family gatherings, no one bats an eye at a whole ham. If you're confused when you go to the market to buy your ham, explain to the butcher that you need a ham as I've described. It usually weighs anywhere from fourteen to sixteen pounds, sometimes more.

Spicy Sugar Glaze

1/4 cup fresh lemon juice

1 cup Steen's 100% Pure Cane Syrup

1/4 teaspoon ground cloves

1/4 teaspoon ground allspice

1 tablespoon coarsely ground black pepper

1/4 cup (packed) light brown sugar

1 teaspoon dry mustard

1. Whisk all ingredients together in a small bowl until well blended. Allow to stand for at least 1 hour before using.

About 1 1/2 cups

Ham

1 cured ham (about 14 pounds)

2. Preheat the oven to 325°F.

3. Remove the ham skin with a sharp knife. Trim the fat to a thickness of 1/4 to 1/8 inch and score it by making long vertical and horizontal cuts. Place the ham, fat side up, on a rack in a shallow roasting pan. Cover loosely with aluminum foil and bake for 30 minutes. Remove from the oven and remove the foil. Spoon 3/4 cup of the glaze over the top

of the ham. Return to oven; bake 30 minutes. Spoon remaining ¾ cup glaze over the ham. Bake about 1 hour, basting occasionally with pan juices.

4. Raise the oven heat to 425° F. and bake for about 15 minutes, to crisp the top of the ham. Remove from the oven and let rest for about 15 minutes before carving.

5. Place the ham on a platter, fat side up, and cut into thin slices. It's best to carve from the smaller end to the wider section. And remember, the ham bone is great for flavoring soups!

16 to 20 servings

Roasted Leg of Lamb

 aster Sunday dinner in Louisiana can be anything from boiled crawfish, baked ham, barbecued chicken to roast leg of lamb. Everyone has a preference and mine is lamb. Many families raise their own Easter lamb; those baby lambs are tender and full of flavor. When the leg is prepared for cooking, the bone is removed, but the socket and ball aren't so the roast will hold its shape. What I especially like about this dish is the spicy bread crumb crust.

1 whole leg of lamb (about 9 to 10 pounds)	½ cup vegetable oil
3 tablespoons chopped garlic	2 cups dried fine bread crumbs
6 tablespoons chopped fresh rosemary leaves	2 tablespoons Rustic Rub (page 9)
4 teaspoons salt	8 medium red potatoes, halved
¾ teaspoon cayenne	3 large carrots, cut into 3-inch pieces (about 2 cups)
1¾ teaspoons freshly ground black pepper	4 medium onions, quartered
3 tablespoons plus ¼ cup Creole or whole-grain mustard	4 celery ribs, cut into 3-inch pieces (about 2 cups)

1. Preheat the oven to 400°F.

2. Line the bottom of a roasting pan with heavy-duty aluminum foil and fit it with a rack.

3. With the butt end of the roast facing you, make about a dozen slits in the fleshy part of the meat with a sharp, pointed knife. In a bowl, mix together the garlic, 3 tablespoons of the rosemary, 1 teaspoon of the salt, ¼ teaspoon of the cayenne, ¼ teaspoon of the black pepper, and 3 table-spoons of the mustard to make a paste. Using your fingers, insert equal amounts of the paste into the holes. Tie the leg crosswise with kitchen twine, at 3-inch intervals. Season the outside of the lamb with 1 teaspoon of the salt, ½ teaspoon of the black pepper, and the remaining ½ tea-spoon cayenne.

4. Heat 3 tablespoons of the vegetable oil in a pan large enough to accom-modate the lamb over high heat. Sear the lamb for about 3 minutes on all sides. Remove the lamb from the skillet and set aside. Combine the bread crumbs, the remaining 3 tablespoons rosemary, the rub, and ¼ cup of the oil in a bowl. Rub the top and sides of the lamb with the remaining ¼ cup mustard. Using your fingers, press the bread crumb mixture evenly and firmly onto the mustard-covered area. Place the lamb on the rack in the roasting pan and roast for 1 hour.

5. Toss the potatoes, carrots, onions, and celery with the remaining 2 tea-spoons salt, remaining 1 teaspoon black pepper, and 1 tablespoon oil. Remove the pan from the oven and place the vegetables on the rack around the lamb. Return the pan to the oven and roast for about 1 hour, or until the internal temperature of the lamb registers 160°F. on a meat thermometer for a delicate pink center. If you prefer the lamb to be medium-rare, roast for about 1 hour 45 minutes, or until a meat thermometer reg-isters 140° to 145°F. Remove the roast and let it rest for 20 to 30 minutes before carving.

6. Serve with the vegetables.

10 to 12 servings

Crusted Tenderloin of Rabbit

he tenderloin of the rabbit is considered a real prize. This preparation makes a flavorful appetizer when served on a bed of White Beans (page 228) and drizzled with Emeril's Worcestershire Sauce (page 7). You may prefer to put the tenderloins on a bed of Southern Greens (page 242), or even on a mound of salad greens. Either wild or farm-raised rabbit can be used for this dish.

1/4 cup dried fine bread crumbs

1/4 teaspoon dried basil

1/4 teaspoon dried oregano

2 teaspoons Rustic Rub (page 9)

1 tablespoon freshly grated parmesan

2 rabbit tenderloins (about 2 ounces each)

1 tablespoon Creole or whole-grain mustard

3 tablespoons vegetable oil

1. Preheat the oven to 400°F.

2. Mix together the bread crumbs, basil, oregano, 1 teaspoon of the rub, and the cheese in a small bowl. Season the tenderloins with the remaining 1 teaspoon rub. Rub the tenderloins with the mustard to coat evenly.

3. Heat the oil in a skillet over medium-high heat.

4. Dredge the tenderloins in the bread crumb mixture. Panfry the tenderloins, cooking for 2 to 3 minutes on each side. Transfer the tenderloins to a pie tin and roast for 2 to 3 minutes.

5. Cut the tenderloins into 1-inch slices and serve warm.

2 first-course servings

Roasted Saddle of Rabbit

 **wise woman once told** me that one can easily live off the land in Louisiana—the marshes, swamps, fields, and gardens. With her ingenuity and a few simple ingredients, she can create a superlative meal like this.

1 saddle of rabbit (about ¾ pound)

1½ teaspoons Rustic Rub (page 9)

2 tablespoons vegetable oil

3 ribs celery

1 large parsnip, cut into 3 × ¼-inch sticks

1 large carrot, cut into 3 × ¼-inch sticks

1 medium beet, quartered

1 medium turnip, quartered

1 large onion, peeled and cut into 1-inch wedges

4 medium red potatoes, quartered (1 pound)

6 garlic cloves

2 tablespoons olive oil

½ teaspoon salt

¼ teaspoon freshly ground black pepper

1 teaspoon dried rosemary

1. Preheat the oven to 400°F.

2. Season the saddle of rabbit with 1 teaspoon of the rub. Heat the oil in a skillet over medium-high heat. Place the rabbit in the oil, skin side down, and cook for about 2 minutes. Turn it over and cook for 2 minutes more. Turn the saddle on one side, then the other, and cook for 1 minute on each side so that the saddle is evenly browned.

3. Line the celery ribs on the bottom of a shallow roasting pan as a rack. Combine the vegetables and garlic in a large bowl; toss with the remaining 1 teaspoon rub, olive oil, salt, black pepper, and rosemary. Spread the vegetables evenly over the celery. Roast for about 45 minutes, or until the vegetables are slightly tender. Place the rabbit on top of the vegetables and roast for 30 minutes for medium, 40 minutes for medium–well done.

4. To serve, cut the saddle crosswise across the back bone into 6 pieces. Serve with the vegetables.

2 main-course servings

CHAPTER 8

Charcuterie

ANDOUILLE

SAUSAGE, TASSO,

BOUDIN,

COUNTRY PÂTÉ,

AND MORE

harcuterie refers to the numerous preparations of cured meat, fresh or smoked sausage, pâté, boudin, and sausage meat. Originally limited to pork, charcuterie has come to include other meats, such as duck and rabbit, as well. Practically all of the peoples—French, Spanish, Acadians, Germans, Italians, and those from the Caribbean—that eventually settled in Louisiana contributed to the charcuterie that is such an integral part of the cuisine. But it was perhaps the Acadians who had the most influence. Because they had to raise most of their foodstuffs at home, the Acadians held a boucherie, or pig killing. A couple of times a year several families gathered to slaughter a pig. From early in the morning until late in the evening, men and women worked at large outdoor tables, turning out headcheese, boudin blanc, boudin rouge, fresh pork sausages, cracklings, and stuffed ponce, or stuffed pig's stomach. Other sausages, like andouille and chaurice, were smoked to be used later. Tasso, once made with

spiced, dried, and smoked trimmings and now made with ham, was, and still is, used to season vegetables and stews. Since the advent of modern refrigeration, boucheries are rarely held. Meat markets and some supermarkets scattered throughout the state, especially in south Louisiana, now provide most of these items for the home kitchen. Marcelle took me to Hebert's, an old-fashioned meat market near Abbeville, where we stood in line with the locals to get our share of tasso, chaurice, boudin, bags of crisp cracklings, and a pig's stomach packed with ground pork and seasonings. Mr. Hebert took me to the back of the shop where workers skillfully butchered the pigs on immaculately clean tables and blocks. At other such markets, I've watched men and women stuff ropes of sausages, stir huge caldrons of cracklings, and chop and mince ingredients for headcheese. The clatter, aroma, and cheerful conversations you find at these markets are infectious. Happy customers load up their carts while visitors from neighboring states bring ice chests and pack them with Louisiana charcuterie unavailable to them elsewhere. Although some of these regional specialties are now available throughout the States or by mail order (see page 342), I have included recipes for several of them that can be duplicated in your home kitchen.

How to Stuff Sausage

Most of the sausages in this chapter can be cooked as patties, but others do have to be stuffed. You can do this easily at home with a funnel or a sausage stuffer. Many heavy-duty mixers have an optional sausage-stuffing attachment. Sausage casings can be purchased at local butcher-supply companies and by mail order (see page 342). Natural casings—hog, beef, lamb, or goat intestines—range in size from 1/2 inch to 3 to 4 inches in diameter. Synthetic casings also exist, but I don't recommend them. Casings are available fresh, salted, or frozen. They usually come 100 yards to the case. How much you need at any one time depends on the amount of filling you have and whether you are making links or a simple coil, with links requiring more casing. If you have more than you need, store the remainder in the refrigerator or freezer. Following is a step-by-step guide to stuffing sausages at home. Be sure to keep everything—food, equipment, work surfaces, and your hands—clean. The sausage mixture and all equipment should be chilled. Work in a cold kitchen, if possible.

1. Soak the casings in warm water until soft and pliable, at least 1 hour. Run lukewarm water through the casings to remove any salt.
2. Tie a double knot in one end of the casing, then cut off a length of casing. Gather all but a couple of inches of the casing over the nozzle of the sausage stuffer or funnel.
3. Start pressing the sausage mixture through, supporting the casing with your other hand. Pack the sausage as tight as you can, but not to the point of bursting. When you have filled almost all the casing (or used up all the stuffing), slip the casing off the nozzle.

4. For a coil, tie the sausage where the stuffing ends. To make links, use one of these methods:

Using butcher's twine, tie the rope of sausage at intervals.

Pinch the rope into links and twist in alternating directions at the indentations.

5. Randomly prick the casings with a thin toothpick or the tines of a fork to release any air that's trapped.

6. Cook, refrigerate, or smoke the sausage.

Hot-Smoking Sausages

If you don't own or have access to a smoker, you can use a kettle grill, such as a Weber grill.

1. Soak 2 cups of hickory chips (oak, apple, pecan, and mesquite can also be used) for 1 hour prior to use. Mound 2½ pounds of charcoal briquettes in the center of the grill and light them. Let burn for 40 minutes. Add the chips and allow them to smoke for about 10 minutes. The interior temperature of the grill should be 300°F.

2. Place the raw sausages around the outermost part of the grill rack. This is to avoid direct heat. You want the sausages to absorb the maximum amount of smoke flavor before it is fully cooked. Check the interior temperature from time to time. If it exceeds 325°F., remove the cover for about 2 minutes and spray the embers with a mild vinegar solution, 1 part vinegar to 7 parts water. Spray as often as necessary, but remember smoke escapes each time the grill is uncovered.

Boudin

oudin, a popular sausage made with bits of pork, fluffy white rice, and seasonings is the breakfast choice in Acadiana. Wrapped in a paper napkin or tucked into a slice of bread and washed down with a cup of dark coffee, it carries you through the morning. It's not necessary to stuff the sausage into casings. You can plunk a heaping spoonful of the mixture on a thick slice of Home-Style French Bread (page 286) or any bread for that matter, not just for breakfast, but any time. I like to drizzle some Steen's 100% Pure Cane Syrup on it too. The mark of a good boudin is lots of chopped parsley and green onions.

2½ pounds pork butt, cut into 1-inch cubes

1 pound pork liver, rinsed in cool water

2 quarts water

1 cup coarsely chopped onions

½ cup coarsely chopped bell peppers

½ cup coarsely chopped celery

4¼ teaspoons salt

2½ teaspoons cayenne

1½ teaspoons freshly ground black pepper

1 cup chopped parsley

1 cup chopped green onions, green parts only

6 cups cooked medium-grain white rice

1. Put the pork, liver, water, onions, bell peppers, celery, 1 teaspoon of the salt, ¼ teaspoon of the cayenne, and ¼ teaspoon of the black pepper in a large heavy pot. Bring to a boil over high heat. Reduce the heat and simmer for about 1½ hours, or until the pork and liver are tender. Remove from the heat and drain, reserving 1½ cups of the broth.

2. Grind the pork and liver together with ½ cup of the parsley and ½ cup of the green onions in a meat grinder fitted with a ¼-inch die. Or, put the pork and liver together with ½ cup of the parsley and ¼ cup of the green onions in a food processor fitted with a metal blade and pulse several times to coarsely grind the mixture. It should not be pureed into a paste.

3. Transfer to a large mixing bowl. Add the rice, the remaining salt, cayenne, black pepper, parsley, and green onions and mix well. Add the broth, ½ cup at a time, and mix thoroughly.

4. Either stuff the mixture into prepared 1½-inch-diameter casings and make 3-inch links or form it into balls the size of walnuts.

5. Serve warm. The sausage can be reheated in a 325°F. oven.

About 4½ pounds

Pork Breakfast Sausage

 n Louisiana, we put sausage on poor boys, in gumbos and jambalayas, and next to eggs for breakfast. Breakfast sausage is one of my favorites, especially when seasoned with fennel seeds, but since I don't like biting down on the seeds, I decided to make the sausage with an essence of fennel. This sausage is wonderful with Pain Perdu (page 295) or Skillet Corn Bread (page 284) for breakfast, but it also can be used in stuffings and dressings. Stuffed into casings, divided into one-pound packages, or shaped into 3-inch patties, the sausage can be stored in the freezer until needed. Tell the butcher you want pork that is 85 percent lean and 15 percent fat, or as close to that as possible.

3 tablespoons fennel seeds

1 cup water

3½ pounds boneless pork butt, cut into 1-inch cubes

4 teaspoons salt

½ teaspoon cayenne

2 teaspoons onion powder

2 teaspoons garlic powder

1 teaspoon freshly ground black pepper

continued

1. Put the fennel seeds and water in a small saucepan and bring to a boil.

2. Reduce the heat and simmer for about 8 minutes. Strain and reserve the liquid, about 3 tablespoons. Discard the seeds.

3. Season the pork with the salt, cayenne, onion powder, garlic powder, black pepper, and the fennel essence. Using your hands, mix well. Grind the pork mixture through a meat grinder fitted with a $\frac{1}{4}$-inch die. Or, put the pork mixture in a food processor fitted with the metal blade and pulse several times to coarsely grind the meat. It should not be pureed into a paste.

4. Either stuff the mixture into prepared $\frac{1}{2}$-inch-diameter casings or divide it into small portions. It can be frozen indefinitely.

About 3 $\frac{1}{2}$ pounds

Andouille Sausage

ndouille, Louisiana's famous sausage, is used in gumbos, jambalayas, and dressings. It gives pizazz to any dish. Andouille is a smoked sausage; if you don't have a smoker, use a kettle grill. I use both garlic powder and fresh garlic to intensify the flavor.

1 boneless pork butt, cut into 1-inch cubes (about 5 pounds)	2 teaspoons freshly ground black pepper
½ cup Rustic Rub (page 9)	1 teaspoon ground cumin
1½ teaspoons chili powder	1½ teaspoons crushed red pepper
¼ cup paprika	2 teaspoons garlic powder
1½ teaspoons filé powder	¼ cup chopped garlic

1. Put the pork and the rest of the ingredients in a large bowl, tossing to coat the meat evenly. Cover and refrigerate for at least 24 hours.

2. Remove from the refrigerator and put the mixture through a meat grinder using a ½-inch die. Or, coarsely grind the meat in a food processor fitted with the metal blade.

3. Stuff the mixture into the prepared 1½-inch-diameter casings, each piece about 10 inches long. It can be frozen indefinitely.

About 5 pounds

Chaurice

ike many other dishes in this cuisine, the preparation of chaurice, a sausage similar to the Spanish chorizo, varies from cook to cook, from butcher to butcher. In some parts of south Louisiana, especially around Lafayette, you'll find some versions with the pork cut into small chunks, rather than being coarsely ground. At outdoor cookouts and barbecues, a few links are often cooked on the grill. The sausages are cut into rounds and passed around on toothpicks as hors d'oeuvres. Sometimes the links are put between two thick slices of French bread and dabbed with Creole mustard to make one heck of a sandwich. Chaurice is sometimes substituted for andouille. The sausage can be eaten fresh or smoked; it's sold both ways in many meat markets.

2½ pounds pork butt, cut into 1-inch cubes

¼ cup chopped garlic

5 teaspoons chili powder

4 tablespoons paprika

1½ teaspoons cayenne

2 teaspoons ground cumin

1½ teaspoons salt

½ teaspoon crushed red pepper

½ teaspoon dried oregano

½ teaspoon dried thyme

½ teaspoon freshly ground black pepper

1 teaspoon onion powder

½ teaspoon garlic powder

---

1. Put the pork in a large mixing bowl. Combine the rest of the ingredients in a small bowl and mix well. Add this mixture to the pork and toss to coat the meat evenly. Cover and refrigerate for 24 hours.

2. Grind the meat twice in a meat grinder fitted with a ¹/₂-inch die. Or, coarsely grind the meat in a food processor fitted with the metal blade.

3. Stuff into prepared 1¹/₂-inch-diameter casings. Form into links or leave in ropes. To hot-smoke the sausage, if desired, follow the directions on page 201, smoking for 20 to 25 minutes, flipping the sausage once every 10 minutes of cooking time.

4. The sausage, fresh or smoked, will keep indefinitely in the freezer.

About 2³/₄ pounds

Tasso

ong ago, tasso was made from the trimmings after a hog was butchered at a boucherie. The strips, much like jerky, were dried and smoked and used to flavor vegetables, gumbos, stews, and rice dishes. Today, tasso has been raised to new heights, being made with good quality lean pork. Tasso is easily made, and I suggest making a batch or two to keep in the freezer to use throughout the year.

2 tablespoons salt

4 teaspoons freshly ground
   black pepper

1¹/₂ tablespoons cayenne

5 tablespoons paprika

1 tablespoon garlic powder

1¹/₂ teaspoons onion powder

2¹/₂ pounds lean pork butt,
   cut into 1-inch-thick
   slices, 4 to 5 ounces each

1. Combine the salt, black pepper, cayenne, paprika, garlic powder, and onion powder in a shallow bowl. Dredge each slice of pork in the spice mix.

2. Using your fingers, press the spice mix well into each piece. Pack in plastic wrap, about four to a pack. Wrap securely. Refrigerate for at least 3 days or up to 1 week to allow the spices to seep into the meat.

3. To smoke the strips, follow the directions on page 201. Place the strips around the outermost part of the grill rack and hot-smoke for 15 minutes, without flipping.

4. Pack the tasso in ¹/₂-pound packages and store in the freezer indefinitely.

About 2¹/₂ pounds

Country Pâté

urprisingly, I found few pâtés in country meat markets in the southern part of the state. When I asked about this, I got several answers. One butcher explained that it was too labor-intensive for his relatively small operation. Another, with a twinkle in his eye, said that the cooks in his area all believe that their homemade pâtés are better than they can find in any store. And still another told me that he supplies his customers with the ingredients they need to make pâtés. Making pâtés keeps them entertained, he said, and busy in their home kitchens. He wouldn't want to take their fun away. Indeed, these people like to putter around in their kitchens. No, putter is not a good word. They spend a lot of time in the kitchen—it's probably the most used room in the house. Oftentimes, there are even two kitchens, one for everyday cooking and one for preparing food for special occasions when extra burners and ovens are required. One day, I was invited to spend the afternoon with a friend. Bernard explained he wanted company while he made his pâtés for an upcoming party. I was further enticed with the promise that he would share a bottle of good red wine that he had been saving for just such an occasion. Once the pâtés were made, I was invited back the next day for a taste, to be enjoyed with yet another bottle of good wine and some French bread. I was not disappointed. This is an uncommonly good pâté, much like one you would find in the country-side of France. The recipe has been handed down from generation

to generation in this gentleman's family, which came to Louisiana a long time ago. I like to serve the pâté spread with Creole mustard and topped with Onion Marmalade (page 15).

1 pound veal round, cut into 1-inch cubes	1/2 teaspoon cayenne
1/2 pound boiled ham, cut into 1-inch cubes	1/2 teaspoon freshly ground black pepper
2 pounds pork butt, cut into 1-inch cubes	1/2 cup chopped celery
	1 cup chopped onions
1/2 pound chicken livers, well trimmed	2 tablespoons chopped garlic
	1/2 cup brandy
11 bay leaves	1 cup port wine
2 1/2 teaspoons salt	2 egg whites
1/4 teaspoon dried thyme	1/4 cup chopped parsley
1/4 teaspoon dried oregano	24 slices bacon

1. Combine the veal, ham, pork, and chicken livers in a large mixing bowl. Add 3 of the bay leaves, the salt, thyme, oregano, cayenne, black pepper, celery, onions, garlic, brandy, and port. Toss to mix well. Cover and refrigerate for 24 hours.

2. Remove from the refrigerator and drain the mixture for 2 to 3 minutes in a colander in the sink, discarding the juices. Remove the bay leaves. Grind the meat once in a meat grinder fitted with a 1/2-inch die. Transfer to a large bowl. Add the egg whites and parsley and mix well.

3. Preheat the oven to 350°F.

4. Line the bottom and sides of two 6-cup rectangular pans (8 1/2 × 4 1/2 × 2 1/2-inch metal or glass bread pans or an earthenware terrine with a cover), using 12 strips of bacon for each pan. Leave enough of the bacon overlapping all sides of the pan so that the bacon will completely cover the top of the pâté mixture when folded over. Divide the pâté mixture equally between the 2 pans, pressing down with your fingers. Fold the overlapping bacon slices over the mixture to encase it. Top each pâté with 4 bay leaves.

continued

5. Set the pans in a roasting pan large enough to accommodate both and place in the oven. Pour boiling water into the roasting pan to come three quarters of the way up the sides of the loaf pans. Bake for 1½ hours, or until the internal temperature reaches 170°F. with an instant-read thermometer.

6. Remove from oven and carefully drain off any excess fat, by pouring or by using a bulb baster. Cover the pans with aluminum foil, then place a 2- to 3-pound weight or a brick wrapped in aluminum foil on top of each pâté. Do not use a can. Return to the oven and bake for 1 hour.

7. Remove from the oven and with the weight or brick still on each pâté, refrigerate for at least 8 hours before serving. Remove the bay leaves.

8. Cut into ½-inch slices to serve. The pâté will keep for 7 to 10 days in the refrigerator.

2 pâtés, 12 to 14 first-course servings

Duck Pastrami

n the planning stages of my restaurant NOLA in the French Quarter, I wanted to include some real and rustic dishes on the menu. Assisted by sous chefs David McCelvey, Sean Roe, and Michael Jordan, I began experimenting with curing meats. Then, when I journeyed around the countryside of Louisiana, I realized that this curing process is used quite often there. I experimented with quite a few items, and this cured duck was the one we liked the best. Pastrami is usually made with beef. But since we serve a lot of duck dishes at the restaurant, I thought it would be interesting to apply the preparation of pastrami to our feathered friends. Generally, the meat is smoked. In this particular rendition, however, I found the taste excellent without smoking. It takes a little time to prepare, but it's good, oui. For a snack, first course, or light supper, serve it on thin slices of Home-Style French Bread (page 286) spread with Creole mustard and Onion Marmalade (page 15). This recipe can be doubled.

1 tablespoon black
  peppercorns

2 teaspoons dried thyme

3 bay leaves, crumbled

1 teaspoon whole cloves

1 tablespoon minced garlic

1 teaspoon whole juniper
  berries, plus 1/3 cup
  crushed juniper berries

4 cups water

1/2 cup (packed) light brown
  sugar

1/2 cup kosher salt

1 whole duck breast,
  split in half
  (2 1/4 to 2 1/2 pounds)

1/4 cup coarsely ground
  black pepper

1. Combine the peppercorns, thyme, bay leaves, cloves, garlic, and whole juniper berries in a small mixing bowl and set aside. Combine the water, sugar, and salt in a saucepan over medium-high heat. Bring to a boil and stir to dissolve the sugar and salt. Remove from the heat and add the dry spice mixture. Steep for 1 hour.

2. Place the duck breast pieces in a glass or plastic container. Pour in the seasoned brine to cover the breasts completely. Cover and refrigerate for 48 hours, turning the duck 2 to 3 times.

3. Remove the duck breasts from the brine and rinse thoroughly with cool water. Pat dry with a towel.

4. Preheat the oven to 250°F.

5. Combine the crushed juniper berries and ground black pepper in a small bowl. Using the palm and heel of your hands, press two thirds of the berry and pepper mixture into the underside of the breasts. Press the remaining mixture onto the skin side. Place the breasts, skin side down, on a rack in a roasting pan and bake for 1 hour. Remove and let cool for 30 minutes.

6. Wrap the breasts tightly in plastic wrap and place in an airtight container. Store in the refrigerator for at least 1 week before using.

7. To serve, remove the meat from the bones and slice thin.

6 servings

Duck Confit

onfit, a French preparation, is one of the oldest forms of preserving meat. Pork, goose, duck, or turkey is cooked in its own fat, and then stored in the fat to preserve it. This technique was practiced in Louisiana on a large scale until modern refrigeration was introduced in the rural areas of the state not too long ago. Marcelle remembers her grandfather, who was a sugarcane farmer, storing meats packed in fat to feed the family during the winter. This recipe is similar to the classic French method; the addition of garlic, thyme, and bay leaves is what makes it so very Louisiana. It is a two-day procedure, but you don't have to do anything while the duck marinates and cooks. Once the confit is made, it can be turned into Duck Rillettes (page 214) or added to Cassoulet (page 189).

4 duck leg portions with thighs attached, excess fat trimmed and reserved (about 2 pounds)

1 tablespoon plus 1/8 teaspoon kosher salt

1/2 teaspoon freshly ground black pepper

10 garlic cloves

4 bay leaves

4 sprigs of fresh thyme

1 1/2 teaspoons black peppercorns

1/2 teaspoon table salt

4 cups olive oil

1. Lay the leg portions on a platter, skin side down. Sprinkle with 1 tablespoon of the kosher salt and the black pepper. Place the garlic cloves, bay leaves, and sprigs of thyme on each of 2 leg portions. Lay the remaining 2 leg portions, flesh to flesh, on top. Put the reserved fat from the ducks in the bottom of a glass or plastic container. Top with the sandwiched leg portions. Sprinkle with the remaining 1/8 teaspoon kosher salt. Cover and refrigerate for 12 hours.

2. Preheat the oven to 200°F.

3. Remove the duck from the refrigerator. Remove the garlic, bay leaves, thyme, and duck fat and reserve. Rinse the duck with cool water, rubbing off some of the salt and pepper. Pat dry with paper towels.

4. Put the reserved garlic, bay leaves, thyme, and duck fat in the bottom of an enameled cast-iron pot. Sprinkle evenly with the peppercorns and salt. Lay the duck on top, skin side down. Add the olive oil. Cover and bake for 12 to 14 hours, or until the meat pulls away from the bone.

5. Remove the duck from the fat. Strain the fat and reserve.

6. Pick the meat from the bones and place it in a stoneware container. Cover the meat with some of the strained fat, making a 1/4-inch layer.

7. The duck confit can be stored in the refrigerator for up to one month. The excess oil can be stored in an airtight container in the refrigerator and used like butter for cooking. The tinge of duck taste in the oil is wonderful and I use the oil to roast potatoes, cook green beans, and panfry veal.

Note: If you are going to prepare the Duck Rillettes, reserve the garlic cloves.

About 2 cups

Duck Rillettes

For rillettes, duck, pork, or rabbit, confit is shredded or pounded until almost smooth. Spread on thin slices of French bread, it can be served as a cold hors d'oeuvre. I like to make it during the Christmas holidays to have on hand when guests drop by. Serve it with a dry red wine, or champagne for a festive treat.

1 recipe Duck Confit
(page 212)

¼ cup minced onions

1 tablespoon minced parsley

10 garlic cloves reserved
from the confit

1 tablespoon Cognac

½ stick (4 tablespoons)
butter

½ teaspoon freshly ground
black pepper

¼ teaspoon salt

2 tablespoons fat reserved
from the confit

1. Combine all of the ingredients in the bowl of an electric mixer fitted with the dough hook. Beat at medium speed for about 1 minute, or until everything is well mixed. Or use a food processor, taking care not to puree the mixture or let it turn into a paste. The texture should be like finely chopped meat.

2. Use immediately or place in an airtight container, drizzle some of the reserved olive oil over the top, and store in the refrigerator for up to 1 week.

About 2 ¼ cups

Rabbit Sausage

ike most hunters, I believe that you should kill only what you will eat. But sometimes during the rabbit hunting season, we have more meat than we can eat at one time. I came up with this rabbit sausage to use up the extras. It can be served with Onion Marmalade (page 15) on sliced French bread for a snack or appetizer. I have also used it in Cassoulet (page 189), and it adds a touch of flavor to stews. Pecan pieces give it a nice texture. Wild or domestic rabbit can be used.

1 rabbit, deboned and cut into 1-inch cubes (about 2½ pounds)	½ teaspoon freshly ground black pepper
6 slices bacon	1 teaspoon dried thyme
½ cup pecan pieces	¼ cup chopped green onions
1 teaspoon salt	¼ cup chopped parsley
½ teaspoon cayenne	1 tablespoon Rustic Rub (page 9)

1. Mix all of the ingredients in a large bowl. Grind the mixture in a meat grinder fitted with a ¼-inch die or coarsely grind in a food processor fitted with a metal blade.

2. Either stuff the mixture into the prepared ½-inch-diameter casings and make 3-inch links or form into 3-inch patties, ¼ inch thick. Fry the links in a nonstick skillet for about 10 minutes, turning them to cook evenly. Fry the patties in a nonstick skillet, about 3 minutes on each side.

3. The links or patties can be stored in the freezer indefinitely.

About 2 pounds

CHAPTER 9

Rice, Beans, and Grains

JAMBALAYA,

RED BEANS AND

RICE, BAKED

CHEESE GRITS,

AND MORE

ccording to the history books, rice came to America accidentally. In 1686, a ship from Madagascar docked in Charleston, South Carolina, for repairs. In return for the repairs and in appreciation of the hospitality extended to the crew, the ship's captain, John Thurber, presented Henry Woodward, Charleston's first settler, with a bag of rice. Rice has been grown in America ever since. It is believed that rice made its way to Louisiana a hundred years or so later, and it continues to thrive in the swampy lowlands of the southwestern part of the state, especially in the parishes of Cameron, Acadia, and Jefferson Davis. Louisianians consume as much rice in one year as other Americans eat in five. Served in gumbos and stews, as the basis of jambalaya, and served with creamy red beans for the tradi-

tional Monday lunch, rice is economical, nutritious, versatile, and bland enough to make other foods taste better. In Louisiana, parboiled or converted rice is a no-no. The preference, especially in south Louisiana, is medium-grain white rice, which is more glutinous and is used primarily in jambalaya and boudin. Long-grain and extra-long-grain white rice is more common in the areas east of the Mississippi River and in the northern section of the state. Red beans and white beans, both cooked to a creamy consistency, are prepared on a weekly basis, with bits of ham or andouille, which gives them the taste for which the cuisine has come to be known. Corn, in one guise or another, is the grain of choice in southern cooking. In Louisiana, you'll find it in Baked Cheese Grits, Sweet Corn Pudding, and Corn Maque Choux, all hearty side dishes that are a welcome change from potatoes.

Rice

Cooking rice is such an everyday occurrence that no one gives much thought to it. When I asked a sweet elderly lady for her recipe, she seriously explained it this way: "Cher, put your rice in a heavy saucepan. Then put enough water so that when you put your little finger in the pot, the water comes to the first joint of your little finger, sprinkle in some salt and a spoon or two of butter or oleo. Turn on the fire and when it begins to boil, lower the fire, cover the pot with a tight-fitting lid, and cook until all of the water is gone." When I inquired about how much rice, she laughed and replied, "As much as you will need for the day." Seriously, it's a very simple method. It's a one to two ratio, one of rice (medium-grain, long-grain, or extra-long-grain) to two of water. Unlike converted rice, the grains do not come out separated. They kind of stick together—not gooey or gluey, but definitely glutinous.

Steamed Rice

Put the 1 cup rice and 2 cups water in a heavy saucepan. Add 1 teaspoon salt and 1 tablespoon butter, margarine, or vegetable oil. Bring to a boil. Reduce the heat to medium-low, cover, and cook for about 20 minutes, or until the water is completely absorbed. This makes 3 cups cooked rice.

Andouille and Chicken Jambalaya

 ambalaya, like gumbo and Crawfish Pie (page 95), is one of the famous dishes of Louisiana. It is believed that the word comes from the French *jambon*, meaning ham, the African *ya* meaning rice, and the Acadian language where everything is *à la*. There are as many recipes as there are bayous that crisscross the state. In Gonzales (a small town southeast of Baton Rouge), proclaimed by the Louisiana legislature to be the jambalaya capital of the world, it is an article of faith that jambalaya should—must—be brown, like this recipe. The brown color is achieved by caramelizing the onions and browning the sausage and chicken in a black cast-iron pot. In New Orleans and some other parts of the state, jambalaya is often red, made so by the addition of tomatoes. That version may have, instead of chicken, ham and shrimp as well as sausage. Then again, you might find a jambalaya made with beef, pork ribs, duck, and even crawfish, depending on what is available. The only common ingredient is rice. No matter which of the jambalayas you choose to make, the secret to tender, moist rice is the two-to-one ratio of liquid to rice.

½ cup vegetable oil

3 cups chopped onions

1 cup chopped bell peppers

3 teaspoons salt

1¼ teaspoons cayenne

1 pound andouille, chorizo, or other smoked sausage, cut crosswise into ¼-inch slices

1½ pounds boneless white and dark chicken meat, cut into 1-inch cubes

3 bay leaves

3 cups medium-grain white rice

6 cups water

1 cup chopped green onions

1. Heat the oil in a large cast-iron Dutch oven over medium heat. Add the onions, bell peppers, 2 teaspoons of the salt, and 1 teaspoon of the cayenne. Stirring often, brown the vegetables for about 20 minutes, or until they are caramelized and dark brown in color. Scrape the bottom and sides of the pot to loosen any browned particles. Add the sausage and cook, stirring often for 10 to 15 minutes, scraping the bottom and sides of the pot to loosen any browned particles.

2. Season the chicken with the remaining 1 teaspoon salt and remaining ¼ teaspoon cayenne. Add the chicken and the bay leaves to the pot. Brown the chicken for 8 to 10 minutes, scraping the bottom of the pot to loosen any browned particles.

3. Add the rice and stir for 2 to 3 minutes to coat it evenly. Add the water, stir to combine, and cover. Cook over medium heat for 30 to 35 minutes, without stirring, or until the rice is tender and the liquid has been absorbed. Remove the pot from the heat and let stand, covered, for 2 to 3 minutes. Remove the bay leaves.

4. Stir in the green onions and serve.

10 to 12 servings

Shrimp and Ham Jambalaya

ere's the shrimp and ham version of jambalaya, flavored with a good amount of tomatoes, and accented with onions, garlic, spices, and herbs.

2 tablespoons vegetable oil	1 tablespoon chopped garlic
1½ cups chopped onions	1 teaspoon salt
½ cup chopped bell peppers	½ teaspoon cayenne
½ cup chopped celery	¼ teaspoon freshly ground black pepper
1 pound medium shrimp, peeled and deveined	¼ teaspoon dried thyme
4 bay leaves	1 cup long-grain white rice
1 pound boiled ham, cut into ½-inch cubes	¼ cup chopped green onions
1 can (14½ ounces) whole tomatoes, chopped, with juice	

1. Heat the oil in a large cast-iron Dutch oven over medium heat. Add the onions, bell peppers, and celery and sauté for 7 to 8 minutes, or until golden and soft. Add the shrimp and bay leaves and sauté until the shrimp turn pink, about 2 minutes. Add the ham and sauté for 2 to 3 minutes. Add the tomatoes with their juice, the garlic, salt, cayenne, black pepper, and thyme. Cook for about 10 minutes, stirring often. Add the rice and stir to mix. Cover and cook over medium heat for 25 to 30 minutes, or until the rice is tender and the liquid has been absorbed.

2. Remove from heat and let stand, covered, for about 5 minutes. Remove the bay leaves.

3. Stir in the green onions and serve.

6 servings

Wild Pecan Rice Dressing

ike Davis, president of the Conrad Rice Mill in New Iberia, produces quality rice products under the Konriko Brand. I especially like Wild Pecan Rice, which is grown in the moist soil of Iberia Parish and nowhere else. The story goes that a young rice miller, searching for an unusual flavor that only nature could provide, experimented with this seed. As his special rice was being milled gently, to retain some of the bran coating, the smell began to tell the tale. As the rice cooked, the kitchen filled with a rich nutty aroma. When eaten the rice carries a subtle pecanlike flavor.

1 tablespoon butter	1 package (7 ounces) Konriko Wild Pecan Rice
¼ cup chopped onions	2 cups water
¼ cup chopped celery	½ pound bacon, chopped, crispy-fried, and drained
1¼ teaspoons salt	
½ teaspoon cayenne	1 cup chopped boiled ham
½ cup pecan pieces	½ cup chopped green onions
1 unpeeled Granny Smith apple, cored and chopped (about 1½ cups)	3 tablespoons chopped parsley

1. Heat the butter in a large saucepan over medium-high heat. Add the onions, celery, salt, and cayenne. Sauté for 3 to 4 minutes, or until slightly wilted. Add the pecans and cook for about 4 minutes. Add the apple and the rice and stir for 1 minute. Add the water and bring to a boil. Reduce the heat to medium, cover, and simmer for about 20 minutes.

2. Remove from the heat. Add the bacon, ham, green onions, and parsley and stir to mix well.

3. Let sit for about 3 minutes before serving.

6 servings

Rice Dressing

ade with chopped chicken giblets and cooked in dark brown gravy, this rice dressing is also called dirty rice. I've heard the locals describe it as being as soft and moist as the south Louisiana marshlands. Often found on holiday tables, it is served with anything fried, roasted, or baked. Marcelle's mama likes to add a dozen or so oysters with three to four tablespoons of their liquor right before she takes it off the stove. "Just stir them around in the pot until the edges of the oysters curl a bit," she advises.

1 pound chicken gizzards

2 tablespoons vegetable oil

2 tablespoons flour

1 pound ground pork

1 cup chopped onions

½ cup chopped bell peppers

½ cup chopped celery

4 cups cooked medium-grain white rice

2 teaspoons salt

½ teaspoon cayenne

½ cup chopped green onions

¼ cup chopped parsley

1. Boil the gizzards in water to cover in a saucepan over medium heat for about 1 hour, or until tender. Drain, reserving the broth. Finely chop the gizzards in a food processor.

2. Combine the oil and flour in a large heavy saucepan over medium heat. Stirring constantly for 8 to 10 minutes, make a dark brown roux, the color of chocolate.

3. Add the ground pork to the roux and cook for 5 to 6 minutes, stirring constantly. Add the onions, bell peppers, and celery and cook for 5 to 6 minutes, or until the vegetables are wilted. Add the chopped gizzards. Pour the reserved broth into a 1-cup measure. Add enough water to make a full cup. Add this to the pot. Mix in the cooked rice, stirring to coat evenly and break up any clumps.

4. Add the salt, cayenne, green onions, and parsley. Mix well. Cook until the rice is warmed through, stirring occasionally.

5. Serve immediately.

8 servings

Eggplant and Rice Dressing

ouisiana cooks are to be admired, if for no other reason, for their creativity. They are constantly combining ingredients that I wouldn't have dreamed of pairing together. I've heard Louisiana food called the cuisine of ad lib and I have to agree with that. This is a side dish of that order. It goes well with Sunday Roast Chicken (page 132), Chicken Loaf (page 139), and I've also seen it stuffed and baked in garden-fresh bell peppers and tomatoes.

1 tablespoon vegetable oil	1 teaspoon cayenne
1/2 pound ground pork	1 large eggplant, peeled and cut into 1-inch cubes (about 2 pounds)
1/2 pound ground beef	
1 cup chopped onions	1 cup water
1/2 cup chopped bell peppers	6 cups cooked long-grain rice
1/2 cup chopped celery	2 tablespoons chopped parsley
2 1/2 teaspoons salt	

1. Heat the oil in a large saucepan over medium-high heat and brown the pork and beef. Add the onions, bell peppers, and celery and cook for about 5 minutes, or until the vegetables are wilted. Add the salt, cayenne, eggplant, and water. Cook, stirring often, for about 10 minutes. Reduce the heat to medium and cook, uncovered, stirring occasionally, for about 30 minutes, or until the eggplant is very soft. With a spoon, mash the eggplant against the side of the pot.

2. Add the rice and parsley. Mix thoroughly, breaking up any clumps. Heat until the rice is warmed through.

3. Serve immediately.

8 servings

Red Beans and Rice

onday wouldn't be Monday in Louisiana without red beans and rice. Legend has it that since Monday was traditionally wash day, an all-day affair before electric washers and dryers, a pot of red beans spent the morning simmering on the back of the stove. If there was a ham bone left over from Sunday's dinner, it was thrown into the pot of beans. The marrow from the cracked bone and a good amount of herbs and spices made the beans tasty; long cooking made them tender and creamy. When the laundry was done, so were the beans. Red beans ladled over fresh steamed rice with a pile of French bread for sopping up every last drop, this is the dish and the day of the week that transplanted Louisianians miss most. Don't fret if you don't have a ham bone; substitute some smoked sausage.

2 tablespoons vegetable oil

1 cup chopped onions

1/2 cup chopped bell peppers

1/2 cup chopped celery

1 teaspoon salt

1/2 teaspoon cayenne

1/4 teaspoon freshly ground black
pepper

1 teaspoon dried thyme

4 bay leaves

1 pound boiled ham, cut into 1/2-inch
cubes

6 ounces smoked sausage, cut
crosswise into 1/4-inch slices
(1 cup)

1 pound dried red beans, rinsed and
sorted over, soaked overnight and
drained

3 tablespoons chopped garlic

8 to 10 cups water

2 recipes Steamed Rice (page 220)

1. Heat the oil in a large heavy saucepan over medium-high heat. Sauté the onions, bell peppers, celery, salt, cayenne, black pepper, and thyme for about 5 minutes. Add the bay leaves, ham, and sausage and sauté for 5 to 6 minutes. Add the beans, garlic, and enough water to cover the contents in the pot. Bring to a boil. Reduce the heat to medium and simmer, uncovered, stirring occasionally, for about 2 hours. Add more water if the mixture becomes dry and thick.

2. Use a wooden spoon to mash about half of the mixture against the side of the pot. Continue to cook, stirring occasionally, for about 1 1/2 hours, or until the mixture is creamy and the beans are soft. Add more water if it becomes too thick. The mixture should be soupy, but not watery.

3. Remove the bay leaves and serve over steamed rice.

8 servings

White Beans

hite beans, flavored with bits of ham and tweaked with garlic, are served alongside many pork dishes. In Des Allemands, southwest of New Orleans, they are teamed with Batter-Fried Catfish (page 121).

1 tablespoon vegetable oil

1/2 cup chopped onions

1/4 cup chopped celery

1 teaspoon salt

1/2 teaspoon freshly ground black pepper

2 bay leaves

1 cup chopped boiled ham

1 tablespoon chopped garlic

1 pound dried white navy beans, rinsed and sorted over, soaked overnight and drained

8 to 10 cups water

1 teaspoon Tabasco sauce

2 recipes Steamed Rice (page 220)

1. Heat the oil in a large heavy saucepan over medium-high heat. Sauté the onions and celery with the salt, black pepper, and bay leaves for about 5 minutes. Add the ham and garlic and cook for about 4 minutes. Add the beans and cover with water. Add the Tabasco. Reduce the heat to medium and simmer, uncovered, for about 3 hours, or until the beans are soft and creamy. Stir occasionally.

2. Remove the bay leaves and serve over steamed white rice.

8 servings

Andouille-Cheese Grits

ominy grits are made from dried corn. Dried corn kernels are boiled in a weak lye solution, then hulled, washed, and dried. The result is dried whole hominy. Grits are ground hominy. Hominy grits, both white and yellow, are often served for breakfast, steaming hot with lots of melted butter and seasoned with salt and cayenne. Cooked with andouille and cheese as in this dish, they can be topped with a couple of poached or fried eggs for a rib-sticking breakfast. But, then again, I also like grits with fresh pork sausage, Southern Greens (page 242), and Skillet Corn Bread (page 284) for supper. Oh, by the way, if and when you visit down here, don't sprinkle sugar on top of your grits. The locals will look at you funny and know you're not from around these parts.

½ pound Andouille Sausage (page 205), chopped

4½ cups milk

1½ teaspoons salt

¼ teaspoon cayenne

1 tablespoon butter

2 cups quick yellow grits

1 cup grated cheddar (4 ounces)

1. Brown the andouille in a saucepan, over medium-high heat, cooking it for about 4 minutes. Add the milk, salt, cayenne, and butter and bring to a boil. Add the grits and reduce the heat to medium. Stir for 30 seconds, then add the cheese and stir until the cheese melts. Cook, uncovered, for 4 to 5 minutes, or until the grits are tender and creamy.

2. Serve immediately.

4 servings

Baked Cheese Grits

reamy and smooth, these grits are the perfect accompaniment to Grillades (page 167), soaking up every bit of rich gravy. I like them too with Panéed Veal (page 177) or Sunday Roast Chicken (page 132).

2 cups yellow grits, not quick or instant grits	2 tablespoons chopped garlic
1 stick (¼ pound) butter	8 ounces cheddar, grated (about 2 cups)
1½ teaspoons salt	3 eggs
½ teaspoon freshly ground black pepper	1 cup milk

1. Preheat the oven to 350°F.

2. Prepare the grits according to package directions. Add the butter, salt, black pepper, garlic, and cheese. Mix until the butter and cheese melt. Beat together the eggs and milk in a small bowl. Add to the grits and mix well.

3. Pour into a square (8 × 2 inch) baking dish and bake for about 1 hour, or until the mixture sets.

4. Serve immediately.

8 servings

Corn Bread and Andouille Dressing

killet Corn Bread, crunchy and always served hot from the oven, is the basis for this dressing. Combined with bits of spicy andouille sausage, it's one that I've come to prefer with chicken, turkey, and quail. Any leftover dressing can be baked in a separate pan.

1 tablespoon vegetable oil

½ pound Andouille Sausage (page 205), finely chopped

½ cup chopped onions

¼ cup chopped bell peppers

¼ cup chopped celery

4 cups crumbled Skillet Corn Bread (page 284)

2 cups water

¾ teaspoon salt

⅛ teaspoon cayenne

1. Heat the oil in a large skillet over medium heat and brown the andouille about 3 minutes. Add the onions, bell peppers, and celery. Sauté for about 5 minutes, or until the vegetables are wilted. Add the corn bread and water and mix well. Season with the salt and cayenne. Cook, stirring, for 2 to 3 minutes. Remove from the heat.

2. Serve warm or let cool to room temperature if using as a stuffing.

4 servings

Sweet Corn Pudding

O ne hot, steaming summer morning, I accompanied Marcelle and her mother to gather corn in a cousin's field near St. Martinville. I watched them pull on rubber boots, tie their hair back in red kerchiefs, and plunge into a thick tract of corn. Before I could roll up my sleeves and join them, they were crashing through the rows. Ears of corn soared through the air from somewhere in the corn patch. It was then I realized there was method to their madness. Mama picked and tossed the ears; Marcelle scooped them up and tucked them into sacks. I watched in amazement. In what seemed like just a matter of minutes, they emerged from the field, their cheeks rosy-red and wet with perspiration, chuckling over "a real good corn harvest." Back at Marcelle's house, they shucked, cleaned, and deftly shaved the cobs, extracting the kernels and milk. Some were set aside to make this pudding; the rest were going into a big pot of Corn Maque Choux (page 234). The pudding, made with milk, rich cream, eggs, onions, bell peppers, bacon, and a hint of nutmeg is nothing short of incredible.

1 teaspoon plus 2 tablespoons butter

3 tablespoons dried fine bread crumbs

4 ears young corn

2 teaspoons salt

¼ teaspoon cayenne

½ cup chopped bacon

1 cup chopped onions

½ cup chopped bell peppers

2 cups heavy cream

1 cup milk

6 eggs

¼ teaspoon freshly ground black pepper

⅛ teaspoon grated nutmeg

½ cup freshly grated parmesan

½ cup yellow cornmeal

1. Preheat the oven to 375°F.

2. Butter the bottom and sides of an 8 × 2-inch square (8 cups) casserole dish with 1 teaspoon of the butter. Sprinkle the bread crumbs evenly on the bottom and sides of the dish.

3. Cut the corn off the cobs by thinly slicing across the top of the kernels and then cutting across a second time to release the milk from the corn. Scrape the cob once or twice to extract any remaining milk. You should have about 2 cups of corn with milk.

4. Heat the remaining 2 tablespoons butter in a large skillet over medium-high heat. Add the corn, 1 teaspoon of the salt, and the cayenne. Sauté for about 2 minutes. Add the bacon and sauté for about 4 minutes, or until slightly crisp. Add the onions and bell peppers and cook for about 3 minutes, or until slightly wilted. Remove from the heat.

5. Combine the cream, milk, and eggs in a mixing bowl. Beat with a wire whisk until the mixture is frothy. Add the remaining 1 teaspoon salt, the black pepper, nutmeg, and cheese. Add this to the corn mixture and stir to mix well. Add the cornmeal and mix well.

6. Pour into the casserole dish and bake for about 1 hour, or until golden.

7. Serve immediately.

8 servings

Corn Maque Choux

I asked the cook, a proud elderly lady, what the name of this dish meant. She looked me straight in the eye and with a deadpan expression more than likely reserved for holier-than-thou chefs answered, "It's a dish made of sweet corn, smothered with onions and other seasonings, and one ripe tomato." What I really wanted to know was what did the words themselves mean. With a twinkle in her eyes and a shy smile, she tilted her head and responded, "Well, let's see, mon cher. Corn in French is maïs, so that has nothing to do with it. And choux is cabbage. Mon ami, I really don't know. Just understand that maque choux is good and you're going to love it."

6 ears young corn

1 cup chopped onions

1/2 cup chopped bell peppers

1 1/2 teaspoons salt

1/4 teaspoon cayenne

2 tablespoons vegetable oil

1 cup chopped, peeled, and seeded tomatoes, or 1 cup chopped canned tomatoes

1/2 cup milk

1. Cut the corn off the cob by thinly slicing across the tops of the kernels and then cutting across a second time to release the milk from the corn. Scrape the cob once or twice to extract the milk. You should have about 4 cups of corn with the milk.
2. Season the onions and bell peppers with the salt and cayenne. Heat the oil in a large skillet over medium heat. Add the onions, bell peppers, and the corn, and cook, stirring occasionally, for about 10 minutes. Add the tomatoes and cook, stirring occasionally, for 15 to 18 minutes, or until the corn is tender. Add the milk, stir, and remove from heat.
3. Serve immediately.

4 servings

CHAPTER 10

Vegetables

SMOTHERED

CABBAGE,

BRABANT

POTATOES,

CANDIED YAMS,

AND MORE

n the warm and drowsy air of Louisiana, vegetables grow profusely almost all year round. During the summer, the fields and gardens yield tomatoes, cucumbers, eggplant, bell peppers, okra, corn, and beans. Crops of heartier vegetables such as cabbage, potatoes, yams, and mirliton are prevalent during the cooler months. Everyone has a garden. It might be a couple of acres with rows and rows of corn, okra, and eggplant along the banks of Bayou Lafourche, or a postage-stamp-size garden near the kitchen door. This love of land is a strong, centuries-old tradition. The first French newcomers found themselves at a loss for the traditional ingredients to which they were accustomed. The table in France was, and still is, regarded as a potential source of pleasure, not merely as sustenance. They were not going to do without so they set out gardens to grow what they needed. The Acadians, who had lived off the land in Acadia, provided yet another culture, another influence. They were a hardy people who

knew well how to adapt to their surroundings. Influenced by native Indians, African cooks, Spanish settlers, and traders from the Caribbean, the gardens have evolved into what we have today. Something as simple as Smothered Cabbage, flavored with bacon and onions, is a hearty dish that goes well with pork. Mirliton, a delicate squash, is prepared in any number of ways—pickled, crunchy-fried, or teamed with shrimp. Sweet green bell peppers are stuffed with sausage dressing. Potatoes are mashed or panfried. Summer vegetables—eggplant, squash, and tomatoes—are cooked together and made into a Louisiana-style ratatouille. Yams, or sweet potatoes, are an essential part of holiday buffets and come to the table in casseroles and puddings.

Smothered Cabbage

ccording to historic records, cabbage was a main crop of the Acadians when they first settled in Canada, and they planted it in the dark, rich soil of south Louisiana upon their arrival. Cabbage is found not only in slaws and soups but also "smothered," which means cooked in its own juices until it is tender and soft. It is often served with pork dishes like Pork Chops and Sweet Potato Gravy (page 179).

1 tablespoon vegetable oil

3/4 pound bacon, cut into 1-inch pieces

1 pound ham hock

2 cups chopped onions

1/4 teaspoon freshly ground black pepper

1/2 teaspoon salt

1/4 cup sliced garlic

4 pounds cabbage, cleaned and coarsely chopped

1/2 stick (4 tablespoons) butter

4 cups water

1/2 teaspoon Rustic Rub (page 9)

1. Heat the oil in a Dutch oven over high heat. Fry the bacon until crisp. Add the ham hock, onions, pepper, and salt. Cook, stirring often, for 2 minutes. Add the garlic, cabbage, butter, and water. Cover the pot and cook until the cabbage begins to wilt, 8 to 10 minutes. Reduce the heat to medium and give the mixture a couple of stirs without disturbing the bottom of the pot. Cover and cook for about 30 minutes, or until the cabbage is soft. Remove the lid and stir, scraping the bottom of the pot and mixing well. Cook, uncovered, for about 30 minutes.

2. Remove the ham hock. When cool enough to handle, pick the meat off the bones and add the pieces to the pot. Add the rub, stir, and remove from the heat.

3. Serve immediately.

1 0 s e r v i n g s

Smothered Okra and Tomatoes

hile many of our gumbos are thickened with okra, it can also be served on its own as a vegetable. Many cooks also freeze cooked okra and tomatoes in the summer to use in gumbos during the winter. Before okra can be used in any dish, it must be cooked to remove the slime. Usually this is done in a large pot on top of the stove, but Marcelle showed me this trick for cooking it in the oven. Remember, never cook okra in a cast-iron pot or the okra will turn black.

2 pounds okra

3 cups chopped onions

2 cups chopped celery

3 cups chopped, peeled, and seeded tomatoes, or 3 cups chopped canned tomatoes

5 bay leaves

1/3 cup vegetable oil

1 tablespoon plus 2 teaspoons salt

1/2 teaspoon cayenne

1/2 teaspoon freshly ground black pepper

1 teaspoon dried thyme

2 tablespoons chopped garlic

1. Preheat the oven to 300°F.

2. Wash the okra under cool water. Cut off the stems and slice each pod crosswise into 1/2-inch rounds.

3. Combine the okra and the rest of the ingredients in a large heavy ovenproof pot, not cast iron. Mix well. Cover the pot with a lid. Bake, stirring occasionally, for 1 1/2 to 2 hours, or until the slime has disappeared. Bake, uncovered, for the last 15 minutes of the cooking time. The time will vary, depending on the tenderness of the okra. Remove the bay leaves.

4. Serve immediately or let cool completely and store in freezer containers.

10 servings

Smothered Green Beans and Potatoes

Smothering extracts the very heart of the flavors of whatever is being cooked. Something as simple as green beans and potatoes, smothered in their juices, becomes nothing short of spectacular. Try it with Round Steak and Onions (page 166) for a real treat. A small amount of roux tightens up the liquid in this version.

½ pound bacon, chopped

¼ cup flour

2 cups chopped onions

1½ teaspoons salt

¼ teaspoon cayenne

¼ teaspoon freshly ground black pepper

2 cups water

1½ pounds fresh green beans, trimmed

1 large baking potato, peeled and cut into 1-inch cubes (about ¾ pound)

1. Fry the bacon in a large saucepan over medium-high heat until slightly crisp, 6 to 8 minutes. Remove the bacon with a slotted spoon and drain on paper towels. Set aside.

2. Add the flour to the fat in the pan and stirring constantly for 5 to 8 minutes, make a medium brown roux, the color of peanut butter.

3. Add the onions and cook, stirring often, for about 5 minutes, or until wilted. Add the salt, cayenne, black pepper, and water. Stir until the mixture is smooth and thick. Add the beans and potatoes. Reduce the heat to medium, cover, and cook for about 20 minutes, stirring occasionally. Potatoes should be fork tender. Uncover and cook for about 3 minutes.

4. Fold in the reserved bacon and serve immediately.

6 servings

Southern Greens

 hen I make Skillet Corn Bread (page 284), I have to have some greens. When I make corn bread and greens, I have to fry up a batch of Batter-Fried Chicken (page 138). Then, I'm a happy man.

½ pound bacon, chopped

3 cups sliced onions

2 teaspoons salt

¾ teaspoon cayenne

¾ teaspoon freshly ground black pepper

1 tablespoon chopped garlic

1 can (12 ounces) beer

¼ cup distilled white vinegar

1 tablespoon molasses

6 pounds greens, such as mustard greens, collard greens, turnip greens, kale, or spinach, rinsed well, picked over, and stemmed

1. Fry the bacon in a large heavy pot over medium heat until slightly crisp. Add the onions and cook, stirring occasionally, for 7 to 8 minutes, or until wilted and golden. Add the salt, cayenne, black pepper, and garlic and cook for about 2 minutes. Add the beer, vinegar, and molasses. Mix well.
2. Begin adding the greens, a third at a time, pressing down on the greens as they wilt. They will wilt considerably as they cook. Cook, uncovered, over medium heat, stirring often, for about 1 hour and 15 minutes.
3. Serve immediately.

8 servings

Ratatouille

n summer, when weather conditions are good, we are blessed with a great *récolte*, or harvest, of tomatoes, bell peppers, eggplant, zucchini, and yellow squash. We celebrate by making this fragrant dish that goes well with just about anything, but especially Fillet Steaks (page 165).

3 tablespoons vegetable oil

¼ cup chopped Tasso (page 207) or spiced ham

2 cups chopped onions

1 cup chopped bell peppers

1 cup chopped celery

2 teaspoons salt

½ teaspoon cayenne

½ teaspoon freshly ground black pepper

1 medium eggplant, peeled and cut into 1-inch cubes (about ½ pound)

1 medium zucchini, cut into 1-inch cubes (about ½ pound)

1 medium yellow squash, cut into 1-inch cubes (about ½ pound)

3 cups chopped, peeled, and seeded fresh tomatoes, or 3 cups chopped canned tomatoes

2 tablespoons chopped garlic

½ teaspoon chopped fresh basil or 1 teaspoon dried

½ teaspoon dried thyme

1. Heat the oil in a Dutch oven over medium-high heat. Add the tasso and sauté for about 2 minutes. Add the onions, bell peppers, celery, salt, cayenne, and black pepper. Cook, stirring constantly, for about 3 minutes, or until the vegetables are slightly wilted. Add the eggplant and cook for 4 to 5 minutes, or until slightly tender. Add the zucchini, yellow squash, tomatoes, garlic, basil, and thyme. Reduce the heat to medium and cook, stirring occasionally, for 8 to 10 minutes, or until the mixture is a little soupy. The vegetables should have a little crunch to them.

2. Serve warm or it can be cooked a day ahead. It gains in flavor when reheated.

6 servings

Sausage-Stuffed Bell Peppers

ne summer afternoon, as I watched an elderly gentleman harvest his bell pepper crop, he filled a bushel basket in no time. When I asked him what he was going to do with all those sweet peppers, he grinned and proudly explained that tomorrow he and his wife were going to stuff them for the freezer. He said that when his sons and their families come for Sunday dinner, they always ask for stuffed bell peppers.

½ pound Pork Breakfast Sausage (page 203), crumbled

1 cup chopped onions

½ cup chopped bell peppers

½ cup chopped celery

½ teaspoon salt

¼ teaspoon cayenne

1½ cups cooked long-grain rice

¼ cup chopped green onions

3 tablespoons chopped parsley

4 medium bell peppers, sliced in half lengthwise, seeds removed

¼ cup dried fine bread crumbs

¼ cup freshly grated parmesan

½ teaspoon Rustic Rub (page 9)

1. Preheat the oven to 400°F.

2. Brown the sausage in a dry skillet over medium-high heat for about 3 minutes. Add the onions, bell peppers, celery, salt, and cayenne. Cook, stirring often, for 4 to 5 minutes, or until the vegetables are wilted. Add the rice and mix well. Cook for about 3 minutes. Remove from the heat and add the green onions and parsley. Mix again.

3. Spoon the mixture into the bell peppers. Combine the bread crumbs, cheese, and rub and sprinkle evenly over the tops of the bell peppers. Place the peppers in a shallow pan and add just enough water to cover the bottom. Bake for about 30 minutes, or until the tops are crusty and brown.

4. Serve hot.

4 servings

Stuffed Vegetables

Both Creole and Acadian cooks transform garden vegetables, such as tomatoes, mirlitons, zucchini, eggplants, and bell peppers by stuffing them with chopped vegetable pulp and rice or bread crumbs, with shrimp, crabmeat, beef, ham, sausage—whatever they have on hand. It's an excellent example of the attitude toward food in this state. Use what you have, waste nothing, and by adding a little of this and a little of that, make vegetables extraordinary fare.

Boiled Artichokes

While artichokes are not native to Louisiana, they are very much a part of our cuisine, most likely introduced by Italians who settled in New Orleans and other parts of the state. Boiled in water spiked with Zatarain's Concentrated Crab & Shrimp Boil, these artichokes take on a robust flavor. I like to dip the fleshy part of the leaves and the heart in a garlicky mayonnaise. This makes a wonderful appetizer for any meal on a warm evening.

4 large artichokes, rinsed in cool water

1 tablespoon salt

2 bay leaves

1 medium lemon, halved

3 tablespoons liquid Zatarain's Concentrated Crab & Shrimp Boil

½ recipe One-Egg Mayonnaise (page 29), with 1 minced garlic clove added

1. Trim off the stems and thorny tips of each leaf of the artichokes. Put them in a deep pot and add enough water to cover.

2. Add the salt and bay leaves. Squeeze the lemon over the pot and add the lemon shells. Add the Zatarain's boil and bring to a boil over high heat. Reduce the heat to medium-high and simmer, uncovered, for 20 to 30 minutes, or until the artichokes are tender when pierced with the tip of a pointed knife. Drain.

3. Place the artichokes, stem side down, on platters with puddles of mayonnaise around them.

4 servings

Roasted Stuffed Artichokes

n small neighborhood Italian cafés throughout the state, and especially in New Orleans, one of the specialties is stuffed artichokes. Bread crumbs are seasoned and stuffed in between the leaves. In my version, the artichokes are boiled and quartered, then a bread crumb mixture is piled on the pieces before roasting.

2 Boiled Artichokes (page 246)	2 tablespoons chopped parsley
6 slices bacon, chopped	1/4 cup dry sherry
1/2 cup chopped onions	1 tablespoon fresh lemon juice
2 tablespoons chopped bell peppers	1/2 teaspoon salt
2 tablespoons chopped celery	1/4 teaspoon cayenne
2 teaspoons Rustic Rub (page 9)	1/2 cup dried fine bread crumbs
2 teaspoons chopped garlic	1/4 cup freshly grated parmesan

1. Preheat the oven to 400°F.

2. Trim off the stems and leaf tips of the artichokes. Quarter the artichokes cutting lengthwise. Remove the chokes. Set aside.

3. Fry the bacon in a skillet over medium heat until slightly crisp. Add the onions, bell peppers, celery, and rub. Sauté the mixture, stirring constantly, for about 3 minutes, or until the vegetables are slightly wilted. Add the garlic and parsley and cook, stirring, for about 2 minutes.

4. Remove from the heat. Add the sherry and swish it around in the pan. Add the lemon juice, salt, cayenne, bread crumbs, and parmesan. Mix well.

5. Divide the mixture into 8 equal portions. Place the artichoke quarters on a baking sheet. Mound a portion of bread crumb mixture on each artichoke quarter. Bake for about 15 minutes, or until the bread crumb mixture is light brown.

6. Serve warm, allowing 2 artichoke quarters per person.

4 servings

Jerusalem Artichokes and Potatoes au Gratin

he Jerusalem artichoke, also called sunchoke or topinambour, is a knotty root native to North America. It is both nutritious and versatile. I was surprised to find it in a pot of baked wild duck here in Louisiana, but I learned that it is used often, especially in south Louisiana. The slightly crunchy Jerusalem artichokes and smooth sliced potatoes combined with cheddar cheese are a cooking preparation much favored by the locals. This dish goes well with Cedar Plank Trout (page 126).

---

6 Jerusalem artichokes, peeled and cut into ¼-inch slices (about ¾ pound)

2 large baking potatoes, peeled and cut into ½-inch slices (about 1¼ pounds)

1 teaspoon salt

⅛ teaspoon freshly ground black pepper

¼ teaspoon cayenne

¼ cup olive oil

1 tablespoon butter

½ cup chopped onions

2 teaspoons chopped garlic

¾ cup grated cheddar (3 ounces)

1 tablespoon flour

½ cup milk

1 cup dried fine bread crumbs

2 tablespoons chopped parsley

2 teaspoons Rustic Rub (page 9)

---

1. Preheat the oven to 400°F.

2. Place the Jerusalem artichokes and potatoes in a mixing bowl and season with the salt, black pepper, and cayenne. Mix in 2 tablespoons of the olive oil and toss thoroughly to coat.

3. Butter the bottom and sides of a 2-quart baking dish. Put half of the artichoke-potato mixture in the bottom of the pan, then sprinkle with ¼ cup of the chopped onions, 1 teaspoon of the chopped garlic, and ¼ cup of the cheese, and the flour. Top this with the remaining artichoke-potato mix-

ture. Sprinkle with the remaining ¼ cup onions, 1 teaspoon garlic, and ½ cup cheese. Pour the milk over the mixture.

4. In a bowl, mix together the remaining 2 tablespoons olive oil with the bread crumbs, parsley, and rub. Spread this topping evenly over the mixture. Bake for 1 hour, or until the potatoes are tender.

5. Serve hot.

6 servings

Roasted Garlic

arlic, known for its curative properties, is used quite a bit in Louisiana cooking. When I see ropes of braided garlic at roadside vegetable stands and small-town markets, I get a hankering to roast a batch. I smear the garlic on crackers or French bread drizzled with a bit of olive oil for a quick snack. It's especially good in Potato Salad with Roasted Garlic Dressing (page 266).

6 large heads garlic

1 tablespoon olive oil

½ teaspoon salt

¼ teaspoon freshly ground black pepper

1. Preheat the oven to 400°F.

2. Cut each head of garlic crosswise in half. Toss the garlic heads with the olive oil, salt, and pepper in a bowl. Turn out the garlic heads onto the center of a sheet of aluminum foil. Bring the ends of the foil together to make a small bag or pouch. Roast for 1 hour, or until the garlic is tender.

3. Remove the bag from the oven and open it up a bit. Return to the oven for about 10 minutes more. Remove the flesh by squeezing each half clove with your thumb and index finger.

4. Use immediately or refrigerate in a little olive oil in an airtight container for 2 to 3 days.

About 1 cup

Baked Garlic Onions

nions stuffed with pork sausage or tiny shrimp show up on holiday buffets. They are delicious, but I like to spoon garlic puree into hollowed-out onions. A real beauty of a dish for garlic lovers.

6 cups water, or enough to cover the onions

2 teaspoons salt

1/4 teaspoon cayenne

2 bay leaves

4 medium to large onions, peeled and hollowed out, leaving a 1/2-inch shell, onion pulp reserved (about 1 1/4 pounds)

1/2 recipe Roasted Garlic (page 249)

1/4 cup chopped parsley

3 tablespoons extra-virgin olive oil

1/4 teaspoon freshly ground black pepper

1/4 cup dried fine bread crumbs

1/4 cup freshly grated parmesan

1 tablespoon vegetable oil

1 teaspoon Rustic Rub (page 9)

1. Preheat the oven to 400°F.

2. Combine the water, 1 1/2 teaspoons salt, cayenne, and bay leaves in a large saucepan. Add the onions and bring to a boil. Cook, uncovered, for 8 to 10 minutes, or until the onions are slightly tender. Drain.

3. Combine the garlic, onion pulp, and parsley in a food processor and puree. With the motor running, pour the olive oil through the feed tube in a steady stream. Add the remaining 1/2 teaspoon salt and the black pepper and pulse a couple of times to mix well.

4. Place the onions in a shallow baking dish. Divide the garlic mixture evenly and spoon some into the center of each onion.

5. Combine the bread crumbs, cheese, vegetable oil, and rub in a small mixing bowl. Spoon the mixture evenly on top of each onion. Bake for about 30 minutes, or until the tops of the onions are lightly brown.

6. Serve hot.

4 servings

Smashing Smashed Potatoes

s much as rice is consumed in Louisiana, there are times when folks opt to serve potatoes with their meal. For me, such is the case when I serve Crispy-Fried Redfish (page 123) to friends on lazy, warm Sunday afternoons. There's nothing subtle about these potatoes. Boiled potatoes, in their jackets, are mashed and tossed with lots of garlic, butter, and cream—smashing! If you want something even more sinful, pour the smashed potatoes into a casserole dish and top with one cup of grated cheddar. Bake at 375°F. until the cheese melts completely.

1½ pounds small red potatoes, quartered

1³/4 teaspoons salt

½ teaspoon freshly ground black pepper

1 stick (¼ pound) butter

1 cup Roasted Garlic (page 249)

1 cup heavy cream

1. Put the potatoes in a saucepan and cover with water. Season with 1 teaspoon of the salt and ¼ teaspoon of the black pepper. Boil until fork tender, about 20 minutes.

2. Drain and return the potatoes to the pot. Add the butter, garlic, and cream. Using a fork, coarsely mash the potatoes and mix well.

3. Season with the remaining salt and black pepper and serve.

6 servings

Brabant Potatoes

'm not really sure where or when these crispy, fried potatoes were introduced to Louisiana, but I'll bet that a French colonist was responsible. For years, they have been served in both fine restaurants and corner cafés. Sometimes cut into large cubes, other times into small ones, they are often drizzled with butter and sprinkled with salt and parsley. They're Louisiana's version of french fries. Make a nest of these in the center of your dinner plate and plunk a thick grilled steak or Crispy-Fried Redfish (page 123) on top. Drizzle with some of Emeril's Worcestershire Sauce (page 7).

2 medium baking potatoes,
peeled and cut into
1/2-inch cubes
(about 1 pound)

2 tablespoons vegetable oil

1/2 teaspoon salt

1/4 teaspoon freshly ground
black pepper

1/4 cup chopped green onions

2 tablespoons chopped
parsley

1 tablespoon Worcestershire
sauce

1 tablespoon chopped garlic

2 tablespoons butter

1. Put the potatoes in a saucepan and cover with water. Boil for 4 to 5 minutes, or until slightly tender. Drain and cool slightly.

2. Heat the oil in a nonstick skillet over medium-high heat. Add the potatoes, salt, and pepper. Cook, shaking the pan back and forth, for 10 to 12 minutes, or until golden brown and crisp. Add the green onions, parsley, Worcestershire, and garlic. Shake the pan again for about 1 minute. Add the butter and continue shaking the pan until it is melted.

3. Serve immediately.

2 servings

Sweet Potato Pudding

 arcelle's family still teases her about how many sweet potatoes she consumed when she was a child. It earned her the nickname "*Patate Douce*." She says she still eats a goodly amount of sweet potatoes especially when they are prepared like this. Smooth and creamy, this is a colorful and festive dish to serve with Ducks with Fig Glaze (page 156) or Pepper-Stuffed Turkey (page 140).

4 medium sweet potatoes, baked
   (page 255) and peeled
   (about 2 pounds)

3 eggs

1 cup milk

1/8 teaspoon grated nutmeg

1/2 teaspoon ground cinnamon

1 cup pecan pieces

1 cup (packed) light brown sugar

2 tablespoons Steen's 100% Pure
   Cane Syrup

1/4 teaspoon salt

1/4 teaspoon vanilla extract

2 tablespoons bourbon

1/2 stick (4 tablespoons) butter,
   softened

1. Preheat the oven to 350°F.
2. Mash the potatoes in a mixing bowl, until smooth. Add the eggs and milk and mix well. Add the nutmeg, cinnamon, 1/2 cup of the pecans, 1/2 cup of the brown sugar, syrup, salt, vanilla, and bourbon. Mix well.
3. Pour the mixture into a 1 1/2-quart round baking dish.
4. Combine the remaining 1/2 cup pecans and the remaining 1/2 cup brown sugar with the butter and mix well. Dot the top of the potato mixture with spoonsful of the butter mixture. Bake for about 45 minutes, or until bubbly.
5. Serve hot.

6 servings

Candied Yams

n October, the town of Opelousas, in south Louisiana, holds its annual Yambilee Festival, with yams prepared in any number of ways. One of the most popular dishes is Candied Yams. It's best to use fresh sweet potatoes, but canned will do. When using canned, be sure to drain well before using. And don't pour the syrup from the can down the drain. Brush it on pork chops or ham as a glaze. There's an old Acadian saying, *Lâche pas la patate*, which literally translated is "Don't let go of the potato," but means "Don't give up!"

3 quarts water	1 tablespoon sugar
1¼ teaspoons salt	⅛ teaspoon freshly ground black pepper
4 medium sweet potatoes, peeled and cut crosswise into ¾-inch slices (2 pounds)	½ cup pecan pieces
½ stick (4 tablespoons) butter, melted	¼ cup Steen's 100% Pure Cane Syrup
½ teaspoon ground cinnamon	¼ cup (packed) light brown sugar
⅛ teaspoon grated nutmeg	1 cup miniature marshmallows

1. Preheat the oven to 450°F.

2. Bring the water, seasoned with 1 teaspoon of the salt, to a boil in a large saucepan. Add the potatoes. Boil for 7 to 8 minutes, or until fork tender.

3. Remove from the pot with a slotted spoon and transfer to a mixing bowl. Add the butter, the remaining ¼ teaspoon salt, the cinnamon, nutmeg, sugar, pepper, pecans, and syrup and toss.

4. Pour into a casserole. Sprinkle the top with the brown sugar and the marshmallows. Bake for about 20 minutes, or until the marshmallows melt and turn light brown.

5. Serve hot.

6 servings

Sweet Potatoes

Sweet potatoes are a tuberous root. The root acts as a storage area, with the plant's food reserves stored as starch. When freshly dug sweet potatoes are cooked, they have a bland taste. The vegetable must be cured and stored to convert the starch to sugar. To cure, the fresh potatoes are subjected to a temperature of 85° to 90°F. and a relative humidity of 85° to 95°F. for at least four to seven days. (Some experts say up to two weeks.) The curing process helps to protect the potato from bruising and results in sugar formation. It's best to buy properly cured sweet potatoes because the high temperature and humidity required for the curing process are not easily attainable in home conditions. Properly cooking the sweet potato is necessary to get syrupy sweet potatoes. Start with a washed potato. There is no need to oil or butter the skin and do not prick the potato with a fork. Do not cut in half. Bake at 400°F. for 30 minutes. Reduce the heat to 375°F. and bake for 45 minutes or until tender. Check for doneness by squeezing a potato. If it is soft, it's done. Sweet potatoes will not cook properly in a microwave. The Beauregard variety (and a few others) was developed by the Louisiana Agricultural Experiment Station, a part of LSU's Agricultural Center, and is one of the major varieties planted by Louisiana growers since it was developed for our soil and climate conditions. These sweet potatoes (or yams) are distinguished physically by its copper skin, its deep orange flesh, and its smooth and syrupy texture when cooked. The word "yam" was a trade name for south Louisiana's moist and sweet potatoes in the 1930s and 1940s to differentiate them from drier, mealy, less tasty varieties grown in other locations. Over time, the trade name has become a common name. Sweet potatoes are believed to have originated in the West Indies and Central America. Some varieties were being grown by Indians when Columbus arrived.

Lyonnaise of Mirliton

 dish prepared à la lyonnaise is made with onions; the best known lyonnaise is with potatoes. But when the vines are heavy with mirlitons in the late summer and early fall, I find that this one is a nice change of pace. The subtle flavor of the mirliton is enhanced by the onions. The dish makes a delicious accompaniment to Chicken Loaf (page 139).

---

3 medium mirlitons, peeled, seeded, and cut into ½-inch cubes (about 1½ pounds)

2 large onions, peeled, halved, and cut lengthwise into ½-inch slices

2½ teaspoons salt

¼ teaspoon freshly ground black pepper

⅛ teaspoon cayenne

2 tablespoons vegetable oil

2 tablespoons butter

---

1. Put the mirlitons in a saucepan and cover with water. Boil, uncovered, for 30 to 35 minutes, or until fork tender. Drain and cool under tap water. Set aside.

2. Season the onions with the salt, black pepper, and cayenne. Heat the oil in a large skillet over medium-high heat, add the onions, and sauté for about 5 minutes, or until caramelized and golden. Add the butter and mirlitons and cook, stirring constantly, for about 5 minutes. Remove from the heat.

3. Serve immediately.

4 servings

Mirliton with Shrimp

ouisiana cooks transform vegetables into something extraordinary. I've seen tomatoes filled with beef and eggplant and bell peppers piled with pork or shrimp stuffing. But mirliton hollowed out and filled with a mashed pulp, bread crumbs, and shrimp is definitely unique.

3 medium mirlitons (about 1½ pounds)	½ teaspoon chopped garlic
2 tablespoons butter	½ pound large shrimp, peeled, deveined, and cut into 3 pieces each
½ cup chopped onions	
¼ cup chopped bell peppers	½ cup dried fine bread crumbs
¼ cup chopped celery	3 tablespoons freshly grated parmesan
1 teaspoon salt	
½ teaspoon cayenne	

1. Put the mirlitons in a saucepan and cover with water. Boil, partially covered, for 40 to 45 minutes, or until fork tender. Drain and cool.

2. Preheat the oven to 350°F.

3. When the mirlitons are cool enough to handle, cut them lengthwise in halves. Remove the seeds and hollow out each half with a spoon, leaving a ¼-inch shell. Reserve the pulp. Set aside shells and pulp separately.

4. Heat the butter in a skillet over medium-high heat. Sauté the onions, bell peppers, and celery for about 5 minutes, or until soft and golden. Add the salt, cayenne, garlic, shrimp, and reserved pulp. Sauté, stirring, for about 4 minutes. Add the bread crumbs and the parmesan and stir to mix well. Remove from the heat.

5. Divide the mixture into 6 equal portions and fill each mirliton shell. Bake for about 30 minutes, or until the tops are brown.

6. Serve immediately.

6 servings

Mirliton Fritters

irlitons make delicious fritters that can be served as an appetizer accompanied by Creole Tartar Sauce (page 28).

1 medium mirliton, peeled, seeded, and cut into ½-inch cubes (about ½ pound)

3 eggs

1½ teaspoons salt

½ teaspoon cayenne

5 teaspoons baking powder

1 cup milk

2¼ cups flour

½ cup chopped onions

¼ cup chopped bell peppers

Solid vegetable shortening, for deep-frying

¼ teaspoon Rustic Rub (page 9)

1. Put the mirliton in a saucepan and cover with water. Boil, uncovered, for 30 to 35 minutes, or until fork tender. Cool under tap water and drain thoroughly. Mash slightly with a fork and set aside.

2. Combine the eggs, salt, cayenne, and baking powder in a mixing bowl and mix well. Add the milk and whisk for a few seconds.

3. Beat in the flour, ¼ cup at a time, until all of it is incorporated and the batter is smooth. Add the mirliton, onions, and bell peppers and mix well.

4. Heat at least 2 inches of the shortening in a large, deep-frying pan to 360°F. Drop the batter, a tablespoonful at a time, into the hot oil. When the fritters pop to the surface, roll them around in the oil using a long-handled spatula or tongs until they are evenly browned.

5. Drain on paper towels. Sprinkle with the rub and serve.

About 24

Smothered Mirliton and Shrimp

ome say the mirliton is a simple vegetable; others claim it is exotic. Try this dish and judge for yourself. This is a dish that is prepared often in south Louisiana, but I never tire of it. The combination of the subtle sweetness of the vegetable and the delicate flavor of the shrimp is enhanced by the ham and garlic. The mixture can be served over steamed rice or toasted slices of French bread.

6 tablespoons butter	1 cup chopped ham
4 tablespoons flour	2 teaspoons chopped garlic
2 medium mirlitons, peeled, seeded, and chopped (about 1 1/4 pounds)	2 cups water
	1 teaspoon salt
1/2 cup chopped onions	1/4 teaspoon cayenne
1/4 cup chopped bell peppers	1 pound medium shrimp, peeled and deveined
1/4 cup chopped celery	

1. Heat the butter in a large skillet over medium-high heat. When the foam subsides, add the flour. Stirring constantly for 10 to 12 minutes, make a blond roux, the color of sandpaper.

2. Add the mirlitons, onions, bell peppers, and celery. Sauté for about 5 minutes, or until the vegetables are wilted. Add the ham and garlic and cook, stirring, for 2 minutes. Add the water, salt, and cayenne. Reduce the heat to medium and simmer uncovered for about 10 minutes. Add the shrimp and cook for 10 minutes more.

3. Serve hot.

4 servings

Spinach Cakes

hese savory little cakes are spiked with Pernod, an anise-flavored liqueur that sharpens the flavor of the spinach. Moist and fragrant, they're excellent with Fried Soft-shell Crabs (page 81) and Shrimp Pernod (page 86), or any of the oyster dishes.

½ stick (4 tablespoons) butter

½ cup flour

½ cup chopped onions

1 cup milk

4 cups cleaned and stemmed fresh spinach (about 6 ounces)

1¼ teaspoons salt

⅛ teaspoon cayenne

¼ teaspoon ground white pepper

¼ teaspoon grated nutmeg

2 teaspoons chopped garlic

½ cup dried fine bread crumbs

2 tablespoons freshly grated parmesan

1 tablespoon Pernod

1/4 cup vegetable oil

2 teaspoons Rustic Rub (page 9)

1. Heat the butter in a skillet over medium-high heat. Add ¼ cup of the flour. Stirring constantly for 5 to 6 minutes, make a blond roux, the color of sandpaper.

2. Add the onions and cook, stirring, for about 2 minutes, or until slightly wilted. Add the milk and stir until the mixture thickens, 3 to 4 minutes. Add the spinach, salt, cayenne, white pepper, nutmeg, and garlic and cook, stirring, for about 4 minutes.

3. Remove from the heat. Add the bread crumbs, parmesan, and Pernod and mix well. Let cool for about 30 minutes. Divide the mixture into 4 equal portions and shape into patties.

4. Heat the oil in a nonstick skillet over medium-high heat. Combine the remaining ¼ cup flour and the rub. Dredge the patties, coating evenly, in the flour. Fry the cakes for about 1½ minutes on each side, or until golden.

5. Transfer to a warm platter and keep warm until ready to use. The cakes can be reheated by placing them in a pie tin in a 400°F. oven for 4 to 5 minutes.

6. Serve warm.

4 cakes

CHAPTER 11

Salads and Salad Dressings

ool salads, either as accompaniments to other dishes or as main courses, are enjoyed year round in the subtropical climate of Louisiana. The ingredients are not exotic, but just what's available from the gardens, fields, farms, and waterways of our state. And like all Louisiana cuisine, the salads are richly flavored, some with Creole mustard, others with creamy mayonnaise, and most with a healthy dose of herbs and spices. During the summer months, tender okra pods are panfried and drizzled with a tangy Green Onion Dressing and served as a Sunday dinner side dish with roast or fried chicken. For large family gatherings, tart, cool Maw-Maw's Slaw or chunky Real Potato Salad tossed with both Creole mustard and creamy mayonnaise are traditional favorites with fried seafood or grilled meats.

CRAB SALAD,

FRIED OKRA

SALAD, GREEN

ONION DRESSING,

AND MORE

Because of the abundance of crab, shrimp, and crawfish, seafood salads are common. The Crab Salad with bits of celery, onions, parsley, and mayonnaise can be dressed up and served as a first course on a bed of shredded lettuce or spooned on thick slices of plump juicy tomatoes. In the spring, when crawfish are plentiful, a crisp Fried Crawfish Salad is an ideal main course for an informal supper. I pile the crunchy crustaceans on top of cool salad greens, accompanied by lots of warm French bread. An old standby here in the South is chicken salad, tucked into tomatoes or piled on French bread. For a powerful main course with a lot of bite and substance, the Beef and Horseradish Salad is a personal favorite.

Maw-Maw's Slaw

food is taken seriously here in Louisiana, even by young children. At a fish-fry at a camp on the levee that contains the Atchafalaya River Basin, a swamp of incredible beauty in the southern part of the state, I overheard two ten-year-olds discussing the merits of the cole slaw that was part of the buffet. Étienne, who was on his second helping, was telling his cousin Monique that he "couldn't ever" get enough of the stuff. Monique replied that "Maw-Maw," their grandmother, sure knew how to make good slaw. One taste made me agree. I went in search of Maw-Maw and asked her to share her secret.

½ pound white cabbage, shredded (about 2 cups)

½ pound red cabbage, shredded (about 2 cups)

½ pound assorted greens, such as mustard greens, collards, or spinach, trimmed, washed, and shredded (about 2 cups)

1 cup thinly sliced red onions

1 cup chopped green onions, green parts only

½ cup chopped parsley

1 recipe One-Egg Mayonnaise (page 29)

¼ cup Creole or whole-grain mustard

1 teaspoon salt

¼ teaspoon freshly ground black pepper

¼ teaspoon cayenne

2 teaspoons sugar

1. Place the white cabbage, red cabbage, greens, red onions, green onions, and parsley in a large salad bowl. In a small bowl, combine the mayonnaise, mustard, salt, black pepper, cayenne, and sugar. Mix well. Add the mixture to the greens and toss to mix thoroughly. Cover and refrigerate for at least 1 hour.

2. Serve chilled. The slaw can be made (or chilled) three hours ahead.

8 servings

Potato Salad with Roasted Garlic Dressing

n Louisiana garlic, used with a heavy hand, is just one of the ingredients that make the cuisine so robust. The sweet yet penetrating taste of roasted garlic works quite well with potatoes boiled in their jackets in a salad that can go to the Sunday dinner table with Batter-Fried Chicken (page 138) or to the camp to serve with Campfire Steaks (page 162).

Roasted Garlic Dressing

½ recipe Roasted Garlic (page 249)

½ cup chopped parsley

¾ cup olive oil

½ teaspoon salt

¼ teaspoon cayenne

1. Combine the garlic and parsley in a food processor and puree until smooth. With the motor running, pour the oil through the feed tube in a steady stream. Add the salt and cayenne and pulse a couple of times to mix well.

Potato Salad

2½ pounds medium red potatoes, scrubbed, boiled, and quartered

½ cup thinly sliced onions

1 teaspoon salt

⅛ teaspoon freshly ground black pepper

2. Combine the potatoes, onions, salt, and black pepper in a salad bowl. Add the garlic dressing and toss to coat thoroughly.

3. Let sit at room temperature or chill for 30 minutes before serving.

6 servings

Real Potato Salad

otato salad is the traditional accompaniment to fried seafood and fried chicken, and in the southern part of the state, particularly along Bayou Teche, the locals like it so much they even put a spoonful or two in their chicken and sausage gumbo. There are two secrets to this potato salad—cut the potatoes into chunks, and no mayonnaise will do but homemade. It's so tasty, I've seen people make a sandwich of it.

1½ pounds medium red potatoes, scrubbed

4 hard-boiled eggs, coarsely chopped

½ teaspoon salt

¼ teaspoon cayenne

¼ teaspoon freshly ground black pepper

¼ cup chopped celery

1 tablespoon chopped green onions

1 tablespoon chopped parsley

½ recipe One-Egg Mayonnaise (page 29)

2 tablespoons Creole or whole-grain mustard

1. Put the potatoes in a saucepan and add enough water to cover. Bring to a boil. Cook, partially covered, for 25 to 30 minutes, or until fork tender.

2. Drain and cool. Peel and cut the potatoes into 1-inch chunks. Put the potatoes in a salad bowl. Add the eggs, salt, cayenne, black pepper, celery, green onions, and parsley. Combine the mayonnaise and mustard and add to the bowl. Toss to mix well.

3. Serve immediately or refrigerate and serve slightly chilled.

4 servings

Creole Rice Salad

ouisianians eat rice every day, with gumbos and red beans, or in jambalayas and puddings. This rice salad is particularly good when piled into hollowed-out tomatoes and served for lunch on a hot summer's day.

3 cups cooked long-grain rice, at
  room temperature

1/2 cup finely chopped celery

1/4 cup finely chopped bell peppers

1 tablespoon finely chopped parsley

3 tablespoons finely chopped green
  onions

1/2 cup finely chopped yellow onions

1/4 cup extra-virgin olive oil

1/4 cup sliced pimiento-stuffed green
  olives

1 tablespoon apple cider vinegar

2 tablespoons Creole or whole-grain
  mustard

3/4 teaspoon salt

1/4 teaspoon freshly ground black
  pepper

1/2 teaspoon Tabasco sauce

1/4 cup finely chopped Pickled
  Banana Peppers (page 19)

4 hard-boiled eggs, coarsely chopped

1. Combine all of the ingredients in a salad bowl and toss to mix well. Refrigerate for at least 2 hours before serving.

2. Serve chilled.

4 servings

Fried Okra Salad

ust about everyone in Louisiana has a summer garden. And no matter how small or large, it will usually harbor
a few bushes of okra. While some of it makes its way into
gumbos, there's always extra for pickling and for salads.

1/4 cup buttermilk

1 egg

4 teaspoons Rustic Rub
  (page 9)

16 okra pods, washed and
  cut in half lengthwise

1/4 cup flour

1/4 cup yellow cornmeal

1 cup solid vegetable
  shortening, for frying

4 cups assorted salad greens

1 recipe Green Onion
  Dressing (page 280)

1. Beat together the buttermilk and egg in a small
bowl. Add 2 teaspoons of the rub and stir to blend.
Add the okra and turn to coat evenly. Let sit for 30
minutes.

2. In another bowl, combine the flour, cornmeal,
and 1 teaspoon of the rub.

3. Heat the shortening in a skillet. When it is hot,
place the okra, split side down, in the oil and fry,
turning once, for about 2 minutes, or until lightly
golden.

4. Drain on paper towels. Sprinkle the okra with the
remaining 1 teaspoon of rub.

5. Divide the greens into 4 equal portions. Top each
with okra and drizzle with dressing.

6. Serve immediately.

4 first-course servings

Beef and Horseradish Salad

n south Louisiana, when people have a craving for a particular dish, they say they have an *envie*. When I have an *envie* for some beef, this spicy salad fills the bill. The rub and grated horseradish give it a kick.

1½ pounds beef tenderloin or sirloin, cut into 1-inch chunks

1 tablespoon Rustic Rub (page 9)

1 tablespoon vegetable oil

1 large yellow onion, cut in half and thinly sliced

3 tablespoons chopped parsley

3 tablespoons chopped green onions

1 tablespoon chopped garlic

1 tablespoon fresh lemon juice

½ teaspoon Worcestershire sauce

½ teaspoon Tabasco sauce

1¼ cups olive oil

¾ teaspoon salt

¼ teaspoon freshly ground black pepper

Dressing

1 egg

½ cup freshly grated horseradish or 1 teaspoon prepared horseradish

1. Combine the beef, rub, and vegetable oil in a bowl and toss to coat.

2. Brown the beef evenly in a large skillet over medium-high heat for 4 to 6 minutes. Do not crowd the beef in the skillet. Transfer the beef to a large bowl and add the onion, parsley, and green onions. Set aside to cool.

3. To make the dressing, combine the egg, horseradish, garlic, lemon juice, Worcestershire, and Tabasco in a food processor. Process until smooth. With the motor running, pour the olive oil through the feed tube in a steady stream. The mixture will thicken. Add the salt and pepper and pulse once or twice to blend.

4. Add the dressing to the beef mixture and toss to coat thoroughly. Cover and refrigerate for at least 1 hour before serving. Serve chilled.

6 servings

Great Chicken Salad

ne of the social rules in the South is that a young bride should know how to cook. If she can make nothing else, she should, at the very least, know how to prepare a great chicken salad. In Louisiana, chances are good that she learned at her mother's knee how to make a good Chicken Broth (page 11) and then to use the leftover chicken to prepare chicken salad. Children like it spread between two pieces of French bread. Adults stuff it into plump, ripe tomatoes for lunch. Me . . . well, when I bake Brioche (page 288), I do a batch of brioche muffins. Then I dig a hole in the center of a muffin and stuff it with this salad.

2 cups diced cooked chicken	1 teaspoon Rustic Rub (page 9)
1 hard-boiled egg, finely chopped	1/8 teaspoon freshly ground black pepper
1/2 cup chopped celery	1/2 teaspoon salt
1/2 cup chopped onions	1/2 cup One-Egg Mayonnaise (page 29)
1 tablespoon minced garlic	
3 tablespoons Creole or whole-grain mustard	

1. Combine the chicken, egg, celery, and onions.

2. Mix together the garlic, mustard, rub, pepper, salt, and mayonnaise in a serving bowl.

3. Add to the chicken mixture and mix well. Refrigerate for at least 1 hour before serving.

4. Serve chilled.

4 servings

Spiced Shrimp Salad in Artichokes

both the shrimp and artichokes are boiled in water seasoned with Zatarain's Concentrated Crab & Shrimp Boil, a mixture of herbs and spices. No subtleness here. You wouldn't think anything so simple could taste so good. There is enough of the shrimp mixture to stuff into four medium artichokes or two large ones. Either way, the dish is a good lunch or light supper.

Shrimp Salad

½ pound medium shrimp, peeled and deveined

1 teaspoon Rustic Rub (page 9)

3 quarts water

1 lemon, halved

3 bay leaves

1 ¼ teaspoons salt plus a pinch

3 tablespoons Zatarain's Concentrated Crab & Shrimp Boil

¼ cup chopped yellow onions

1 tablespoon chopped parsley

¼ cup chopped celery

¼ cup chopped green onions

2 tablespoons Creole or whole-grain mustard

3 tablespoons One-Egg Mayonnaise (page 29)

⅛ teaspoon ground white pepper

2 large or 4 medium Boiled Artichokes (page 246), cooled

3 cups assorted salad greens

1 tablespoon olive oil

Pinch of black pepper

1. Season the shrimp with the rub. Pour the water into a large saucepan and add the juice of the lemon and the lemon shells, bay leaves, 1 teaspoon salt, and the crab and shrimp boil. Bring to a boil over high heat for 5 minutes. Add the shrimp and remove from the heat. Let sit for 2 minutes. With a slotted spoon, remove the shrimp. Let cool slightly.

2. Coarsely chop the shrimp and mix together with the onions, parsley,

celery, and green onions. Mix $\frac{1}{4}$ teaspoon salt, the mustard, mayonnaise, and white pepper. Add to the shrimp mixture and mix well.

3. To prepare the artichokes, lay each artichoke on its side on a cutting board. Evenly trim the base and cut off about 1 inch of the top. Sit the artichoke on its base, spread apart the outer leaves, and carefully remove and discard the center section, including the choke.

4. Divide the shrimp salad into equal portions and spoon into the center of the artichokes.

5. Toss the greens with a pinch of salt, the olive oil, and black pepper. Divide into equal portions and arrange on plates.

6. Place the artichokes on top of the greens and refrigerate for at least 15 minutes or up to 1 hour.

7. Serve chilled.

2 to 4 servings

Crab Salad

 hen the call goes out in late spring–early summer that "the crabs are running," everyone, from commercial fishermen armed with huge crab traps to families carrying small round hand nets, heads to the Gulf and adjoining waterways to try their hand. With any luck, baskets and hampers filled to the brim will be brought home by evening. Then the big decision is what to do with the catch. Should we make a gumbo? Or should we have an outdoor crab boil? When the crabs are fresh and sweet, I opt for a cool salad, piled on thick slices of ripe tomatoes or on crisp salad greens for a first course. Ah, *laisser le bons temps rouler*—let the good times roll.

½ pound lump crabmeat, picked over for shells and cartilage (about 1 cup)	2 tablespoons finely chopped yellow onions
¼ teaspoon salt	4 large pimiento-stuffed green olives, chopped
⅛ teaspoon freshly ground black pepper	2 teaspoons chopped parsley
2 tablespoons finely chopped celery	1 tablespoon chopped green onions
	2 tablespoons One-Egg Mayonnaise (page 29)

1. Combine all of the ingredients in a serving bowl and mix well. Refrigerate for 1 hour.
2. Serve chilled.

2 servings

Fried Crawfish Salad

During the crawfish season, which runs roughly from January to June, these tasty crustaceans find their way into just about everything that is prepared for the dinner table. It might be an étouffée or bisque, or something like this—crunchy-fried crawfish coupled with Creole Mustard Dressing—served as a main course for lunch or supper.

1 egg

¼ cup milk

1 pound peeled crawfish
tails

4 teaspoons Rustic Rub
(page 9)

1 cup yellow cornmeal

½ cup flour

Solid vegetable shortening,
for deep-frying

4 cups assorted salad greens

Pinch of salt

Pinch of freshly ground black
pepper

1 recipe Creole Mustard
Dressing (page 278)

¼ cup freshly grated
parmesan

1. Beat together the egg and milk in a mixing bowl. Add the crawfish tails and 2 teaspoons of the rub. Turn to coat the tails evenly. Let sit for 10 minutes.

2. In another bowl, combine the cornmeal, flour, and the remaining 2 teaspoons of rub.

3. Using your hands, remove the crawfish tails from the egg-milk mixture and add to the cornmeal-flour mixture. Toss to coat evenly. Shake off the excess.

4. Heat the shortening to 360°F. in a deep-fryer or deep pot. Deep-fry the crawfish tails a few at a time until they pop to the surface and are golden, 1½ to 2 minutes. Remove and drain on paper towels.

5. Toss the greens in a bowl with the salt, pepper, and 1 cup of the dressing. Divide the greens among 4 salad plates. Divide the crawfish into 4 equal portions and place on top of the greens.

6. To serve, spoon a tablespoon or so of dressing on top of each serving and sprinkle each with 1 tablespoon of the cheese.

4 servings

Warm Tuna Salad

W ith Louisiana's proximity to the Gulf of Mexico, fresh tuna is popular. Seared tuna on a bed of crisp salad greens with some Green Dressing is an easily prepared main course.

4 tuna steaks, 3/4 inch thick
(about 4 ounces each)

4 teaspoons Rustic Rub
(page 9)

8 cups assorted salad greens

1 cup thinly sliced onions

3 tomatoes, quartered

6 tablespoons Green Dressing
(page 279)

1. Season each tuna steak with 1 teaspoon of the rub.

2. Sear the steaks in a nonstick skillet over high heat, 1 1/2 to 2 minutes on each side, less if you prefer it on the rare side. Remove and let cool for about 5 minutes. Flake the tuna with a fork.

3. Divide the salad greens and onions among 6 salad plates. Divide the tuna evenly into 6 portions and place on the greens. Garnish with tomato wedges. Top each with 1 tablespoon of the dressing.

6 servings

Egg Salad

Louisiana is basically a rural state so it's not unusual to find chicken coops. Yard eggs, with brown shells and golden yellow yolks, are common. Cécile, a happy lady with a weathered face, gathers her eggs each morning and showed me how she makes this salad. Cher, this is no drab concoction. The chopped eggs are perked up with lemon juice, onions, Tabasco sauce, and mixed with homemade mayonnaise. The result can be tucked in between two thick slices of French bread for a quick lunch on a warm day or spread on slices of cool cucumbers or tomatoes for a snack.

6 hard-boiled eggs, coarsely chopped	¼ teaspoon salt
¼ cup chopped celery	2 tablespoons chopped parsley
¼ cup chopped onions	½ recipe One-Egg Mayonnaise (page 29)
1 teaspoon fresh lemon juice	⅛ teaspoon Tabasco sauce
Pinch of freshly ground black pepper	

1. Combine the eggs, celery, and onions in a mixing bowl.
2. In another bowl, combine the lemon juice, pepper, salt, parsley, mayonnaise, and Tabasco.
3. Add to the egg mixture and mix well. Refrigerate for at least 1 hour.
4. Serve chilled.

4 servings

Creole Mustard Dressing

he combination of sparky Creole mustard and honey makes this a great dipping sauce for fried crawfish, shrimp, or oysters as well as a dressing for salad greens.

1 egg

3 tablespoons Creole or whole-grain mustard

1 cup olive oil

1 tablespoon honey

⅛ teaspoon cayenne

½ teaspoon salt

2 tablespoons chopped parsley

1 tablespoon distilled white vinegar

1. In a food processor or blender, process the egg and mustard until blended. With the motor running, slowly pour the oil through the feed tube in a steady stream. The mixture will thicken. Add the honey, cayenne, salt, parsley, and vinegar and pulse to blend.

2. Transfer to an airtight container and refrigerate for at least 30 minutes before using. This is best used within 24 hours.

1 ½ cups

Green Dressing

reen onions, known elsewhere as scallions, play an important flavor role in Louisiana cooking, so important that I have included two dressings using green onions. This one, made in a food processor, results in a thick, creamy dressing similar to mayonnaise. Usually the entire green onion is used, but in this recipe we use only the green part. The dressing is great on Warm Tuna Salad (page 276) or on slices of cold chicken or beef. Marcelle uses it as a dabbing sauce for boiled shrimp.

½ cup chopped green onions, green parts only	1 egg
¼ cup chopped parsley	½ teaspoon salt
1 teaspoon lemon zest	¼ teaspoon freshly ground black pepper
2 tablespoons fresh lemon juice	¾ cup vegetable oil
1 teaspoon chopped garlic	

1. Combine the green onions, parsley, lemon zest, lemon juice, garlic, egg, salt, and pepper in a food processor or blender and process until smooth. With the motor running, pour the oil through the feed tube in a slow steady stream. The mixture will thicken.

2. Transfer to an airtight container and refrigerate for 30 minutes before using. Best used within 24 hours.

1 ½ cups

Green Onion Dressing

arcelle has a buddy, T-Coon, who has a restaurant and catering business in Lafayette in the heart of Acadiana. He uses so many green onions that he grows several acres himself. T-Coon says that if you bite into a piece of boudin and don't chew on a piece of green onion, there isn't enough. That's my kind of cook.Toss this dressing, made with only the green part of the onion, with salad greens to accompany Monday's traditional fare of Red Beans and Rice (page 226). Or spoon it on chilled Boiled Artichokes or slices of avocado. Personally, I like it on Fried Okra Salad (page 269).

1 cup olive oil	3 tablespoons distilled white vinegar
¼ cup chopped parsley	¾ teaspoon salt
½ cup finely chopped green onions, green parts only	½ teaspoon freshly ground black pepper
1 tablespoon chopped garlic	¼ teaspoon dry mustard
1 tablespoon fresh lemon juice	½ teaspoon sugar

1. Combine all of the ingredients in a bowl and whisk for 2 to 3 minutes to blend. Or put the ingredients in a jar fitted with a lid and shake vigorously for 15 seconds. Refrigerate for at least 1 hour before serving.

2. The dressing will keep for several days in the refrigerator.

about 1 ¼ cups

CHAPTER 12

Bread

SKILLET

CORN BREAD,

HOME-STYLE

FRENCH BREAD,

BRIOCHE, AND

MORE

rom corn bread to French bread, the breads of Louisiana are simple and satisfying. Corn bread in Louisiana is prepared in a cast-iron skillet. It is crunchy and dense—ideal for lathering with sweet butter and dark, rich cane syrup or to be used for stuffings and dressings. The French settlers brought with them their French bread, which has undergone many changes. Due to the high humidity in the southern part of the state and the primitive ovens used for baking, French bread here is light, white, and tender inside, with a thin, crisp crust. It is eaten at practically every meal. Brioche, also of French origin, is buttery and light. When a day old, it is used to make Pain Perdu for breakfast topped with something sweet and accompanied by spicy sausage. Born out of necessity and made with on-hand ingredients were Rice Bread, Sweet Potato Bread, and Crackling Bread, which are still favorites in the rural communities in the southern part of the state.

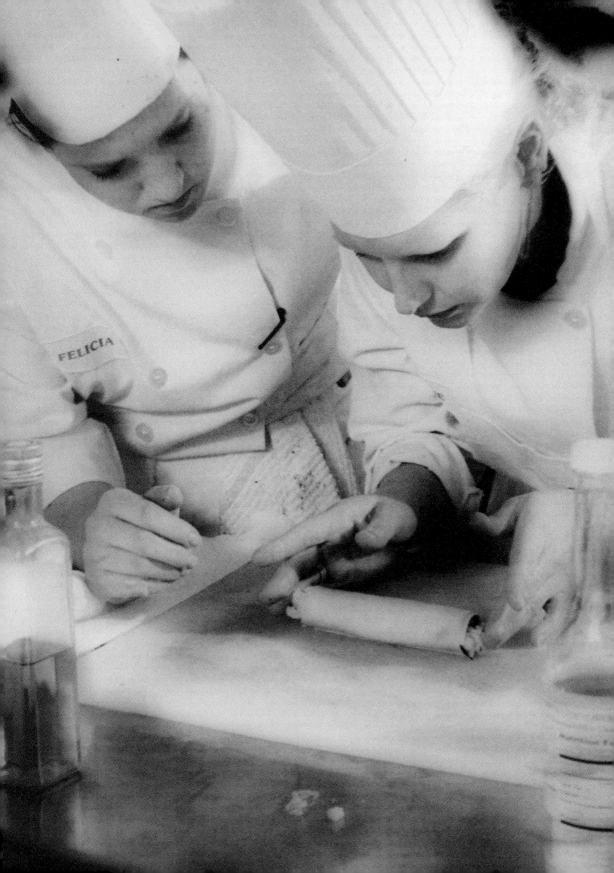

Skillet Corn Bread

n the months of October, November, and December during *la roulaison*, the sugarcane harvest, the air is filled with the sickly sweet smell of cane being burned in the fields and processed at the sugar mills. The farmers and their crews are usually in the fields before dawn and warm themselves around small fires built on the headlands. Many bring with them a chunk of crusty corn bread drenched with butter and a link of spicy boudin for breakfast. It is all washed down with rich, dark, steaming coffee brought along in thermos bottles. I, too, enjoy my corn bread early in the morning, and I daresay it's just as good in my warm, cozy kitchen, drowning in thick cane syrup.

2 cups yellow cornmeal	1½ cups milk
1 cup flour	½ cup whole-kernel corn, canned or frozen
1½ teaspoons salt	
1 tablespoon sugar	½ cup chopped onions
1 teaspoon baking powder	3 tablespoons lard or solid vegetable shortening
¼ teaspoon cayenne (optional)	
1 egg, beaten	

1. Preheat the oven to 400°F.

2. Combine the cornmeal, flour, 1 teaspoon of the salt, sugar, baking powder, and cayenne, if using, in a mixing bowl. Add the egg and milk and mix well, but do not beat. Fold in the corn and onions.

3. Heat the lard or shortening in a 10-inch cast-iron or other ovenproof skillet over medium-high heat until almost smoking. Pour in the batter and cook for 3 to 4 minutes, or until the edges begin to turn golden. Place the skillet in the oven and bake for 45 minutes, or until golden brown. Sprinkle the top with the remaining ½ teaspoon salt. Let cool for about 5 minutes.

4. Slice into wedges to serve. The corn bread can be stored, wrapped in plastic wrap or foil, for up to three days in the refrigerator. To reheat, sprinkle the bread with a little water and place in the oven.

6 to 8 servings

Rice Bread

his old-fashioned bread is similar to corn bread, but much finer in texture. Day-old rice is pureed to give substance to the bread. It makes breakfast a real meal. Dab it with small pieces of Preserved Pears (page 23) and serve it with Pork Breakfast Sausage (page 203).

2 tablespoons butter

3 eggs

2½ cups milk

2 cups yellow cornmeal

2½ teaspoons baking powder

1 teaspoon salt

1 cup cold cooked medium-grain white rice

1. Preheat the oven to 400°F.

2. Butter a 9-inch cake pan with 1 tablespoon of the butter and lightly flour it.

3. Beat the eggs until light and frothy. Gradually add 2 cups of the milk and mix well. Add the cornmeal, baking powder, and salt.

4. Melt the remaining 1 tablespoon butter and combine with the remaining ½ cup milk and the rice in a food processor or blender and process to make a paste.

5. Add the rice mixture to the cornmeal mixture, stirring to mix thoroughly. Pour into the cake pan and bake for about 45 minutes, or until light golden. Let cool for several minutes.

6. Slice into wedges to serve. The bread can be wrapped in plastic wrap and stored in the refrigerator for up to three days. To reheat, sprinkle with a little water before putting it in the oven.

6 to 8 servings

Home-Style French Bread

throughout Louisiana, loaves of French bread wrapped in white cloth or nestled in a small basket are as much a part of the table setting as plates, knives, and forks. The goodness of the bread is often measured by how many crumbs fall to the table, for it is important that the crust be thin and crisp. Just about every good waiter in the city is armed with a crumber to clean the table from time to time during the course of a meal. In the country, servers keep a napkin or cloth tucked in their aprons to dust the table. The bread is more often than not spread with butter and used as a pusher to get every last morsel on the dinner plate onto the fork or to sop up every last drop of gumbo, gravy, or red beans at the bottom of the bowl. No one stands on formality.

2 envelopes (1/4 ounce each) active
   dry yeast

1 1/2 tablespoons salt

1 tablespoon plus 2 teaspoons sugar

2 cups warm water (about 110°F.)

5 cups flour

4 tablespoons yellow cornmeal

1 egg yolk mixed with 1 tablespoon
   water

1. Combine the yeast, salt, sugar, and water in a large mixing bowl. Whisk with a fork until the yeast is dissolved. Mix in the flour, 1/4 cup at a time, until the dough comes away from the sides of the bowl and forms a ball. (This procedure can be done with an electric mixer fitted with a dough hook. Add the flour all at once with the mixer on low speed and beat until combined. Put the mixer on high speed and mix until the dough climbs up the hook, about 3 minutes.)

2. Lightly oil the inside of a large bowl. Place the dough in the bowl. Turn the dough to oil all sides. Cover the bowl with a clean cloth and put in a warm, draft-free place. Let rise until it doubles in size, about 1 1/2 hours.

3. Remove the dough from the bowl and invert it onto a heavily floured surface. Divide the dough into 2 equal portions. Pat each portion into a large rectangle, about 3/4 inch thick. Roll up the dough, beginning with the short side and stopping after each full turn to press the edge of the roll firmly into the flat sheet of dough to seal. Press with your fingertips. Tuck and roll so that any seams disappear into the dough.

4. Sprinkle a baking sheet evenly with 2 tablespoons of the cornmeal. Place the loaves on the baking sheet, about 3 inches apart. Sprinkle with the remaining 2 tablespoons cornmeal. Cover the loaves with a cloth and let rise until doubled in size, about 1 hour.

5. Preheat the oven to 400°F.

6. With a sharp knife, make diagonal slashes, about 1 inch apart, on the top of each loaf. With a pastry brush, brush the egg wash evenly over each loaf. Place a cup of hot water in an ovenproof container on the baking sheet with the loaves. Bake for 45 minutes, or until the bread is golden brown. Remove from the oven and cool on a rack.

7. Slice to serve. The bread is also delicious reheated. Place, uncovered, in a 350°F. oven for about 15 minutes, or until heated through.

2 large loaves

Brioche

Much loved in New Orleans and in Acadiana as well, this brioche is a soft bread or roll made from a yeast dough enriched with butter and eggs. Unlike other types of brioche, this one is not formed. The dough is simply dropped into pans or muffin tins. In the old days, it was common for the ladies of the house or their cooks to rise in the wee hours of the morning to prepare this bread so that it would be popping out of the oven when the household gathered for breakfast. Light and airy, it's heavenly when generously spread with Preserved Pears (page 23) or any kind of jelly or jam. For lunch or a snack, brioche rolls can be stuffed with Great Chicken Salad (page 271). When it's baked in loaf form, I like to use day-old slices to make Pain Perdu (page 295).

Starter

3 envelopes (¼ ounce each) active dry yeast

½ cup warm milk (about 110°F.)

1 cup flour

Combine the yeast and milk in a small bowl and stir to dissolve the yeast. Add the flour and mix to blend well. Let sit at room temperature in a warm, draft-free place for about 2 hours to allow fermentation.

Dough

4 cups flour

6 eggs

½ cup warm water (about 110°F.)

3 tablespoons sugar

2 teaspoons salt

3 sticks (¾ pound) plus
2 tablespoons butter, at room
temperature

1 egg yolk, beaten

1. Put 2 cups of the flour into a large mixing bowl. Add 4 of the eggs, one at a time, beating thoroughly into the flour using a wooden spoon with each addition. The dough will be sticky, thick, and spongy. Add the water, sugar, and salt and mix well, beating vigorously. Add 3 sticks of the butter and work it into the dough with your hands until it is well blended. Add the remaining 2 eggs and mix well into the dough. Add the remaining 2 cups flour and blend into the dough, breaking up any lumps with either the back of the wooden spoon or your fingers.

2. Add the starter. Using your hands, knead and fold the starter into the dough. Continue kneading and folding until all is well mixed, about 5 minutes. The dough will be sticky and moist.

3. Cover with a clean cloth and let rise in a warm, draft-free place until it doubles in size, about 2 hours.

4. To make loaves, lightly butter two 9 × 5 × 3-inch loaf pans with the remaining 2 tablespoons butter. To make the rolls, butter 12 standard-size muffin cups.

5. Punch the dough lightly with your fingers. For loaves, divide the dough into 2 equal portions and place in the pans. For rolls, divide the dough into 12 equal portions and gently drop into the muffin cups. Brush the tops with the egg yolk. Cover and let rise in a warm, draft-free place until it doubles in size, about 1 hour.

6. Preheat the oven to 400°F.

7. Bake loaves for 25 to 30 minutes and bake rolls for about 20 minutes, or until deep golden brown. Place the pans on a wire rack to cool for several minutes. Turn the loaves and rolls out of the pans and let cool completely on the wire rack.

8. Slice and serve.

2 loaves or 12 brioche rolls

Spinach Bread

ysters Rockefeller, the signature dish at the famous Antoine's in New Orleans, was created in 1899 by Jules Alciatore, who combined fresh local oysters with a puree of mixed green leafy vegetables, none of which was spinach, despite what most people think. He named the dish after one of the wealthiest men in the United States, John D. Rockefeller, because the dish was so rich in taste. Since then, many dishes have been created in New Orleans that combine salty oysters with mellow spinach, which happens to be in season at the same time. This wonderful spinach-flecked bread can be served with just about any oyster dish. Here's my recommendation: Spread two slices with Creole Tartar Sauce (page 28) and tuck in a few Skillet Oysters (page 108). C'est bon, oui.

1 cup water	1 tablespoon sugar
2 cups (tightly packed) cleaned and stemmed fresh spinach	1 teaspoon salt
4 tablespoons plus 1 teaspoon butter	1/8 teaspoon freshly ground black pepper
2 envelopes (1/4 ounce each) active dry yeast	3 3/4 cups flour
1 egg	1 teaspoon kosher salt
	1 tablespoon freshly grated parmesan

1. Place the water and spinach in a saucepan over medium heat. Wilt the spinach, pressing down with the back of a spoon, for about 45 seconds. Drain the spinach well, reserving the liquid. Squeeze the spinach to get as much liquid out as possible. (You should have about 1 cup spinach water and ½ cup spinach.)

2. Pour the liquid into a mixing bowl and add 4 tablespoons of the butter. The butter will melt and cool down the liquid to about 110°F. Add the yeast and stir to dissolve. Beat the egg into the mixture. Add the sugar, salt, and black pepper. Finely chop the spinach and add to the yeast mixture.

3. Add the flour and mix well with a wooden spoon until the dough comes away from the sides of the bowl. Using your hands, form the dough into a ball. Lightly oil a bowl. Place the dough in the bowl. Turn the dough to oil all sides. Cover with a clean cloth and set aside to rise in a warm, draft-free place until it doubles in size, about 1 hour.

4. Butter an 8½ × 4½ × 2½-inch loaf pan with the remaining butter.

5. Invert the dough onto a floured surface and punch it down with your fist. Fold each side in and tuck the ends into the center. Repeat. Put the dough, seam side down, into the pan. With the tip of a sharp knife, make 3 slashes lengthwise down the center of the dough.

6. Sprinkle the dough with the kosher salt and cheese. Cover and let rise in a warm, draft-free place until it doubles in size, about 1 hour.

7. Preheat the oven to 375°F.

8. Bake for about 40 minutes, or until golden. Remove the pan from the oven and place on a wire rack to cool before removing from the pan.

9. Slice to serve warm or at room temperature.

1 loaf

Crackling Bread

Grattons or cracklings are little chunks of fried pork skin. People in these parts eat cracklings like other Americans eat popcorn. Grattons can be bought just about every day at country grocery stores or meat markets throughout south Louisiana, and at a boucherie there's always a batch cooking in a large cast-iron caldron. The commercial kind, found in bags like potato chips, are available at many supermarkets. They're lighter and airier than the local kind, but they'll work just fine in the recipe. Serve this bread with Country Pâté (page 208) or crumble it up and toss it in a green salad.

2 envelopes (¼ ounce each) active dry yeast

1 cup warm water (about 110°F.)

1 teaspoon salt

1 teaspoon sugar

¼ teaspoon freshly ground black pepper

½ stick (4 tablespoons) butter, melted

½ cup cracklings or commercial fried pork skins, coarsely crushed

3 cups flour

1. Combine the yeast and water in a mixing bowl and whisk to dissolve. Add the salt, sugar, black pepper, butter, and cracklings. Work the flour, 1 cup at a time, into the yeast mixture with a rubber spatula or wooden spoon, turning (or mixing) the mixture until the flour is incorporated (or well blended) and the dough leaves the sides of the bowl. Form the dough into a ball.
2. Place the dough in a lightly oiled bowl, turning it to oil all sides. Cover with a clean cloth and let rise in a warm, draft-free place until it doubles in size, about 2 hours.
3. Preheat the oven to 375°F.
4. Place the loaf (or ball of dough) in the center of a lightly oiled baking sheet. Bake for about 1 hour, or until golden brown. Remove the pan from the oven and place on a wire rack to cool.
5. Serve slightly warm or at room temperature.

1 loaf

Sweet Potato Bread

during the time when the Acadians were carving a home for themselves out of the prairies, swamps, and marshlands of south Louisiana, their cuisine was influenced by the Africans who arrived from the West Indies after the Haitian revolution in 1791. It is likely that the use of sweet potatoes was introduced around this time. The sweet potato is a versatile vegetable. Baked in bread, it develops an excellent flavor. Golden and fresh from the oven, this bread is delicious with Pork Breakfast Sausage (page 203) and a strong cup of coffee.

2 envelopes (¼ ounce each) active dry yeast	3 tablespoons butter, melted
½ cup warm water (about 110°F.)	2 eggs, beaten
¼ cup sugar	1 small sweet potato, baked (see page 255), peeled, and mashed or ½ cup canned sweet potato puree
1 tablespoon salt	
¼ teaspoon freshly ground black pepper	3¼ cups plus 1 tablespoon flour

1. Dissolve the yeast in the water in a mixing bowl. Add the sugar, salt, pepper, and butter. Mix well and let sit for 15 minutes. Add the eggs and sweet potato. Add the flour, ½ cup at a time, and work with your hands, until the flour is incorporated and the mixture comes away from the sides of the bowl. Form the dough into a ball. Sprinkle the dough with the remaining 1 tablespoon flour.

2. Place the dough in a lightly oiled bowl, turning it to oil all sides. Cover the bowl with a clean cloth and let rise until it doubles in size, about 1½ hours.

continued

3. Punch the dough down and roll it into an oval loaf about 8 by 3 inches. Place the loaf in the center of a lightly oiled baking sheet. Cover and let rise until it doubles in size, about 45 minutes.

4. Preheat the oven to 350°F.

5. Bake for about 40 minutes, or until golden. Remove the baking sheet from the oven. Transfer the loaf to a wire rack to cool until just slightly warm.

6. Slice and serve.

1 loaf

Black Pepper Drop Biscuits

 particularly like these drop biscuits, seasoned with black pepper, with stews or dishes with a thick gravy. They're great for sopping up every last drop. These have a little kick to them. If you prefer regular biscuits, don't add the black pepper. The recipe can be doubled if you want to make a larger batch.

1 cup flour	2 tablespoons plus 1 teaspoon solid vegetable shortening
1 teaspoon baking powder	¼ cup plus 1 tablespoon milk
⅛ teaspoon baking soda	2 teaspoons coarsely ground black pepper
¼ teaspoon salt	

1. Preheat the oven to 400°F.

2. Lightly oil a pie tin.

3. Combine all of the ingredients in a mixing bowl and mix well. The dough will be slightly sticky.

4. Divide the dough into 4 equal portions and drop into the pie tin. Bake for 25 to 30 minutes, or until lightly browned.

5. Serve right from the oven.

4 biscuits

Pain Perdu

ain perdu, literally lost bread in French, is French toast. Innovative and thrifty cooks in Louisiana do not like to see good food go to waste. I like to make Pain Perdu with Brioche when it's a day old, but any kind of day-old bread can be used. Children and adults both like it with cane syrup, Fig Preserves (page 22), or any kind of jelly and powdered sugar.

1 large orange

3 eggs

3/4 cup milk

1/2 teaspoon ground cinnamon

1/8 teaspoon grated nutmeg

2 tablespoons sugar

1/2 tablespoon vanilla extract

1 stick (1/4 pound) butter

8 slices Brioche (page 288) or any kind of sliced bread

Powdered sugar, for dusting

1. Grate the orange rind until you have about 1 tablespoon zest. Cut the orange in half and squeeze it. Mix 1/4 cup of the juice with the zest in a mixing bowl. Use the rest for another purpose.
2. Add the eggs, milk, cinnamon, nutmeg, sugar, and vanilla. Whisk together to dissolve the sugar.
3. Heat 2 tablespoons of the butter in a nonstick skillet over medium-high heat. Dip 2 slices of the bread into the egg-milk mixture, coating evenly. Fry in the butter until golden brown, 2 to 3 minutes on each side. Repeat until all the butter and bread is used.
4. Sprinkle with powdered sugar and serve hot.

4 servings

Ruth's Banana-Nut Bread

ew Orleans is a busy banana port. Not surprisingly, bananas are used in many desserts like this banana bread that my mother-in-law makes. Unlike others, this one is soft and rich.

½ cup solid vegetable shortening	1 teaspoon baking soda
1 cup sugar	½ teaspoon salt
2 eggs	1¼ cups flour
¾ cup mashed ripe bananas	½ cup chopped pecans or walnuts

1. Preheat the oven to 350°F.

2. Grease and flour a 9 × 5 × 3-inch loaf pan.

3. In a mixing bowl, cream the shortening and the sugar. Add the eggs, one at a time, mixing together between each addition. Add the bananas and mix well. Add the baking soda, salt, flour, and nuts and mix thoroughly. The dough will be sticky.

4. Pour into the loaf pan. Bake for about 1 hour, or until it shrinks slightly away from the sides of the pan, is firm to the touch, and is a rich brown. Remove pan from the oven and cool completely on a wire rack.

5. Slice to serve.

1 loaf

CHAPTER 13

Cakes and Pies

PEACH UPSIDE-

DOWN CAKE,

PRALINE POUND

CAKE, PECAN

PIE, AND MORE

The people of Louisiana love cakes and pies. At weddings and other festive occasions, there is a designated "sweet" table, which is filled with family favorites. Aunt Marie brings her gâteau de sirop, a smooth-textured cake made with cane syrup. Aunt Mignon and cousin Thérèse bring pies. In the winter, it's pecan; in the warmer months, it's strawberry or blueberry. Fruit cobblers are always part of the spread. Customarily, guests will peruse the sweet table, seeking old favorites or making inquiries about new delights. Irritable children are often consoled with a small slice of pound cake. There's always plenty left over for guests to take home, many times with a handwritten recipe tucked into the package.

Gâteau de Sirop

his simple classic country cake is found on tables throughout Louisiana. What makes it special is the slight molasses flavor of the cane syrup. Like gumbo and jambalaya, there are endless versions of this cake, but this one is my favorite. Wash it down with a glass of cold milk or a cup of hot coffee. With or without the sugar-cinnamon topping, it's a winner.

Cake Batter

⅓ cup cake batter plus 1 tablespoon solid vegetable shortening

⅓ cup sugar

⅓ cup Steen's 100% Pure Cane Syrup

⅓ cup boiling water

1 egg, beaten

½ teaspoon baking powder

¾ teaspoon ground cinnamon

1 teaspoon salt

1½ cups flour

¾ teaspoon grated nutmeg

½ teaspoon baking soda

1. Preheat the oven to 350°F.
2. Grease a 9-inch cake pan with 1 tablespoon of the shortening.
3. Cream together the remaining shortening, the sugar, and syrup in a mixing bowl. Add the water and mix well. Add the egg and mix again.
4. Mix together the baking powder, cinnamon, salt, flour, nutmeg, and baking soda and beat until smooth.
5. Pour into the pan and bake for 35 minutes, or until the cake sets and slightly shrinks from the side of the pan. Remove and cool slightly.

Sugar-Cinnamon Topping

⅓ cup (packed) light brown sugar

2 teaspoons ground cinnamon

3 tablespoons flour

3 tablespoons solid vegetable shortening

⅓ cup pecan pieces

6. Combine all the topping ingredients in a mixing bowl and mix well.

7. After the cake has cooled slightly, spread the topping evenly over the cake and return the cake to the oven. Bake for 10 minutes, or until the topping melts.

8. Cut into wedges to serve. It can be served warm or at room temperature.

One 9-inch cake, 6 to 8 servings

Peach Upside-down Cake

 n the late spring and early summer, people make a special trip to Ruston, in the northern part of the state near the Arkansas border, to pick or buy bushels of luscious, sweet peaches for preserves, pies, and other delights such as this moist cake. It is ideal for picnics and backyard get-togethers.

Topping

1½ pounds peaches, peeled, pitted, and sliced (about 2½ cups)

½ teaspoon ground cinnamon

¼ teaspoon grated nutmeg

1 tablespoon sugar

1. Toss the peaches, cinnamon, nutmeg, and sugar in a mixing bowl to coat evenly. Set aside.
2. Preheat the oven to 350°F.

Cake Batter

1 stick (¼ pound) butter, softened

1½ cups sugar

1 teaspoon baking powder

1 teaspoon baking soda

1 teaspoon salt

2 eggs

1 teaspoon vanilla extract

1 teaspoon ground cinnamon

½ teaspoon grated nutmeg

1 cup milk

2¼ cups flour

3. Combine the butter, sugar, baking powder, baking soda, salt, and eggs in a mixing bowl. Blend the mixture, working it with the back of a wooden spoon to break up any lumps, until it is smooth. Add the vanilla, cinnamon, nutmeg, and milk. Mix well. Add the flour and beat until smooth.

Syrup

½ stick (4 tablespoons)
   butter

½ cup sugar

4. In a 10½-inch ovenproof skillet (or an 8 × 11½ × 2-inch baking pan), combine the butter and the sugar over medium-high heat. Stir with a wooden spoon until the mixture caramelizes and becomes syrupy.

5. Spread the peaches evenly in the bottom of the skillet or pan. Remove from the heat. Pour the cake batter into the skillet or pan and spread evenly over the peaches.

6. Bake for about 40 minutes, or until the cake is golden and pulls away slightly from the sides of the skillet or pan. Remove from the oven and cool for about 30 minutes, then invert over a large platter.

7. Slice to serve.

One 8- to 9-inch cake, 12 servings

Praline Pound Cake

People in Louisiana don't wait for an invitation, but are always dropping in and visiting each other. Why, some could spend the better part of a day visiting and do so every chance they get. Late in the afternoon, however, is when just about everyone spends time with neighbors, friends, or family members. In the city, people sit on the front stoop. In the country, they make themselves comfortable on swings or rockers on the porch or in the yard. Something sweet, like a pound cake, is usually offered, and I find this one comes in handy at such times. I usually make two at a time since they keep well. One is baked plain for topping with whatever berries—strawberries, blackberries, blueberries—are in season. The other one is dressed up with crumbled pralines and rum for dessert after a late-evening dinner.

continued

4 sticks (1 pound butter)
minus 1 heaping
tablespoon, cut into chips
and softened

1 pound sugar (about
2½ cups)

10 eggs, separated

2 teaspoons vanilla extract

1 pound flour (about
3½ cups)

1 teaspoon baking powder

Pinch of salt

1 teaspoon grated lemon zest

1 cup crumbled Creamy
Pralines (page 328)

2 tablespoons dark rum

1. Preheat the oven to 350°F.

2. Butter two 9 × 5 × 3-inch loaf pans, using the heaping tablespoon of the butter.

3. Cream the remaining butter and the sugar in the bowl of an electric mixer on low speed until light and fluffy. Scrape down the sides with a rubber spatula.

4. In a separate mixing bowl, beat together the egg yolks with the vanilla until light and frothy. With the electric mixer on medium-low, gradually add the egg yolk mixture to the butter and sugar mixture and mix for about 4 minutes.

5. In another bowl, combine the flour, baking powder, and salt. With the electric mixer on medium speed, alternately add the flour mixture, a third at a time, and the egg whites, a third at a time, to the butter and egg mixture, beating for 2 minutes between each addition. Scrape down the sides of the bowl as you mix. Add the lemon zest during the last 2 minutes of mixing.

6. Divide the batter equally between the pans. To one of the cakes, add the crumbled pralines and the rum with the batter and gently stir to mix evenly; leave the other plain. Bake the plain cake for about 1 hour, the praline cake for about 1 hour and 10 minutes. Both should be golden when done and firm to the touch.

7. Serve either or both. The cakes can be stored by wrapping them in wax paper, then in plastic wrap, then in foil. They do not need to be refrigerated.

2 9-inch loaf cakes, 8 to 10 servings

Praline Cream Pie

he French Quarter in New Orleans is filled with shops that sell thousands of pralines each day. The aroma of the sugar melting in the huge kettles is intoxicating, especially on a blustery, cold afternoon when the winds sweep off the levee holding back the Mississippi River. I especially like to munch a few while I walk through the produce market gathering ingredients for a Sunday afternoon meal. The idea for this praline cream pie came to me on just such a day when I got a whiff of the pralines as I was pondering what to have for dessert. Crushed pralines are used to make the crust and are folded into the pastry cream. The filling is made with milk, eggs, sugar, vanilla, and dark cane syrup. You just can't go wrong with that combination!

Crust

1½ cups graham cracker crumbs

½ cup crumbled Creamy Pralines (page 328)

1 stick (¼ pound) butter, melted

1. Preheat the oven to 400°F.

2. Combine the graham cracker crumbs with the crumbled pralines in a 9-inch pie dish, using your hands to work them together. Drizzle in the butter and using your fingers, work the crumb mixture with the butter until it binds together. Spread and press the mixture evenly on the bottom and sides of the dish to make the crust.

3. Bake for 8 to 10 minutes, or until brown. Remove from the oven and cool completely on a rack.

continued

Filling

2½ cups milk

3/4 cup sugar

1 teaspoon vanilla

1 tablespoon Steen's 100% Pure
Cane Syrup

5 egg yolks

½ cup cornstarch

½ cup crumbled Creamy Pralines
(page 328)

4. Combine the milk, sugar, vanilla, and syrup in a nonreactive saucepan over medium heat. Stir slowly to dissolve the sugar and heat just long enough to scald the milk. Remove from the heat.

5. Combine the egg yolks and cornstarch in a mixing bowl and mix well. Add the milk mixture, ¼ cup at a time, to the egg mixture, blending between additions, until all is combined. Pour the mixture into a saucepan and place it over medium heat. Cook, stirring constantly, for 1 to 2 minutes, removing the pan from the heat from time to time to keep the mixture from getting too hot. Stir until smooth and thick. Remove from the heat and put through a fine sieve to remove any lumps.

6. Pour the mixture into a small bowl and place the bowl in a larger bowl filled with ice and water to cool down the mixture. Stir occasionally while it's sitting in the ice and water bath.

7. When it has cooled, fold in the crumbled pralines. Carefully spread the mixture evenly in the pie crust. Refrigerate for at least 2 hours, or until it sets.

Topping

1 cup heavy cream

3 tablespoons sugar

1 tablespoon Steen's 100%
Pure Cane Syrup

¼ cup crumbled Creamy
Pralines (page 328)

8. With an electric mixer, whip the cream and sugar until soft peaks form.

9. To serve, spread the cream evenly over the top of the pie. Drizzle with the syrup and sprinkle with the crumbled pralines.

One 9-inch pie

Pecan Pie

n the center of the state, around Natchitoches, there are thousands of acres of prime pecan orchards. The nuts are harvested from October to December, and everyone buys pounds of what the locals call the crown prince of nuts to keep on hand. The pecan pieces or halves are used to make candy, pralines, and pecan pie. In my version, cane syrup adds a hint of molasses flavor. Top the pie with vanilla ice cream, if you like, while the pie is still warm.

1/2 recipe Basic Sweet Pie Crust (page 313)

1 1/2 cups pecan pieces

4 eggs, beaten

1/2 cup granulated sugar

1/2 cup (packed) light brown sugar

1/4 cup Steen's 100% Pure Cane Syrup

3/4 cup light corn syrup

1/2 teaspoon vanilla extract

1/8 teaspoon salt

1/2 stick (4 tablespoons) butter, melted

1 tablespoon flour

1. Preheat the oven to 375°F.

2. Place the pie shell in the bottom of a 9-inch pie pan. Spread the pecan pieces evenly on the bottom.

3. Combine the eggs, sugar, brown sugar, cane syrup, corn syrup, vanilla, salt, butter, and flour in a mixing bowl. Mix well. Pour the mixture over the pecans.

4. Bake for about 1 hour, or until the filling sets and the pastry is nicely browned.

5. Cool for 10 minutes before slicing to serve. It can also be served at room temperature.

One 9-inch pie

Strawberry Pie

n Pontchatoula, north of New Orleans, across Lake Pontchartrain, the sweetest strawberries in the world are grown. In the spring, families pick their own for ice cream, cakes, jams, and, my favorite, strawberry pie. Chilled and topped with whipped cream, it makes a wonderful dessert to serve on a warm evening.

---

1 cup graham cracker crumbs

½ stick (4 tablespoons) butter, melted

5 cups strawberries, rinsed, hulled, and halved

1 cup plus 3 tablespoons sugar

½ teaspoon vanilla extract

3 tablespoons cornstarch

3 tablespoons brandy

1 cup heavy cream

---

1. Preheat the oven to 375°F.

2. Mix the crumbs and butter together in the bottom of a 9-inch pie pan. Press the mixture against the bottom and sides of the pan to form a crust. Bake until golden and crisp, 7 to 8 minutes. Remove from the oven and cool completely on a rack.

3. Combine the berries, 1 cup of the sugar, and the vanilla in a saucepan over medium-high heat. Stir until the sugar dissolves. Combine the cornstarch with the brandy in a cup and add to the berry mixture. Cook, stirring occasionally, until the mixture thickens, about 5 minutes. Remove from the heat and let cool. Pour into the pie crust. Cover and refrigerate for at least 6 hours, or until the filling sets.

4. When ready to serve, whip the cream with the remaining 3 tablespoons sugar, using an electric mixer, until soft peaks form. Spread evenly over the top of the pie to serve.

One 9-inch pie

Blueberry Pie

lueberries grow wild along rural roads and in vacant lots all over the state during late spring and early summer. Youngsters, carrying pails and buckets, swarm through the patches to collect the berries. But in recent years, blueberry farms have been popping up here and there, and we're finding these plump berries to be a good alternative for pies and cobblers.

4 cups fresh blueberries, rinsed in cool water

1/2 teaspoon ground cinnamon

1/4 teaspoon grated nutmeg

1/2 cup sugar

1 teaspoon vanilla extract

1 tablespoon cornstarch

1 tablespoon water

1 recipe Basic Sweet Pie Crust (page 313)

1 egg, beaten

Vanilla ice cream, for serving

1. Preheat the oven to 375°F.

2. Combine the blueberries, cinnamon, nutmeg, sugar, and vanilla in a saucepan over medium heat. Cook, stirring for 7 to 8 minutes, or until the juice begins to form a syrup. Dissolve the cornstarch in the water and add to the blueberry mixture. Stir until it thickens slightly, 2 to 3 minutes. Remove from the heat and let cool.

3. Line a 9-inch pie pan with the pie crust. Pour the blueberry mixture into the crust. Carefully place the top crust over the filling and crimp the edges together. Brush the crust and edges with the beaten egg. With a pointed knife, make 3 small slashes in the center of the crust.

4. Place the pie in the center of a baking sheet and bake for about 45 minutes, or until the crust is golden. Let cool for 10 to 12 minutes.

5. To serve, cut into wedges and top each with a scoop of ice cream.

One 9-inch pie

Ruston Peach Crumb Pie

weet, ripe peaches flavored with brown sugar, cinnamon, and nutmeg, then topped with crunchy pecans, make for a delectable summertime pie.

Crust

1¼ cups flour

1 teaspoon sugar

½ teaspoon salt

1 stick (¼ pound) butter,
    cut into small pieces

1 tablespoon ice water

1. Combine the flour, sugar, and salt in a mixing bowl. Add the butter and work it into the dry ingredients using your hands until the mixture resembles coarse crumbs. Mix in the water. Form into a flattened ball, wrap in plastic wrap, and refrigerate for about 1 hour.

2. Pat out the dough on a lightly floured surface and dust it lightly with flour. Roll the dough into a circle, 12 inches in diameter and ⅛ inch thick. Place the crust in a 9-inch pie pan. Crimp the edges. Refrigerate until ready to use.

Filling

1½ cups water

¼ cup (packed) light brown sugar

2 tablespoons cornstarch

½ teaspoon salt

1 teaspoon ground cinnamon

½ teaspoon grated nutmeg

Pinch of black pepper

2 pounds peaches, peeled, pitted, and
    cut into wedges (about 3 cups)

3. Combine the water, brown sugar, cornstarch, salt, cinnamon, nutmeg, and pepper in a saucepan over high heat. Bring to a boil and whisk until smooth. Remove from the heat.

4. Put the peaches in a bowl and pour the syrup over them. Toss to coat evenly. Let cool for about 10 minutes.

Topping

½ cup (packed) light brown sugar

½ cup flour

1 cup pecan pieces

½ stick (4 tablespoons) butter, cut into small pieces

¼ teaspoon ground cinnamon

¼ teaspoon grated nutmeg

5. Preheat the oven to 350°F.

6. Combine the sugar, flour, pecans, butter, cinnamon, and nutmeg in a mixing bowl. Using your fingers, work the mixture together. Form into a ball.

7. Remove the pie crust from the refrigerator. Pour in the peach mixture and spread evenly. Crumble the topping evenly over the top of the peaches.

8. Bake for 1 hour, or until the crust and top are nicely browned.

9. Cool for 10 to 15 minutes before slicing to serve.

One 9-inch pie

Blueberry-Peach Cobbler

Cobblers are popular in the South, especially during spring and summer when berries are abundant and the blueberry and peach crops peak at the same time. The royal blue of the berries and the golden yellow of the peaches make this a real beauty of a dish.

2 cups fresh blueberries	1 teaspoon salt
¾ cup granulated sugar	1 egg
2 tablespoons butter	1 tablespoon baking powder
2 pounds peaches, peeled, pitted, and coarsely chopped (about 3½ cups)	1 cup flour
	1 tablespoon vanilla extract
¼ cup (packed) light brown sugar	½ cup milk
¼ teaspoon grated nutmeg	Vanilla ice cream, for serving
1 teaspoon ground cinnamon	

1. Preheat the oven to 375°F.

2. Combine the blueberries, ½ cup of the sugar, and the butter in a small saucepan over high heat. Cook, stirring until a syrup forms, for 6 to 7 minutes. Remove from the heat.

3. Toss the peaches with the brown sugar, nutmeg, cinnamon, and salt in a mixing bowl.

4. Spread the peach mixture in a 3-quart rectangular casserole dish. Spoon the blueberry mixture evenly over the peaches.

5. Mix the remaining ¼ cup sugar and the egg in a bowl and beat. Add the baking powder, flour, vanilla, and milk. Beat well with a wire whisk until the mixture is smooth and resembles a cake batter. Pour this mixture evenly over the blueberries.

6. Bake for 30 to 35 minutes, or until golden brown.

7. Cool for 10 minutes before serving. Serve warm with ice cream.

8 servings

Basic Sweet Pie Crust

his recipe makes enough for a nine-inch double crust. If you need only a single crust, cut the ball of dough in two and freeze half. Defrost the frozen dough thoroughly before rolling it out. Or halve this recipe if you want to make a single crust. Be careful not to overhandle the dough.

2 cups flour

½ teaspoon salt

1½ teaspoons sugar

¾ cup solid vegetable shortening

3 to 4 tablespoons ice water

1. Combine the flour, salt, and sugar in a mixing bowl. Add the shortening and work it in with your hands until the mixture resembles coarse crumbs. Add the water, 1 tablespoon at a time, and work it in with your hands. Add only as much as you need for a smooth ball of dough. Wrap the dough in plastic wrap and refrigerate for at least 30 minutes.

2. Remove the dough from the refrigerator and place it on a lightly floured surface. For 2 crusts, cut the dough in two and put the second half back in the refrigerator. For each crust, roll out the dough on the floured surface into a circle about 12 inches in diameter and ⅛ inch thick. Gently fold the circle of dough in half and then in half again so that you can lift it without tearing it, and unfold into a 9-inch pie pan.

3. Fill and proceed as directed in the recipe.

Two 9-inch pie crusts

Basic Savory Pie Crust

ie is not worth eating unless the crust is flaky and delicately crisp. This one, made with lard, gives our savory pies the taste that Southerners expect. Remember to use as little flour as possible when rolling out, as the dough will grow tough the more you work it. This recipe makes enough for a nine-inch double crust. If you need only one crust, cut the ball of dough in two and freeze half.

3¼ cups flour

1 teaspoon salt

1⅓ cups cold lard or solid vegetable shortening

4 to 5 tablespoons ice water

1. Combine the flour and salt in a bowl. Add the lard and work it in with your hands until the mixture resembles coarse crumbs. Add the water, 1 tablespoon at a time, working it in with your hands. Add only as much as you need to make a smooth ball of dough. Wrap it in plastic wrap and refrigerate for at least 30 minutes.

2. Remove the dough from the refrigerator and place it on a lightly floured surface. For 2 crusts, cut the dough in two and put the second half back in the refrigerator. For each crust, roll the dough out on the floured surface into a circle about 12 inches in diameter and ⅛ inch thick. Gently fold the circle of dough in half and then in half again so that you can lift it without tearing it, and unfold into a 9-inch pie pan.

3. Fill and proceed as directed in the recipe.

Two 9-inch pie crusts

Puddings, Custards, and Ice Cream

he desserts I've encountered in my sweeps through the state are simple but uncommonly good. Pudding, as it is known here, is usually sweet, like Bread Pudding and Rice Pudding, but there are also savory puddings like Andouille Pudding (page 188). Years ago, the word "pudding" applied to all boiled dishes; it has the same origin as the French *boudin*, or blood sausage. This blood sausage was made often at a boucherie, but because of strict health regulations, it is rarely found today. The custards are creamy, but not too sweet. When I asked Aunt Git in Lafayette, who shared with me her recipe for Caramel Cup Custard, why there weren't more elaborate desserts, she smiled and replied, "*Mon cher*, our gumbos, étouffées, and stews are so good, so filling and robust, we only need a *goûteé*, a small taste of

dessert to complete our meal and satisfy our palates. We don't want to ruin a good meal!" And you know, I think she's right. But I'm such a lover of sweets, I sometimes overindulge. You'll have to try these sweet *entremets* and decide for yourself which you like the best.

Marcelle's Bread Pudding

unt Te, Marcelle's great-aunt, was known far and wide for her light-as-a-cloud bread pudding. Aunt Te owned a small café across the street from the school in Loreauville in Iberia Parish. During the lunch hour, it was standing room only: Not only the locals and the schoolchildren but high-powered executives from the oil industry ate elbow to elbow. During the oil boom in the 1960s and 1970s, a Texas oilman would send his chauffeur early in the morning to pick up bread pudding and gallons of her famous crawfish étouffée. Then the driver would rush back to the Lone Star State so that his boss could have a dinner party that evening for his wealthy friends. Rhena, Marcelle's mama, says that bread pudding should be just that—pudding. It shouldn't be so firm that you have to cut it with a knife like some bread puddings I've known. Make the bourbon sauce shortly before serving.

6 eggs, separated

6 cups milk

2 teaspoons vanilla extract

3/4 cup plus 6 tablespoons sugar

1/2 teaspoon ground cinnamon

1/4 teaspoon grated nutmeg

1/2 pound (about 8 thick slices) bread, cut into 1-inch cubes (about 8 cups loosely packed)

1/2 stick (4 tablespoons) butter, cut into small pieces

1. Combine the egg yolks, milk, vanilla, 3/4 cup of the sugar, cinnamon, and nutmeg and whisk until the sugar dissolves. Place the bread pieces in a large 10-cup rectangular or oval casserole dish. Pour the yolk and milk mixture over the bread and let it sit for about 30 minutes, mashing the bread occasionally with a fork.

2. Preheat the oven to 300°F.

3. Dot the top of the bread and milk mixture with the butter. Place the casserole in a larger baking dish or roasting pan and fill the dish with enough water to come halfway up the sides of the casserole.

4. Bake for about 1 1/2 hours, or until the pudding sets and a knife inserted into the pudding comes out clean. Remove the pudding from the oven and remove from the water bath.

5. Beat the egg whites with the remaining 6 tablespoons sugar until they form stiff peaks for a meringue.

6. Increase the oven temperature to 425°F.

7. Spread the meringue evenly over the top of the pudding, going all the way to the edges of the casserole. Return the casserole to the oven. Bake for about 15 minutes, or until the meringue is lightly browned.

8. Remove from the oven and cool on the counter for about 15 minutes.

About 10 servings

Bourbon Sauce

1/2 stick (4 tablespoons) butter

1/2 cup sugar

1/4 cup bourbon

4 egg yolks, beaten

9. Melt the butter in a double boiler over simmering water. Add the sugar and whisk to dissolve. Add the bourbon and whisk for 1 minute.

10. Remove from the heat and drizzle in the egg yolks, whisking constantly.

11. Return the double boiler to the heat and continue whisking until the sauce is pale and slightly thickened, 3 to 4 minutes.

12. Spoon the sauce over the pudding and serve immediately.

Rice Pudding

hese people never tire of rice. I would not have believed that a rice pudding could be so tasty. I'm told that small children in south Louisiana are practically raised on it, but I have also observed a goodly number of adults enjoying this creamy dessert. Served chilled, it's refreshing and nourishing. Marcelle's Tante May had this often for the children as an after-school treat.

1 quart milk

½ cup plus 2 tablespoons uncooked
   long-grain white rice

Pinch of salt

½ cup plus 1 tablespoon sugar

2 egg yolks

1 teaspoon vanilla extract

¼ teaspoon ground cinnamon

⅛ teaspoon grated nutmeg

¼ cup raisins

½ cup heavy cream

1 tablespoon dark rum (optional)

1. Combine the milk, rice, and salt in a saucepan over medium heat. Simmer for about 30 minutes, or until the rice is tender.

2. Combine ½ cup of the sugar, the egg yolks, vanilla, cinnamon, and nutmeg in a bowl.

3. When the rice is done, stir the raisins and the sugar and egg mixture into the rice pot. Cook over medium heat stirring constantly, for about 4 minutes, or until the mixture thickens. Remove from the heat and let cool.

4. Mix together the cream, the remaining 1 tablespoon sugar, and the rum, if using, in a large mixing bowl. Using a handheld electric mixer, beat until soft peaks form. Fold in the cooled rice mixture.

5. Spoon the mixture into six 4-ounce custard cups and refrigerate for at least 1 hour.

6. Serve chilled.

6 servings

Caramel Cup Custard

For years, every respectable restaurant or café in and around New Orleans had this smooth custard on the menu. And hostesses included it at one or even several dinner parties held during the social season. Similar to flan, it's not too heavy or too rich, but a satisfying way to end any meal. In some of the small towns of south Louisiana, the custard was baked in a casserole, rather than in individual ramekins. It was made at the beginning of the week, and family members helped themselves to it after lunch or supper until there was no more.

1¼ cups sugar

1 tablespoon fresh lemon juice

3 eggs

1 cup heavy cream

¾ teaspoon vanilla extract

1. Preheat the oven to 350°F.

2. Combine 1 cup of the sugar and the lemon juice in a heavy nonreactive saucepan over medium heat. Cook, stirring constantly, for about 10 minutes, or until the sugar dissolves and turns smooth and brown. Remove from the heat. Spoon 1 tablespoon of the caramel into each of four 6-ounce custard cups.

3. Combine the eggs, cream, vanilla, and the remaining ¼ cup sugar in a small mixing bowl. Whisk to dissolve the sugar.

4. Evenly divide the mixture among the custard cups. Place the cups in a baking pan large enough to hold them comfortably. Fill the pan with enough water to reach three quarters of the way up the side of the cups.

5. Bake for about 1 hour, or until the custard sets and a knife inserted in the custard comes out clean. Let cool, then refrigerate for at least 4 hours.

6. When ready to serve, use a thin knife to loosen the custard around the edges of the cup. Invert onto chilled dessert plates.

4 servings

Peach Custard with Macaroons

 have always been partial to macaroons, which I learned to make when I was a boy. When I discovered several old Louisiana macaroon custard recipes, which were popular at the turn of the century, I was elated. The addition of peaches is my idea.

3 eggs

2 cups heavy cream

½ teaspoon ground cinnamon

¼ teaspoon grated nutmeg

½ cup (packed) light brown sugar

½ teaspoon vanilla extract

1 tablespoon butter

6 large ripe peaches, peeled, pitted, and cut in half (about 3¼ pounds)

1½ cups crumbled Almond Macaroons (page 331)

1. Preheat the oven to 350°F.

2. Whisk together the eggs, cream, cinnamon, nutmeg, brown sugar, and vanilla in a mixing bowl.

3. Butter a deep 8-inch round baking dish.

4. Arrange the peach halves, standing them each on end, in the baking dish. Pour the egg mixture over the peaches.

5. Bake for about 1½ hours, or until the custard sets and a knife inserted in the custard comes out clean. Remove from the oven and sprinkle with the crumbled macaroons. Return to the oven and bake for 15 minutes.

6. Serve immediately.

8 servings

Creole Cream Cheese Ice Cream

n farms in Louisiana, everyone had at least one milk cow to provide fresh milk daily for the family. Remember the kind that had cream floating on the top? There wasn't a meal at which homemade butter did not make an appearance. Or pitchers of sweet cream to pour over fresh berries or figs. The milk left after the butter was churned and removed was, of course, buttermilk, which was used for drinking, cooking, or baking. But perhaps one of the best milk products was the mystical Creole cream cheese. Raw milk was clabbered and strained. Fresh cream was added to the curds. The final product was then sprinkled with sugar, or salt and pepper, or topped with fresh strawberries, blackberries, or figs. For years, Creole cream cheese was found difficult to make in other parts of the country, probably because of the absence of certain bacteria either in the milk or the air. Thanks to modern science, however, Creole cream cheese is now produced commercially. It's readily found in and around New Orleans, and Starflake Foods Co. in Columbus, Ohio, also has a good product that I use at my restaurant from time to time. Ask the manager of your local supermarket if he can get it, or a similar product, for you. Some homemakers are still making their own cheese. During the dog days of August in Louisiana, when the heat builds and builds during the day, the old ice cream freezer is dragged out and a batch of ice cream cools us down. Marcelle's Aunt Grace used to make a cream cheese ice cream and store it in ice cube trays in

the freezer. The children were allowed to pop a couple of cubes out whenever they worked up a sweat. I can't begin to describe the incredibly delicious flavor and richness of this concoction. We've added Louisiana strawberries to ours, but you can use any kind of fresh fruit—berries, peaches, bananas. We froze ours in a glass loaf dish, but you can use wax-coated disposable cups or any freezer containers you have. If you want to dress up the mold to serve at a formal dinner party, top it with whipped cream and drizzle with strawberry sauce. You can also make it in an ice cream freezer. Follow the manufacturer's instructions.

---

2 cups heavy cream

1/2 cup sugar

1/2 teaspoon vanilla extract

1/8 teaspoon salt

5 egg yolks

2 3/4 cups Creole cream cheese or drained ricotta or small curd cottage cheese

1 pint fresh strawberries, rinsed, hulled, and quartered

---

1. Combine the cream, sugar, vanilla, and salt in a nonreactive saucepan over medium-high heat. Stir to dissolve the sugar. Bring the cream to the boiling point to scald it. Remove from the heat.

2. Beat the egg yolks in a bowl. Add the cream mixture, about 1/4 cup at a time, to the beaten eggs, whisking in between each addition, until all is used. Pour the mixture into a saucepan, and cook, stirring, over medium heat, for 2 to 3 minutes, or until the mixture becomes thick enough to coat a wooden spoon. (Tip: If the mixture separates, pour it slowly through the feed tube of a food processor with the motor running. It should recombine and you can continue.) Remove from the heat.

3. Add the cream cheese to the egg mixture and whisk until thoroughly mixed. Add the strawberries.

4. Pour the mixture into a glass 9 × 5 × 3-inch loaf dish or decorative mold and cover with plastic wrap. Freeze for at least 8 hours. The ice cream should be quite firm.

5. To unmold, dunk the bottom of the container in a pan of hot water to loosen, then invert onto a serving platter. Let stand for a few minutes before slicing into serving portions.

12 to 14 servings

Strawberry Sauce

1 pint fresh strawberries, rinsed, hulled, and quartered

¼ cup sugar

2 tablespoons brandy

6. Combine the berries, sugar, and brandy in a saucepan over medium-high heat. Bring to a boil. Cook, stirring occasionally, until the sugar dissolves, about 5 minutes.

7. Remove from the heat and let cool for several minutes. Puree in a blender or food processor.

8. Chill for at least 30 minutes before using.

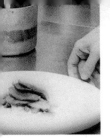

CHAPTER 15

Lagniappe

PRALINES,

PIG'S EARS,

DIRTY MARTINIS,

AND MORE

ere in Louisiana, there is a tradition of giving lagniappe, a little something extra. Sometimes it's an extra doughnut or beignet at the bakery, or it could be a few extra grattons, or perhaps a few more shrimp than you ordered. For my lagniappe, I've included recipes for drinks to help the food go down; pralines, a Louisiana mainstay; and cookies: almond macaroons and a favorite butter cookie recipe of mine. Cookies are not a strong part of the Louisiana heritage. It's more the same old, same old. In fact, Marcelle doesn't remember her mother making a lot of cookies. She made pig's ears, pralines, maybe fudge sometimes. She does remember an old aunt making sugar cookies with fig topping. In New Orleans, the cookies of choice are pecan lace cookies and bâtons de noisettes, or nut sticks. The praline is a descendant of a confection invented by Lassagne, a chef to the Duc du Plessis-Praslin, in the 1600s. Almonds, rather than pecans that are used here, were coated with

caramelized sugar. The pralines were believed to help in avoiding indigestion. The praline that is common now in Louisiana is a sugary, sometimes creamy, sometimes crunchy candylike sweet. Long ago, the candies were cooked in large vats in the open air of the French Quarter, and today there are still several praline shops there. The aroma as the sugar cooks is quite tantalizing.

Creamy Pralines

Pralines (pronounced praw-leens), a sweet concoction made primarily with pecans and sugar, are a favorite treat especially around the Christmas holidays. Years ago, the pralines were peddled in the streets of the French Quarter and good little children were rewarded with one neatly wrapped in a square of wax paper. Nowadays, when pecans are plentiful, there's no reason not to have them year round.

1 cup granulated sugar	Pinch of salt
1 cup (packed) light brown sugar	½ cup sweetened condensed milk
2 tablespoons light corn syrup	1 teaspoon vanilla extract
2 tablespoons butter	1½ cups pecan pieces

1. Combine the sugar, brown sugar, corn syrup, butter, salt, and condensed milk in a heavy saucepan over medium heat. With a wooden spoon, stir until the sugar dissolves. Continue to cook, stirring, until smooth and light brown, about 8 minutes. Add the vanilla and pecans and continue to cook, stirring, until the mixture reaches 234° to 240°F. on a candy ther-

mometer or the soft ball stage, that is, when a bit dropped into cold water forms a soft ball that flattens.

2. Remove from the heat and drop by the spoonful onto wax paper. Let cool. Remove from the paper with a thin knife.

3. Pralines can be stored in an airtight container at room temperature for up to 2 weeks.

About 1 ½ dozen

Crunchy Pralines

n the first clear and cold day of each winter, Marcelle's Aunt Grace makes a batch of these crunchy pralines. It's been their own special ritual since Marcelle was a little girl. The reason it's done on such a day is that, as Aunt Grace says, pralines should never be made on a warm humid day, else the sugar candies won't solidify.

1 pound (packed) light brown sugar (about 2½ cups)

2 tablespoons butter

¼ cup water

2 cups pecan pieces

1. Combine the sugar, butter, and water in a heavy saucepan over medium heat. Stir to dissolve the sugar. Continue to stir for 3 to 4 minutes. The mixture will begin to boil. Add the pecans and continue to stir for about 5 minutes.

2. Remove from the heat. Drop by the spoonful onto wax paper. Let cool. Remove from the paper with a thin knife.

3. Pralines may be stored in an airtight container at room temperature for about 2 weeks.

About 2 dozen

Peanut Butter Pralines

he first time I had a peanut butter praline was on a dreary winter's day when I visited Joe Cahn, who operates the New Orleans School of Cooking and Louisiana General Store in the French Quarter. It brightened my day.

1 cup granulated sugar	1 tablespoon butter
1 cup (packed) light brown sugar	Pinch of salt
½ cup sweetened condensed milk	3 tablespoons creamy peanut butter
2 tablespoons dark corn syrup	1½ cups pecan pieces

1. Combine the sugar, brown sugar, milk, syrup, butter, salt, and peanut butter in a heavy saucepan over medium heat. Stir until the sugar dissolves. Continue to cook, stirring, until the mixture begins to bubble around the edges of the pan, about 12 minutes. Add the pecans and continue to stir until the mixture thickens, about 8 minutes, and reaches 234° to 240°F. on a candy thermometer, or the soft ball stage, that is, when a bit dropped into cold water forms a soft ball that flattens.

2. Remove from the heat and drop by the tablespoonful onto wax paper. Let cool. Lift the pralines off the paper with a thin knife.

3. Pralines can be stored in an airtight container at room temperature for up to 2 weeks.

About 1½ dozen

Almond Macaroons

sweet lady in Lafayette offered me some of her homemade macaroons one afternoon as we sipped our coffee in delicate demitasse cups. She recalled how her mother took a break from her housework when her husband came in from work. There was always something sweet to munch on while they discussed the day. Those macaroons we enjoyed reminded me of when I was a boy learning to bake. I loved the aroma of macaroons baking in the oven. My teacher, Mr. Amarillo, told me that the secret to making perfect macaroons was to rub the almond paste and sugar together so fine that the mixture resembled clouds in the sky.

1 can (8 ounces) almond paste

1 cup sugar

3 egg whites

Cold water

1. Preheat the oven to 325°F.
2. Line a cookie sheet with parchment paper.
3. Crumble the almond paste in a mixing bowl. Add the sugar. Work the mixture with your hands and fingers until there are no lumps and it looks like clouds.
4. In another bowl, beat the egg whites until they form stiff peaks. Add to the almond mixture and combine thoroughly.
5. Spoon the mixture by the tablespoonful about 1 inch apart onto the lined cookie sheet. With a pastry brush, dampen the tops of the cookies with water to prevent the sugar from crystallizing and burning.
6. Bake for 45 minutes, or until delicately brown. Using a metal spatula, transfer to a wire rack to cool.
7. Macaroons can be eaten right away, or cooled and stored in an airtight container at room temperature for up to 5 days.

16 cookies

Spiced Butter Cookies

hese butter cookies, with a hint of cinnamon and nutmeg, can be drizzled with melted chocolate or dabbed with Fig Preserves (page 22), which is how I like them. They are made often in sugarcane country.

2 sticks (½ pound) butter, softened

½ cup plus 1 tablespoon sugar

1½ teaspoons vanilla extract

½ teaspoon ground cinnamon

¼ teaspoon grated nutmeg

2 cups flour

Cold water

1. Preheat the oven to 375°F.

2. Line a cookie sheet with parchment paper.

3. Cream the butter in a bowl with an electric mixer. When the butter is soft and whipped, add the sugar, vanilla, cinnamon, and nutmeg. With the mixer on high speed, mix well, scraping the sides of the bowl as you mix. Beating at medium speed, add the flour, about ¼ cup at a time. Stop the mixer from time to time to scrape down the sides of the bowl. The dough will be stiff.

4. Drop the dough by the tablespoonful about 1 inch apart onto the lined cookie sheet. Dip your index finger into the water and press down on the center of each drop of dough to flatten it.

5. Bake for 20 to 25 minutes, or until lightly browned around the edges. Remove from the oven and transfer the cookies with a metal spatula to a wire rack to cool.

6. The cookies can be stored in an airtight container in the refrigerator for up to 1 week.

About 2 dozen cookies

Oreilles de Cochon

hese pastries are twirled and folded as they fry, making them look like pig's ears. They are old-time favorites of the bayou country and were served as a special treat in winter months or as dessert at large family gatherings. Light as puffs, they are drizzled with cane syrup cooked with pecans to give them crunch. Don't try to get these to your mouth with a fork. They are meant to be eaten with your fingers. It takes a little practice to twirl the dough around in the hot oil, but with some patience you will be able to do it. They should come out twisted, folded, and slightly awkward looking. Hey, I never said they were pretty, just good. All will be slightly different in appearance. If you think you can't do it, ask a child to help. Children are wonderful with them. Just follow the directions carefully.

1 cup flour

¼ teaspoon salt

⅛ to ¼ cup water

Solid vegetable shortening, for deep-frying

1 cup Steen's 100% Pure Cane Syrup

½ cup pecan pieces

1. Combine the flour and salt in a bowl. Add just as much water as you need to make a stiff dough.
2. Divide the dough into 12 equal portions, about the size of a pecan or walnut. Roll out each portion on a floured surface with a rolling pin into a very thin round.
3. Heat the shortening to 360°F. in a deep-fryer or deep saucepan. Drop each portion one at a time into the hot oil, then give it a quick twist in the center with a long-handled fork, holding the fork in the dough until it sets slightly. Rotate the fork, flattening the tines against the dough to form an "ear." Remove the fork. Turn the ears around in the oil until golden brown. Drain on paper towels.

4. Combine the syrup and pecans in a saucepan over low heat and cook, stirring, until it reaches 234° to 240°F. on a candy thermometer, or the soft ball stage, that is, when a bit dropped into cold water forms a soft ball that flattens.

5. Drizzle about 1 tablespoon of the syrup onto each of the ears. Serve immediately.

1 dozen

Croquignoles

ong ago, before modern highways, it was near impossible for country children to visit the French Quarter and taste the golden beignets that their city cousins enjoyed. However, they managed quite well with these little fried doughnutlike cakes. The dough for these slightly sweet and chewy doughnuts is cut into diamond shapes, then slashed vertically in the center to give them a festive appearance. Ladies in the country also served them to visitors along with small cups of strong coffee mellowed with a little cream. Sprinkled with sugar, the pastries look as if they are covered with delicate lace. They are not like the classical French croquignoles, which are glazed crunchy biscuits.

3 cups flour	½ cup sugar
1 tablespoon baking powder	2 tablespoons butter, melted
½ teaspoon grated nutmeg	1 tablespoon vanilla extract
½ teaspoon ground cinnamon	Solid vegetable shortening, for deep-frying
½ teaspoon salt	
3 eggs	Powdered sugar, for dusting

1. Combine the flour, baking powder, nutmeg, cinnamon, and salt in a bowl.

2. In another bowl, beat the eggs until light and frothy. Add the sugar and whisk to dissolve. Add the butter and vanilla and continue to whisk for 2 to 3 minutes. Add the flour mixture, about 1 cup at a time, blending together until a stiff dough forms.

3. Lightly flour a work surface and sprinkle the dough with a little flour. Pat the dough into a large rectangle, about $\frac{1}{8}$ inch thick. Using a pastry wheel or a sharp knife, cut out about 12 diamond-shape pieces. Make a slit lengthwise through the center of each diamond.

4. Heat the shortening to 360°F. in a deep-fryer or deep saucepan. Deep-fry the diamonds, two to three at a time, turning them around with a slotted spoon, until they are golden brown and crisp, about 4 minutes. Transfer to paper towels to drain.

5. Dust with powdered sugar and serve immediately.

1 dozen, 6 servings

My Mint Julep

all and cool, there's nothing like a mint julep when the temperature is soaring. Tari, my wife, and I have mint growing in the courtyard at home and keep a jar of simple syrup in the refrigerator. Throughout the South, there are several methods used, each different, but all good. Here's my recipe. The secret is to make juleps one at a time.

6 to 8 fresh mint leaves

1 tablespoon Simple Syrup (page 337)

Crushed ice

2½ ounces bourbon

Sprig of mint for garnish

1. Put the mint leaves and the syrup in the bottom of a tall glass. With the handle of a wooden spoon, crush and mash the leaves to extract the flavor. Fill the glass with crushed (not cubed) ice. Pour in the bourbon.

2. With a long-handled spoon, jiggle (not stir) to chill and mix. Garnish with a sprig of mint. Sip.

1 julep

Marcelle's Milk Punch

ilk punch is a favorite eye-opener served with brunch. It can be made with bourbon, brandy, or dark rum. Marcelle favors bourbon. Never pour this cool and soothing mixture over ice—it waters it down.

1 bottle (750 ml) bourbon

3 quarts half-and-half

4 tablespoons vanilla extract

Simple Syrup

Grated nutmeg

1. Combine the bourbon, half-and-half, and vanilla in a gallon container. Add as much syrup as you need to attain the desired sweetness. Chill thoroughly.
2. Pour into chilled glasses, sprinkle with ground nutmeg, and serve.

4 quarts

Simple Syrup

1 cup sugar

1 cup water

3. Combine the sugar and the water in a small saucepan. Stir and boil until the sugar dissolves and the liquid becomes slightly syrupy. Cool completely before using.
4. The syrup will keep indefinitely in the refrigerator. This makes about 1 cup.

Bloody Mary

old and spiced up with Louisiana's own Tabasco sauce, it's consumed by the gallon at brunches and lunches down here. Omit the vodka for Virgin Marys.

8 cups thick tomato juice	2 tablespoons Worcestershire sauce
1 teaspoon salt	2 teaspoons Tabasco sauce
1 teaspoon celery salt	10 ounces vodka
2 teaspoons freshly ground black pepper	Crushed ice
1 tablespoon fresh lemon juice	Quick Pickled Okra (page 16) or Pickled Mirliton (page 17), for garnish
2 tablespoons fresh lime juice	

1. Pour the tomato juice into a large pitcher. Stir in the salt, celery salt, pepper, lemon juice, lime juice, Worcestershire, Tabasco, and vodka. Chill for at least 1 hour before serving.

2. Fill tall glasses with crushed ice and add the mix. Garnish and serve.

About 10 tall drinks

Rock's Sea Breeze

ock is Marcelle's spouse. He's in his element
when he's in his boat cruising down Bayou Teche,
which flows along their front yard, showing guests
points of interest. "There's a stand of purple-blue
Louisiana iris. Over there are blue herons roosting in the willow
trees. Coming up on our left are wood ducks and mallards. Ahead
of us is a clump of American lotus," he bellows. Once he returns
you to his wharf, there's always a pitcher of something cold and
good. Here's his favorite.

4 cups fresh grapefruit juice

1 cup cranberry juice

6 ounces vodka

Crushed ice

Club soda

1. Combine the grapefruit juice, cranberry juice,
and vodka in a large pitcher. Chill for about 1 hour.
2. Fill tall glasses with crushed ice, add the mixture,
and a splash of club soda. Drink up!

About 6 tall drinks

Dirty Martinis

When we were working together on the cookbook, we put in
many long hours testing recipes. After especially long days, we
rewarded ourselves with a dirty martini. We pulled out a bottle of
vodka that had been chilling in the freezer all day, poured some
over chipped ice in wineglasses, splashed in a little olive juice
from the olive jar, and added a couple of big olives, Quick Pickled
Okra (page 16), and Pickled Mirliton (page 17). Living well is the
best revenge.

Emeril's Coffee

n Louisiana, we like our coffee strong and dark. We serve a lot of this coffee drink at Emeril's after dinner.

2 ounces Kahlúa

1 tablespoon cocoa

1 ounce amaretto

Hot coffee

Whipped cream, for topping

1. Pour 1 ounce Kahlúa into 1 coffee cup saucer. Put the cocoa into another saucer. Dip the rim of an old-fashioned glass first in the Kahlúa, then in the cocoa.

2. Add the remaining 1 ounce Kahlúa and the amaretto to the glass. Fill the glass with hot coffee and top with whipped cream. Sit back and enjoy.

1 drink

Coffee and Other Beverages

Coffee and chicory, served with warm milk—café au lait—is a New Orleans institution. Chicory, a root, was first used in America during the Civil War when coffee was hard to come by, and it continues to be used today. Chicory makes coffee stronger and thicker. Many visitors drinking it for the first time think they are being poisoned since the taste is quite bitter. Even without the addition of chicory, New Orleans coffee is strongly brewed, giving it a powerful taste. It has to be calmed down with warm milk. Elsewhere in the state, and especially in Acadiana, the coffee is pure, thick, and strong, sometimes likened to the crude oil that is pumped out of the marshes. You will often find this rich, black coffee served in a demitasse cup with a few drops of cream and a tinge of sugar to smooth it out. These Acadians drink a lot of coffee—with breakfast, sometimes even mixed together with crumbled corn bread and a little hot milk; at mid-morning; after lunch; mid-afternoon; and after supper or dinner. It's a daily ritual. They make their coffee in small drip pots for themselves and for whoever stops by to visit.

Because of the heartiness of the food, beer—ice cold—is the beverage of choice at seafood boils, fish frys, and other outdoor cookouts. Sometimes you'll be fortunate enough to be offered homemade wines made with muscadines (a type of wild grape), tiny wild cherries, and Louisiana peaches. If a California or French wine is served, it's usually a red one since most white wines do not hold up to the spicy foods. Iced tea is consumed in enormous quantities, both in summer and in the cooler months, always flavored with sugar and lemon.

Real and Rustic Source Guide

With the popularity of Louisiana cooking, many of the ingredients used in this book are available at supermarkets and specialty stores and the following suppliers.

Battistella's Sea Foods Inc.
(504) 949-2724 OR (800) 375-2728
Live crawfish, frozen crawfish tails, frozen seafood, fish

Bruce Foods Corporation
(800) 299-9082
Canned sweet potatoes (yams), canned okra, Louisiana Gold Pepper Sauce and other hot sauces, pickled peppers

Creole Country Sausage Factory
(504) 488-1263
Sausage casings

The C. S. Steen Syrup Mill, Inc.
(318) 893-1654 OR (800) 725-1654
Steen's 100% Pure Cane Syrup

Cajun Chef Products
(318) 394-7112
Pepper sauces, pickled peppers, pickled okra, cayenne, filé powder

Cane River Pecan Co.
(318) 367-3226
Cracked pecans, pecan pieces, shelled pecan halves

Chef John Folse & Co.
(800) 256-2433
Cast-iron pots, burners and butane tanks for seafood boils, sausages, andouille, tasso

Comeaux's Inc.
(800) 323-2492
Sausages, tasso, boudin, catfish, crawfish (boiled and frozen), crabmeat, gumbo crabs, oysters, shrimp, coffee, spices

Crescent City Meat Co.
(800) 375-1956
Andouille, tasso, assorted pork sausages

K-Paul's Louisiana Mail Order
(800) 654-6017
Spices, sausages, andouille, tasso

Konriko Company Store
(800) 551-3245
Rice, Konriko Brand Wild Pecan Rice, spices

Louisiana Seafood Exchange
(504) 834-9395
All types of seafood

Natchitoches Pecans, Inc.
(318) 379-0272 OR (800) 572-5925
(outside Louisiana only)
Cracked pecans, pecan pieces, shelled pecan halves, pralines

New Orleans Fish House
(504) 821-9700 OR (800) 839-3474
Crawfish, shrimp, crabmeat, fish

The New Orleans School of Cooking and Louisiana General Store
(800) 237-4841
Zatarain products (Creole mustard, crab and shrimp boil, spices), Steen's 100% Pure Cane Syrup, rice, hot sauces, spice blends, Tabasco products, coffee, pickled peppers

Randol's Inc.
(800) YO-CAJUN (800-962-2586)
Live crawfish and crabs, fresh and frozen crawfish tails, fresh and frozen crabmeat

The Tabasco Country Store
(800) 634-9599
All Tabasco products

Index